UNIVERSITY OF BIRMINGHAM

The Community Prevention of Coronary Heart Disease

EDITED BY DR KEITH WILLIAMS
Director of Public Health, Coventry Health Authority
Honorary Senior Clinical Lecturer, University of Birmingham
Honorary Visiting Senior Lecturer, University of Warwick

74195

London: HMSO

ISBN 0 11 701623 3

Contents

Introduction

Coronary Heart Disease is the major cause of death in the United Kingdom, accounting for approximately 150,000 deaths annually. Many of these deaths are preventable. This book is a series of essays on the prevention of Coronary Heart Disease, written by experts in the field. It is aimed at offering practical ideas to the primary care team for interventions to be mounted at a local level. Individual authors have deliberately been given considerable freedom in content and style. I hope that you find it interesting and helpful.

KEITH WILLIAMS
January 1992

I
Risk Factors
which can be Modified

Smoking and Coronary Heart Disease

Tim Marshall, Department of Social Medicine, University of Birmingham

1

Coronary heart disease (CHD) is both the largest element of cardiovascular disease and the single most common cause of death of both men and women in all parts of the United Kingdom[1-3]. The relationship between CHD and smoking was comprehensively reviewed in 1983[4]. Since then, further studies have provided much additional information on the smoking - CHD relationship, in particular on the effects of smoking cessation, passive smoking, and the changing constituents of tobacco and hence of tobacco smoke. In this chapter we shall review the studies which have provided our major understanding of the smoking - CHD relationship, and we shall consider recent work in each of the areas mentioned above.

From the methodological point of view it is interesting that two of the earliest studies to throw light on the smoking-CHD relationship were *prospective observational* studies, widely recognised to be both the most expensive type of epidemiological study design and the slowest to provide answers to the research questions posed. Nevertheless, such studies have provided high-quality information for (literally) decades, and have exposed limitations in some more recent studies which have used different research designs.

Hammond and Horn's early study was prospective, but not long-term. Nearly 188,000 white males were asked about their smoking habits early in 1952. The first report, of follow-up to 31 October 1953, identified differences in mortality rates from 'diseases of the coronary arteries' between smokers and non-smokers, with death rates rising more or less in accordance with the amount smoked[5]. This trend was confirmed in a later report after 44 months of follow-up, at which time the age-adjusted relative risk of death from coronary disease for smokers versus

Figure 1 **Age-standard annual mortality rates from Ischaemic Heart Disease of male and female British doctors**
A: Age < 65   B: Age>=65   NB: Note different scales in A and B

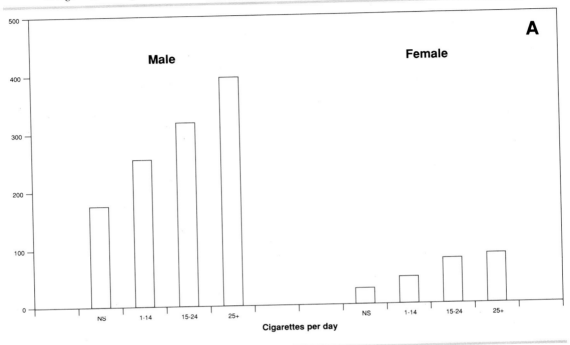

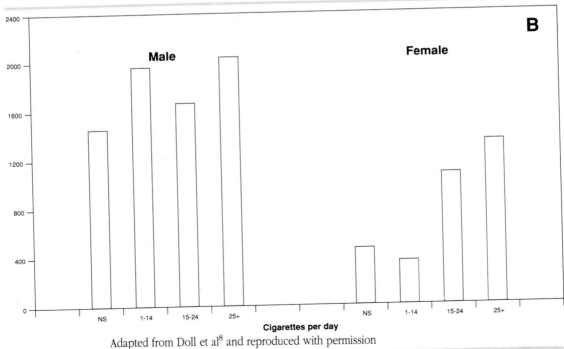

Adapted from Doll et al[8] and reproduced with permission

non-smokers was 1.7 to 1[6].

There are many problems with this study, not least with the representativeness of the sample. Despite this, the results obtained - and obtained quickly, essentially as a consequence of the huge size of the study - are very much in accordance with what has subsequently been found from more rigorously-designed studies with longer follow-up times. Two of these are now reviewed briefly.

The British Doctors study was begun in 1951 with a questionnaire to everyone on the then current British Medical Register. Of the many published reports, we concentrate on two, concerned with 20 and 22 years follow-up of male[7] and female[8] doctors respectively. Figure 1 shows age-standardised annual mortality rates from ischaemic heart disease (IHD) separately for those under and over 65, and for both men and women according to the amount smoked (pipe, cigar and mixed smokers are not shown here). It is clear that

1 with one exception (female smokers of 1-14 cigarettes per day), smokers always have higher mortality rates than non-smokers.
2 in the younger age-group, death rates in both sexes rise consistently with the amount smoked. At ages 65 and above, a simple trend is less clear, but in general higher rates are observed in both sexes amongst the heavier smokers.
3 the extra mortality associated with smoking cigarettes is
    a) greater in absolute terms at older ages
    b) greater in relative terms at younger ages
    and these observations hold for both men and women. It is worth noting that Hammond and Horn's study had similar findings, though they were restricted to men only.

One of the possible drawbacks of this study was that doctors in Britain (and in most other countries) could be perceived as coming from a privileged social group and that neither in their experience of smoking per se, nor in their exposure to other factors influencing CHD would their experience be applicable to the general population. Subject to the limitations of geography the Framingham study avoided these criticisms.

Smaller than both the previous studies mentioned, Framingham began ahead of either and has been under way for longer. The biennial medical examination of subjects initially free of heart disease made it possible to study the incidence rates for smokers and non-smokers in three different age-groups[9]. The findings for men are similar to those of the British doctors study, but those for women reveal no consistent pattern (Figure 2).

A more recent prospective observational study is the British Regional Heart study[10]. Over seven and a half thousand men aged 40-59 were randomly selected from general practices with age-sex registers between January 1978 and June 1980. The intention was to determine the role of individual and environmental risk

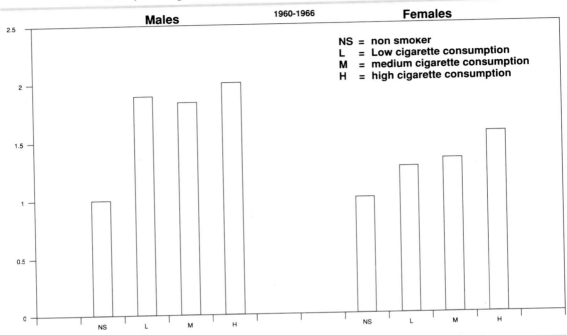

Figure 2   **24 year incidence rate per thousand of coronary heart disease by cigarette-smoking status, Framingham Study**

Adapted from Dawber et al[9] and reproduced with permission

factors, to identify inter-relationships between risk factors and to ascertain the way in which the risks and interactions change over time. After (a mean of) 4.2 years follow-up, the relative odds for ischaemic heart disease of smoking are shown in Figure 3. Apart from the unexpected fall in risk amongst the heaviest smokers (though based on very small numbers), these findings are consistent with the other reports described here. The figure introduces the important concept of adjusting risks for the presence of other risk factors, a concept to which we shall return later in this review.

The fundamental question raised by these and many other similar findings is, of course, whether the observed epidemiological association is causal. There are those who argue that it is not[12], but their alternative thesis - that the observed association is confounded with personality and genotype - has not found widespread acceptance. One way of investigating the putative cause - effect relationship is to find out what happens when people stop smoking. If the relationship were indeed causal, one could hypothesize that incidence and mortality rates amongst former smokers should eventually fall to those of never-smokers - unless smoking induced some irreversible state with a life-long enhanced risk.

Relative odds for ischaemic heart disease according to smoking habit

Figure 3

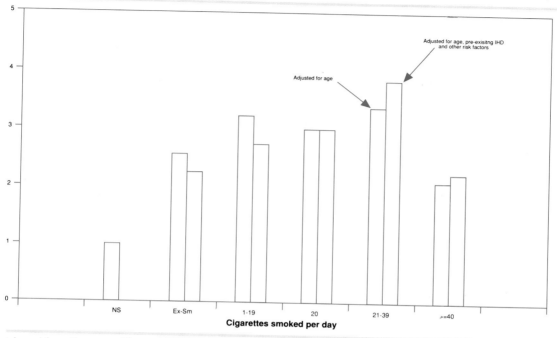

Adapted from Shaper et al[11] and reproduced with permission

Fortunately, many of the long-term prospective studies have been able to address this question. In another huge American Cancer Society study, Hammond and Garfinkel found a steady decline in the risk of death from CHD according to the length of time smoking had been stopped; and that this decline obtained for both light (1-19 per day) and heavy (20+ per day) smokers[13]. These findings suggest that it might take up to 20 years after stopping smoking for the CHD risk to reduce to that of the never-smoking population (Figure 4). It is fair to comment that this decline is likely to be influenced as well by how long people did actually smoke before stopping.

The Framingham study was too small to deduce trends in CHD mortality in relation to the length of time since stopping smoking[14], but both the British Doctors study[7] (deaths) and the British Regional Heart Study[15] (major IHD events) show that the relative risk remains substantially above 1 even after 15 years[7] and 20 years[15] smoking cessation. The doctors study also showed that the benefit of giving up is relatively greater in younger men, i.e. stopping smoking at 30 is likely to result in a relatively greater reduction in mortality from CHD than stopping smoking at 60. This is partly because IHD mortality of non-smokers increases with age, and partly because 30-year old stoppers will have had a shorter smoking history than 60-year old stoppers.

Figure 4

Relative risk of death from CHD according to length of time since giving up smoking; by amount smoked (men only)

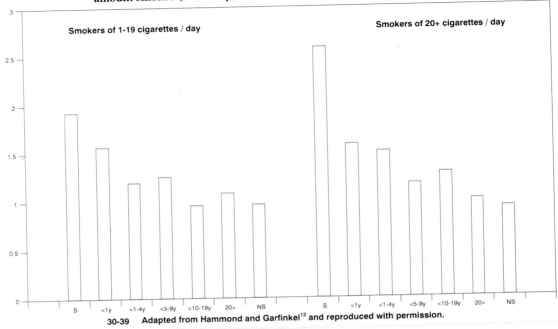

Adapted from Hammond and Garfinkel[13] and reproduced with permission

A more recent report[16] suggests that the reduced risk from giving up smoking might come much quicker than other studies have found. In a case-control study of female survivors of a first myocardial infarction (MI), aged 25-64, Rosenberg and colleagues showed that the odds ratio (relative risk) of an MI was

3.6 (3.0 to 4.4)   for current smokers versus never smokers

2.6 (1.8 to 3.8)   for ex-smokers of less than 2 years cessation versus never-smokers

1.2 (1.0 to 1.7)   for all ex-smokers versus never smokers.

The same pattern obtained irrespective of the amount smoked, smoking duration, age or other factors, and most risk had been dissipated within 3-4 years of stopping. These findings are similar to an earlier study with the same design (case-control), of male survivors of a first MI[17] and have been supported in a recent leading article[18].

The difference between the findings of the prospective and retrospective studies is important both for our understanding of the atherogenic mechanisms and effects of smoking, and for policies and methods of health education in relation to smoking reduction or cessation. In our view, the prospective studies give a more accurate view of the change in CHD risk according to length of time

Relative risks from CHD mortality from smoking low (L), medium (M) or high (H) tar/nicotine cigarettes; by sex and time period

Figure 5

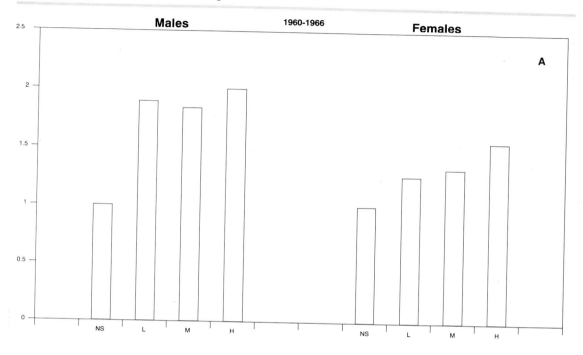

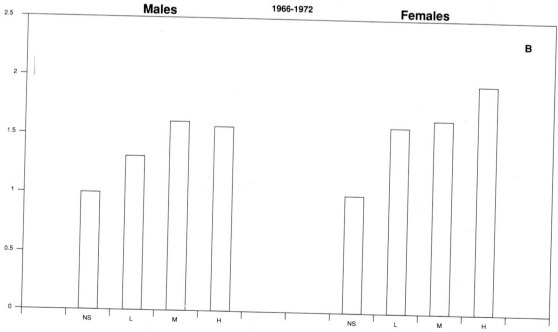

since stopping, essentially because the retrospective studies by definition exclude from the cases those who died from the infarction. A strict interpretation of the retrospective studies is, therefore 'The risk of a non-fatal, first myocardial infarction reduces to that of the level of never smokers within about 4 years of stopping smoking'. Such a statement of course says nothing about the risk of a fatal MI, which all the prospective studies show to be raised above the level of non-smokers for at least another dozen years, or even longer.

Much less work has been done on the long-term follow-up of MI survivors in relation to their smoking habits, and some results seem at first sight anomalous. For example, Daly et al[19] in studying male 2 year survivors of a first MI found that the 13-year actuarial survival of smokers who stopped was greater than that of never-smokers (though both had better survival than continuing smokers). This curious result has been found elsewhere,[20] and is explained by the non-smokers having more of other coronary risk factors than the smokers. Unfortunately, the crude survival rates were not adjusted for these differences, and the data were not presented in such a way as to enable a direct comparison with the other prospective studies to be made.

Notwithstanding these difficulties, the general message obtained from these studies is quite clear: giving up smoking, whether before or after a heart attack, is good for you. Whether this is true for all smokers depends on the assumption that the 'stoppers' can be regarded as a random sample from the entire population, or in other words, just like the 'continuers' save for the fact of their having stopped. This seems inherently implausible, though statistical adjustment for differences on other risk factors can be used to isolate the 'stopping - continuing' effect[15].

The question then arises as to whether a *policy* of persuading people to stop smoking, either before or after a heart attack, could help (a) to increase the numbers of ex-smokers, and thereby (b) to reduce the incidence of IHD events. Such a proposition takes us into health education and health promotion, and into randomised controlled trials to assess the value of intervening.

Principles of primary preventive trials in cardiovascular disease have recently been reviewed by Pocock and Thompson[21]; most of what they have to say is relevant to the more specific area of coronary heart disease, but also to secondary prevention in this field. There is a need to consider whether a 'representative' sample of the whole at-risk population should be used, or only a high-risk group; to decide whether to use a single intervention (e.g. 'stop smoking') or to intervene in several areas (smoking, diet, exercise...); and to decide whether the randomisation should be of individuals or groups (e.g. factories). The first of these points clearly conditions the extent to which the results can be generalised; the second affects the ease with which the intended intervention can be carried out and monitored, and how far the effect of any individual element of the intervention can be isolated; and the third affects both the practicalities of offering intervention to people, and the statistical analysis of the results. Trials illustrating these several components have recently been reviewed by McCormick and Skrabanek[22]. Results for those studies where reduction or cessation of smoking was one of the intervention elements are shown below.

Table 1

Trial	Sample Size	Age group (years)	Duration (years)	Intervention	CHD deaths		Total deaths	
					I	C	I	C
WHO[23]	60,881	40-59	6	D, S, BP, E, W	428	450*	1325	1341*
Goteborg[24]	30,000	47-55	12	D, S, BP	462	461	1293	1318
MRFIT[25]	12,866	35-57	7	D, S, BP	115	124	265	260
Helsinki[26]	1,222	40-55	5	D, S, BP, E, W	4	1	10	5*
Oslo[27]	1,232	40-49	5	D, S	6	13*	16	23*
Whitehall[28]	1,445	40-59	10	S	49	62	123	128

D = Diet, S = Smoking, BP = Blood Pressure, E = Exercise, W = Weight.
*Adjusted for differences in sample size between intervention (I) and Control (C) groups. From McCormick and Skrabanek[22] with permission.

Set alongside the plethora of results from observational studies showing a benefit from smoking cessation, these findings are astonishing. How can it be that voluntarily giving up smoking results in a reduction in CHD risk, but doing so as part of a randomised controlled trial appears to offer no benefit? We have to distinguish between the effects of a policy decision to persuade people to give up smoking, and the effects of actually giving up. The results above show the comparative effects of a policy decision, and in that respect it is clear that the policies i.e. the interventions have been pretty ineffective. We do not not have comparable data relating only to those people who followed the allocated treatment; but even if we did, and the intervention were shown to be beneficial, in order to fit in with the overall results above, we should then have to explain why non-compliance in the intervention group produced worse results than non-compliance in the control group. Unless we follow Eysenck's argument, that it is differences in personality type which condition both giving up smoking and the diseases subsequently experienced[12], we must admit to a lacuna in our knowledge and understanding of the effects of smoking cessation.

One of the problems with attempting to apply these findings to the present population is that many elements of the smoking habit have changed since the early enquiries were begun. These elements - filter-tipped or plain cigarettes, patterns of inhaling and so-called high, middle and low-yield cigarettes (referring variously to tar, nicotine or carbon monoxide) - have provided important insights into the smoking - CHD relationship but in their variation over time have made prediction of future patterns of disease or mortality all but impossible.

In assessing the possible effects of inhalation, a further difficulty arises from the way in which information about inhaling is collected - essentially by self-report. Stepney, for example, showed that measured CO concentrations in exhalate did not differ significantly between subjects in different self-stated inhaling categories[29]. There is, too, the related question of whether people actually understand, when asked, what is meant by inhaling, so that subsequent classification by their answers is meaningful. Nevertheless, there are several reports which *do* indicate differences in CHD rates - either disease prevalence, or mortality - between self-reported inhalers and non-inhalers. Data from a number of these studies are summarised in the following table.

Table 2 Relative risks of cardiac symptoms or CHD death for inhalers compared with non-inhalers.

Study	Condition	Categories and Risks			Statistical adjustments
Doll and Peto[7]	IHD death	Men Aged	<65	>65	Age and amount smoked
			1.57	1.13	
Hawthorne and Fry[30]	Angina	Men	1.37		Age and amount smoked
		Women	1.39		
	Possible infarction	Men	1.32		Age and amount smoked
		Women	1.24		
	IHD death	Men	2.17		Age and amount smoked
Higenbotham, Shipley and Rose[31]	CHD death	Men Smokers of 1-9/d 10-19/d 20+/d grade			Age and employment grade
		1.23	1.04	1.27	

Despite the very different population of these studies - male British doctors, males and females in west Central Scotland, and male Whitehall civil servants - the results are fairly similar, all indicating that inhalers are at greater risk of CHD, or of dying from CHD, than non-inhalers. The British doctors study yet again shows the reducing risk of putatively hazardous behaviour with increasing age, and this is seen also in a comparison of non-inhalers with non-smokers: the relative risk of IHD deaths under 65 is 1.41, and at 65 and over, is 1.31 (derived from reference 7).

The role of filter cigarettes in relation to CHD is much more ambiguous than that of inhaling/not inhaling. The theoretical argument is that smoking can be made less hazardous by reducing or removing entirely through filtration those substances in tobacco smoke most likely to cause cardiovascular disease (and, of course, other diseases). There are huge problems with trying to isolate the 'filter' effect on disease and mortality, both because of the switching of individuals from one to the other type of cigarettes, and because of other contemporaneous changes in cigarette manufacture. These problems have been discussed by Lee and Garfinkel[32], who noted that they exist also when trying to identify the effects of low, medium or high-yield cigarettes.

Hawthorne and Fry[30] found relative risks for plain vs. filter cigarettes of *less* than 1 for the symptoms reported in table 2, though for neither symptom for either sex was the risk significantly different from 1; the same was true for CHD mortality. In the Framingham study, there was no consistent pattern of CHD risk, either elevated or reduced, for plain cigarettes versus filter cigarettes, and none of the relative risks examined was, after adjusting for total cholesterol, systolic blood pressure and age, significantly different from 1.[33]

To some extent the issue of filter versus plain is a proxy for studying the true 'yield' of a cigarette, whether of tar, nicotine or CO. Changes in yield may occur for a variety of reasons, including filtering, changes in the way that cigarettes are smoked - e.g. longer (or shorter) draw, deeper (or shallower) inhalation, more (or fewer) puffs - and changes in the nature of the tobacco itself. From this perspective, filtering is simply one of the methods giving rise to an overall result expressed as the yield.

There are again problems with assessing the reliability of machine-derived 'yields' as indicators of substances received by human smokers (see, for example, Rickert et al[34]), and the changing nature of manufactured cigarettes over time merely compounds these difficulties. One of the first to report, from another huge American Cancer Society study, was Hammond et al[35] whose results, based on over one million subjects, are summarised in Figure 5. This shows clearly that over both time-periods studied, and for both sexes, there was an excess mortality from CHD for smokers of all kinds of yield compared with non-smokers, and that in general the higher the yield, the greater the risk.

Some studies have been able to reproduce these findings, but others have not. Hawthorne and Fry[30] found higher CHD symptom prevalences in smokers of higher tar cigarettes. Higenbottam et al[31] found a fairly consistent pattern of increasing CHD mortality with increasing tar yield, for inhalers within each amount smoked, but no such pattern for non-inhalers. And when the same group studied CO yield after adjusting for age, employment grade, amount smoked and tar yield, the risk of death from CHD was 32% lower in the high yield group (though not statistically significant), whilst amongst inhalers only, death from CHD was 51% lower, and significant at $p<0.01$[36]. The authors concluded that highly complex interactions were involved - which is, perhaps, another way of saying that we do not yet understand it all.

Two more recent studies, both from the USA, have returned to the questionably appropriate case-control approach to address the issue of high/low yield cigarettes. Kaufman et al[37] and Palmer et al[38] found a complete absence of any trend in relative risk for a non-fatal myocardial infarction with increasing levels of nicotine in the 'most recently - smoked cigarettes' in males or females. The same was true for CO levels. This invites the inference that 'If the risks of myocardial infarction among smokers do not vary according to the nicotine or carbon monoxide yields of the cigarettes they smoke, it is possible that these substances are not primarily responsible for the pathogenic effects of cigarette smoke on the cardiovascular system.'[38] What neither study addresses is the issue of fatal MI. Whilst it is technically correct to refer to 'the risk of a non-fatal MI' in relation to these studies, such a limited perspective is unavailable to the individual who may be at risk of an MI of either kind, and wishes to know whether to change brands.

On the other hand, Hammond's huge study seems almost alone in producing consistent results, but these were from a time when tar, nicotine and CO yields were all far higher than those of the more recent studies. It may be that the ambiguities and inconsistencies of these later studies indicate that, within the range of nicotine and CO yields *now* available, there is indeed no lesser risk associated with lower yield brands. If this were so, Kaufman's and Palmer's conclusions - essentially that there is nothing to be gained in terms of reduced CHD risk from switching to low yield brands - would still be correct. Despite a recent symposium devoted to the subject[39], many uncertainties remain.

Summarising so far we have the following:

Smoking is associated with an increased risk of CHD mortality, and there is a dose-response relationship between the amount smoked and the risk. This occurs in both sexes. With increasing age, the relative risk for CHD death declines (though remaining above 1), partly because of the selective elimination of high-risk smokers from the population and partly because of the gradual rise in the 'ordinary' risk of CHD amongst non-smokers.

Giving up smoking is associated observationally with reducing risk of CHD death, and there is again a dose-response relationship where 'dose' = length of time since giving up. It takes at least 15 years, and maybe over 20, of smoking cessation before the risk in ex-smokers reduces to that of never-smokers of the same age. Experimental studies of health education/health promotion where smoking reduction or cessation has been one of the targeted elements of behaviour change have failed substantially to reproduce the findings from observational studies. The reasons for the difference between the results of these two approaches remain unresolved, though personality and other lifestyle factors not so far considered may have a part to play.

Despite difficulties in defining inhaling and in measuring differences in exhalate between self-stated inhalers and non-inhalers, several studies show inhalers to be at greater risk of CHD symptoms or mortality than non-inhalers, who in turn are at greater risk than non-smokers. Filter cigarettes do not appear to be associated with a reduced risk of CHD death. There have been many studies of 'low-yield' cigarettes, but the evidence for a dose-response relationship is equivocal. Early studies showed that low-tar was associated with reduced risk; others have found this to be true only for inhalers. Low CO and nicotine levels have sometimes been associated with lower risk and sometimes not. Proper analysis is complicated by contemporaneous changes in cigarette manufacture, and by the need to take account statistically of many other variables.

Passive smoking is the most recent aspect of the smoking habit to have come under epidemiological scrutiny. Hirayama's early report on non-smoking Japanese women found a significantly elevated risk of IHD amongst those whose husbands smoked compared with those whose husbands did not, and a dose-response relationship between the amount smoked and the risk[40]. Others have tried to replicate these findings on white populations, though not always successfully. Garland studied never-smoking married women aged 50-79 in Southern California in the early 1970s. After a 10 year follow-up, wives of current or ex-smokers had higher crude and age-adjusted death rates from IHD than wives of never-smokers, but the relative risk (2.7) was not at all significant[41]. Svendsen used data originally obtained during the MRFIT study to explore the opposite relationship, smoking/non-smoking wives and husbands' CHD risk[42]. These results and others from a study by Helsing[43] and Sandler[44] exploring the relationship in both directions, are show in abbreviated form in table 3.

Most of these studies suggest a small but (if the study was large enough) statistically significant risk of death from CHD if a non-smoker lived with a smoker. Logically this fits with the findings of the risks to smokers themselves, and they are consistent to the extent that they indicate a lower risk to passive than to active smokers. Precise estimates of the true relative risks (for male smokers on female non-smokers, and vice versa), as well as dose-response relationships and the other matters considered in this review, are obviously more difficult to establish than those to smokers themselves. The whole area seems ripe for some meta-analysis such as has been done in a number of other clinical fields.

Passive smoking has not figured largely in the complex calculations of how many deaths might be attributed annually to the smoking habit. This is because the conventional methods for estimating quantities such as attributable risk percent and population attribution risk percent assume static exposure levels with constant risk, neither of which holds in relation to smoking.

It is nevertheless of considerable public health interest to know, or be able to estimate, the risk of CHD death associated with smoking. To do so it is of course necessary to take account simultaneously of the amount smoked, the length of time since giving up (where relevant), and age. The latter is confounded with

Table 3 Relative risks for IHD disease/death of non-smokers living with smokers

Study	Condition	Subjects	RR	Statistical Adjustments
Svendsen et al[42]	CHD death	Never-smoking husbands	2.11 (0.69-6.46)	Age, baseline blood pressure, cholesterol, weight, education, alcohol consumption.
	CHD death	Never+Ex-smoking husbands	1.45 (0.77-2.73)	
	CHD event	Never--smoking husbands	1.48 (0.89-2.47)	
	CHD event	Never+Ex-smoking husbands	1.19 (0.85-1.65)	
Helsing et al[43] Sandler et al[44]	Death from arterio-sclerotic heart disesease	Non-smoking males	1.31 (1.05-1.64)	Age, housing, schooling, marital status
	Death from arterio-sclerotic heart disease	Non-smoking females	1.19 (1.04-1.36)	

smoking years (since most people who smoke begin to do so within a fairly narrow age range), to which in our view too little attention has been paid. One of the few studies to incorporate this in an analysis was by Cook et al[15], but even this study was not truly prospective in relation to the variables studied (age of starting smoking, number of years smoking, number of years since giving up), and they were unable to address simultaneously the effect of the amount smoked. The findings - that age and smoking-years were adequate predictors of the future IHD risk *without* needing to know the number of years since giving up - are of obvious public health importance, but we still do not know how soon after starting smoking the excess risk of CHD begins to be evident, nor whether this risk varies with the amount smoked.

A complementary approach to the model-building of the British Regional

Heart study is the empirical perspective of Goldman and Cook in assessing the contribution of smoking to the observed decline in CHD mortality in the USA between 1968 and 1976[45]. In a wide-ranging review, they estimated that 24 percent of the reduction in CHD deaths could be attributed to smoking. If true, that is a considerable achievement, albeit very far from asserting that 24 percent of *all* CHD deaths are attributable to smoking. Even so, the achievement is likely to be greater over a longer period of time, since the specific contribution of other factors, particularly medical measures, in earlier periods of time is likely to have been less.

Much of this is speculation since, particularly with preventive measures such as stopping or reducing smoking, the benefits in terms of reduced mortality are seen years, and sometimes decades, after the measures themselves are introduced. The complexities of modelling exposures and consequential changing effects when other risk factors are continually changing have been discussed by Blackburn, who observed that the models we already have are both 'hopelessly complex' and 'not robust'[46]. Smoking may seem a relatively simple factor to alter (though the trials show it is not so simple at all), but modelling the effects of so doing has been, and will remain, extremely complicated.

References

1   Office of Population Censuses and Surveys. (Annual) *Mortality Statistics: Cause*. Series DH2. HMSO, London.

2   Common Services Agency. (Annual) *Scottish Health Statistics*. HMSO, Edinburgh.

3   Registrar General Northern Ireland. (Annual). *Annual Report.* HMSO, Belfast.

4   US Public Health Service. (1983) *The Health Consequences of Smoking: Cardiovascular Disease*. US Department of Health and Human Services, Washington.

5   Hammond, E.C. and Horn D. (1954) 'The relationship between human smoking habits and death rates.' *Journal of the American Medical Association*, 155, 1316-1328.

6   Hammond, E.C. and Horn, D. (1958) 'Smoking and death rates - Report on forty-four months of follow-up of 187, 783 men II Death rates by cause.' *Journal of the American Medical Association*, 166, 1294-1308.

7   Doll, R. and Peto, R. (1976) 'Mortality in relation to smoking: 20 years' observations on male British doctors.' *British Medical Journal*, (ii), 1525-1536.

8   Doll, R., Gray, R., Hafner, B., and Peto, R. (1980) 'Mortality in relation to smoking: 22 years' observations on female British doctors.' *British Medical Journal*, (i), 967-971.

9   Dawber, T.R. (1980) *The Framingham Study: The epidemiology of atherosclerotic disease*. Harvard University Press, Cambridge (Mass) and London.

10 Shaper, A.G., Pocock, S.J., Walker, M., Cohen, N.M., Wale, C.J. and Thomson, A.G. (1981) 'British Regional Heart Study: Cardiovascular risk factors in middle-aged men in 24 towns.' *British Medical Journal*, (ii), 179-186.

11 Shaper, A.G., Pocock, S.J., Walker, M., Phillips, A.N., Whitehead, T.P. and MacFarlane, P.W. (1985) 'Risk factors for ischaemic heart disease: The prospective phase of the British Regional Heart Study.' *Journal of Epidemiology and Community Health*, 39, 197-209.

12 Eysenck, H.J. (1980) *The causes and effects of smoking*. Temple Smith, London.

13 Hammond, E.C. and Garfinkel, L. (1969) 'Coronary heart disease, stroke and aortic aneurysms. Factors in the etiology.' *Archives of Environmental Health*, 19, 167-182.

14 Gordon, T., Kannel, W.B., McGee, D. and Dawber, T.R. (1974) 'Death and coronary attacks in men after giving up cigarette smoking.' *Lancet*, (ii), 1345-1348.

15 Cook, D.G., Shaper, A.G., Pocock, S.J. and Kussick, S.J. (1986) 'Giving up smoking and the risk of heart attacks.' *Lancet*, (ii), 1376-1379.

16 Rosenberg, L., Palmer, J.R. and Shapiro, S. (1990) 'Decline in the risk of myocardial infarction among women who stop smoking.' *New England Journal of Medicine*, 322, 213-217.

17 Rosenberg, L., Kaufman, D.W., Helmrich, S.P. and Shapiro, S. (1985) 'The risk of myocardial infarction after quitting smoking in men under 55 years of age.' *New England Journal of Medicine*, 313, 1511-1514.

18 Higenbottam, T. (1989) 'The search for safer cigarettes.' *British Medical Journal*, (ii), 994-995.

19 Daly, L.E., Mulcahy, R., Graham, I.M. and Hickey, N. (1983) 'Long term effect on mortality of stopping smoking after unstable angina and myocardial infarction.' *British Medical Journal*, (ii), 324-326.

20 Sparrow, D., Dawber, T.R.. and Colton, T. (1978) 'The influence of cigarette smoking on prognosis after a first myocardial infarction.' *Journal of Chronic Diseases*, 31, 425-432.

21 Pocock, S.J. and Thompson, S.G. (1990) 'Primary prevention trials in cardiovascular disease.' *Journal of Epidemiology and Community Health*, 44, 3-6.

22 McCormick, J. and Skrabanek, P. (1988) 'Coronary Heart Disease is not preventable by population interventions.' *Lancet*, (ii), 839-841.

23 WHO European Collaborative Group. (1986) 'European collaborative trial of multi-factorial prevention of coronary heart disease: final report on the 6-year results.' *Lancet*, (i), 869-872.

24 Wilhelmson, L., Bergland. G., Elmfeldt, D. et al. (1986) 'The multi-factorial primary prevention trial in Goteborg, Sweden.' *European Heart Journal*, 7, 271-288.

25 Multiple Risk Factor Intervention Trial Research Group. (1982) 'Multiple risk factor intervention trial. Risk factor changes and mortality results.' *Journal of the American Medical Association*, 248, 1465-1477.

26 Miettinnen, T.A., Huttenen, J.K., Naukkarinen, V. et al. (1985) 'Multi-factorial primary prevention of cardiovascular disease in middle-aged men.' *Journal of the Medical Association*, 254, 2097-2102.

27 Hjermann, I., Velve Byre, K., Holme, I. and Leren P. (1981) 'Effects of diet and smoking intervention on the incidence of coronary heart disease. Report from the Oslo study group of a randomised trial in healthy men.' *Lancet*, (ii), 1303-1310.

28 Rose, G., Hamilton, P.J.S., Colwell, L. and Shipley, M.J. (1982) 'A randomised controlled trial of anti-smoking advice: 10 year results.' *Journal of Epidemiology and Community Health*, 36, 102-108.

29 Stepney, R. (1982) 'Are smokers' self-reports of inhalation a useful measure of smoke exposure?' *Journal of Epidemiology and Community Health*, 36, 109-112.

30 Hawthorne, V.M. and Fry, J.S. (1978) 'Smoking and health: the association between smoking behaviour, total mortality and cardiorespiratory disease in West Central Scotland.' *Journal of Epidemiology and Community Health*, 32, 260-266.

31 Higenbottam, T., Shipley, M.J. and Rose, G. (1982) 'Cigarettes, lung cancer and coronary heart disease: the effects of inhalation and tar yield.' *Journal of Epidemiology and Community Health*, 36, 113-117.

32 Lee, P.N. and Garfinkel, L. (1981) 'Mortality and type of cigarette smoked.' *Journal of Epidemiology and Community Health*, 35, 16-22.

33 Castelli, W.P., Garrison, R.J., Dawber, T.R., McNamara, P.M., Feinleib, M. and Kannel, W.B. (1981) 'The filter cigarette and coronary heart disease: the Framingham study.' *Lancet*, (ii), 109-113.

34 Rickert, W.S., Robinson, J.C. and Lawless, E. (1989) 'Limitations to potential uses for data based on the machine smoking of cigarettes: cigarette smoke contents.' In: *Nicotine, Smoking and the Low Tar Programme*, ed. N. Wald and P. Froggatt, 85-99. Oxford University Press, Oxford.

35 Hammond, E.C., Garfinkel, L., Seidman, H. and Kew, E.A. (1976) ' "Tar" and nicotine content of cigarette smoke in relation to death rates.' *Environmental Research*, 12, 263-274.

36 Borland, C., Chamberlain, A., Higenbottam, T., Shipley, M. and Rose, G. (1983) 'Carbon monoxide yield of cigarettes and its relation to cardiorespiratory disease.' *British Medical Journal*, (ii), 1583-1586.

37 Kaufman, D.W., Helmrich, S.P., Rosenberg, L., Miettinen, O.S. and Shapiro, S. (1983) 'Nicotine and Carbon Monoxide content of cigarette smoke and the risk of myocardial infarction in young men.' *New England Journal of Medicine*, 308, 409-413.

38 Palmer, J.R., Rosenberg, L. and Shapiro, S. (1989) ' "Low yield" cigarettes and the risk of non-fatal myocardial infarction in women.' *New England Journal of Medicine*, 320, 1569-1573.

39 Wald, N. and Froggatt, P. (eds). (1989) *Nicotine, Smoking and the Low Tar Programme*. Oxford University Press, Oxford.

40 Hirayama, T. (1985) 'Passive smoking: a new target of epidemiology' *Journal of Experimental Clinical Medicine*, 10, 287-293.

41 Garland, C., Barrett-Connor, E., Suarez, L., Criqui, M.H. and Wingard, D.L. (1985) 'Effects of passive smoking on ischemic heart disease mortality of non-smokers. A prospective Study.' *American Journal of Epidemiology*, 121, 645-650.

42 Svendsen, K.H., Kuller, L.H., Martin, M.J. and Ockene, J.K. (1987) 'Effects of passive smoking in the Multiple Risk Factor Intervention Trial.' *American Journal of Epidemiology*, 126, 783-795.

43 Helsing, K.J., Sandler, D.P., Comstock, G.W. and Chee, E. (1988) 'Heart disease mortality in non-smokers living with smokers.' *American Journal of Epidemiology*, 127, 915-923.

44 Sandler, D.P., Comstock, G.W., Helsing, K.J. and Shore, D.L. (1989) 'Deaths from all causes in smokers who lived with non-smokers.' *American Journal of Public Health*, 79, 163-167.

45 Goldman, L. and Cook, F. (1984) 'Decline in ischemic heart disease mortality rates.' *Annals of Internal Medicine*, 101, 825-836.

46 Blackburn, H. (1989) 'Trends and Determinants of CHD mortality: Changes in Risk Factors and their Effects.' *International Journal of Epidemiology*, 18, 3 (Supplement), S210-S215.

Diet, Cholesterol and Heart Disease

John Kemm, Senior Lecturer, Department of Social Medicine, University of Birmingham

2

Introduction

This chapter examines the reasons for believing that dietary factors and blood lipids play an important part in causing ischaemic heart disease (IHD). It also reviews the evidence that changing dietary patterns and modifying blood lipid levels will be effective in preventing much of that disease.

The subject will be considered in three sections:

The link between diet and heart disease

The link between blood cholesterol levels and heart disease

The link between diet and blood cholesterol levels

Types of evidence

The types of evidence that can be used to study the links between diet, blood cholesterol level and ischaemic heart disease are listed in Table 1.

Types of evidence linking diet and IHD

Table 1

1. Epidemiological evidence of Association
   - i. Correlations of nutrient intakes and IHD frequency between countries, regions or smaller population groups.
   - ii Secular trends in nutrient intake and IHD frequency
   - iii Studies of migrant groups
   - iv Case control studies
   - v Cohort studies

2. Animal models of IHD like disease caused by diet

3. Demonstration in animals and in humans of dietary influence on mechanisms which may be involved in pathogenesis of IHD

4. Intervention studies in human populations

Diet and heart disease

Several problems complicate the task of identifying dietary causes of IHD. First diet is notoriously difficult to measure accurately[1] and inaccuracies in dietary measurement may conceal underlying relationships. Second the causation of IHD is multifactorial. Many non-dietary factors such as smoking, exercise, psychological factors and family history play a part together with diet in causing heart disease. Great care therefore has to be taken in dietary studies to ensure that the results are not confounded by non-dietary factors. Third, heart disease takes a very long time to develop and the early changes may occur twenty or more years before the disease becomes clinically apparent. This means that it may be necessary to consider the diet eaten many years ago or the average dietary intake over long periods of time.

A short guide to the types of dietary fat

Dietary fat mostly consists of triglycerides which are made up of fatty acids combined with glycerol. The effect of the fat on the body is determined by the type of fatty acid. Fatty acids consist of long hydrocarbon chains with a carboxyl (acid) group at one end. The two important characteristics of the chain are its saturation (the number and location of double bonds) and its length.

The carbon atoms in fatty chains can be linked by single or double bonds. In a saturated fatty acid all the bonds are single. Monounsaturated fatty acids have one double bond in the chain and polyunsaturated fatty acids have two or more double bonds in the chain. Saturated fats cannot be converted to polyunsaturated fats in the body.

Carbon atoms are added onto fatty acid chains in pairs so that the fatty acid chains contain even numbers of carbon atoms.

Longer chain lengths make fats more solid and increasing unsaturation makes them more liquid. The polyunsaturated fats are mostly found in some plant oils (sunflower oil, safflower oil, corn oil) but not all plant oils are good sources. Animal fats tend to be saturated but fish oils contain polyunsaturated oils. The dietary sources of fatty acids are further discussed in Chapter 8.

International comparisons of diet and heart disease

It has long been recognised that the countries with high mortality rates for IHD tended to be the developed countries and that these countries also had high per capita fat intakes. The classical seven countries study of Keys[2] showed a marked correlation between death rates from heart disease in each country and their intake of saturated fat (Figure 1). The same study also showed that the type of fat was also important. There was an even stronger relationship between heart disease rates and the P:S ratio (ratio of polyunsaturated to saturated fatty acids) in the diet (Figure 2). Comparisons of European countries[3] show the same relationship (Figure 3) but the correlations are less strong than in Keys' original study. It should be noted that there are several countries with mortality rates from heart disease very different from that which would be predicted on the basis of the fat intake of their population.

The relation of heart disease death rates and percent of dietary calories supplied by saturated fatty acids in sixteen different populations. (Each population is one cohort of the seven countries studies).

Figure 1

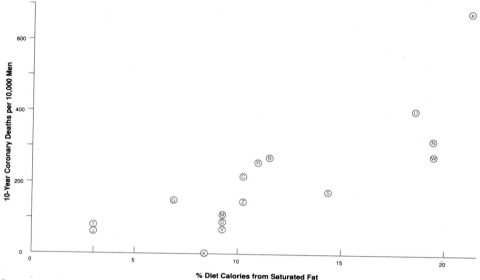

Source: Keys A. (1980). *Seven countries a mutivariate analysis of death and coronary heart disease*. Publ. Havard University Press, Cambridge Mass.

The relation of heart disease incidence to the P:S ratio of the diet in seven countries. P:S ratio is ratio of polyunsaturated to saturated fats in the diet. Incidence rates are for men aged 40-59.

Figure 2

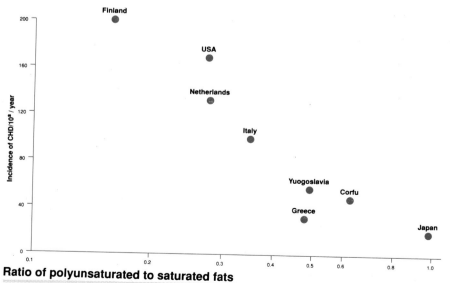

Source: Shaper A.G. & Mann J.W. (1977). *Dietary recommendations for the community towards the postponement of coronary heart disease*. British Medical Journal i, 867-871.

Figure 3

The relation of heart disease death rates to the P:S ratio of the diet in twenty countries. Death rates are for men aged 45-54.

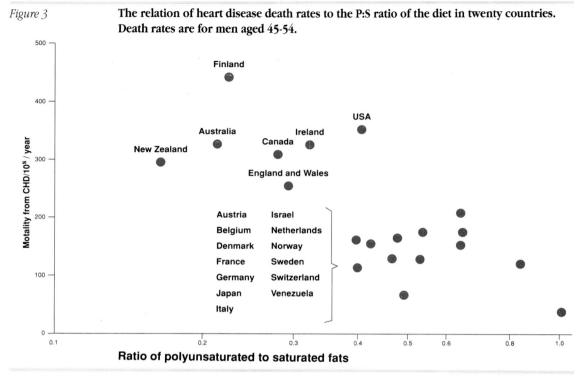

Source: Shaper A.G. & Mann J.W. (1977). *Dietary recommendations for the community towards the postponement of coronary heart disease.* British Medical Journal i, 867-871.

Studies of correlations at a national level have their limitations. They are extremely valuable for suggesting ideas that are worth further investigation (hypothesis generation). However other lines of evidence have to be used in order to test these hypotheses.

Cohort studies of diet and heart disease

There have now been several studies in which the diet of individuals in a population has been characterised and then these individuals have been followed over many years so that their disease risk can be determined. Sometimes these studies (for example the Western Electric study[4]) have shown that individuals with high fat intakes have an increased risk of heart disease. It is notable however that many cohort studies including the best known of them the Framingham study have not shown a relationship between an individual's fat intake and their subsequent risk of heart disease.[5]

The contrast between the consistent and strong relationship between dietary fat intake and heart disease when nations are compared and the difficulty of demonstrating such a relationship at an individual level needs to be explained. Those who reject the fat theory argue that the correlations at a national level are produced by confounding variables and there is no increased risk associated with higher fat intake. Their interpretation is almost certainly wrong.

Alternative explanations as to why many cohort studies have failed to show an association between dietary fat intake and heart disease are available. The methods for estimating dietary intake are very crude and the resulting misclassification of individuals might mask an underlying relationship[6]. The range of dietary variation within a population will be much less than that between populations and non-dietary factors could conceal the effect of small variations in fat intake.

Blood cholesterol and heart disease

In contrast to the difficulty of finding correlations between dietary intake and heart disease the data on blood cholesterol and heart disease are very consistent both at a national level and at an individual level. The seven countries study[2] showed a strong correlation between heart disease rates and mean cholesterol level in each population.

At the individual level, numerous cohort studies have confirmed that risk of heart disease rises as blood cholesterol rises. Figure 4 shows data from a very large American study (MRFIT) in which the risk in the top decile of cholesterol is 3-4 times higher than the risk for the bottom decile[7]. Similar findings have been made in the virtually every cohort study. There is no doubt that total cholesterol is a predictor of individual risk.

Types of cholesterol in blood

Early studies were based on measurement of total cholesterol but recent developments have identified several different cholesterol fractions in blood. About 70% of the cholesterol in the blood is associated with the low density lipoprotein particles (LDL cholesterol). Most of this cholesterol will be taken up in the peripheral tissues. A small percentage of the cholesterol in blood is associated with high density lipoprotein particles (HDL cholesterol). HDL cholesterol is probably cholesterol which has been taken up from the peripheral tissues and is being transported to the liver where it will be broken down. The different types of cholesterol and their functions are described further in more specialised books[8].

Total cholesterol reflects mostly LDL cholesterol. It is therefore not surprising that increases in LDL cholesterol are associated with increased risk of coronary heart disease[9]. The significance of HDL cholesterol is slightly less clear. Several studies found it to be inversely correlated with the risk of heart disease though others did not[10]. If HDL cholesterol is protective against coronary heart disease then it is only weakly so.

Figure 4

Heart disease death rates in men according to serum cholesterol half decile. Death rates are aged adjusted six year death rates per 1,000 men. Data from 361662 men screened for MRFIT study.

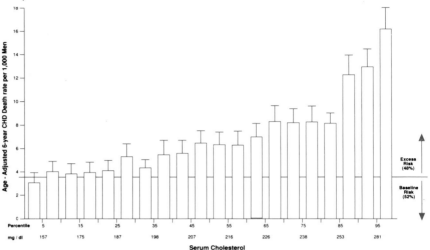

Source: Martin M.J., Hulley S.B., Browne W.S., Kuller L.H and Wentworth D. (1986). *Serum cholesterol, blood pressure and mortality: Implications from a cohort of 361,662 men.* Lancet ii, 933-936.

Diet and blood cholesterol

At a national level there is a correlation between per capita fat intake and mean serum cholesterol (Figure 5) but at an individual level most studies have failed to show this relationship[5,11].

Short term studies in which groups of people are fed different diets under controlled conditions can throw light on the relationship between diet and serum cholesterol. Virtually all studies agree that increasing the saturated fat in the diet increases mean serum cholesterol and that increasing the polyunsaturated fat in the diet decreases mean serum cholesterol (Figure 6). Increasing the cholesterol in the diet causes a small increase in the serum cholesterol[12].

The effect of saturated fatty acids on serum cholesterol depends on their chain length. Saturated fatty acids with less than 12 carbon atoms and saturated fatty acids with more than 18 carbon atoms (stearic acid) or more have little or no effect on serum cholesterol. The saturated fats which have most effect on serum cholesterol have 12, 14 or 16 carbons.

Monosaturated fatty acids were originally believed to have no effect on serum cholesterol but more recent work suggests that in some situations they may be as effective as polyunsaturated fatty acids in lowering serum cholesterol[13].

All these conclusions refer to the effect of dietary change on the mean serum cholesterol of groups of people. Individual people vary considerably in the way their serum cholesterol reacts to dietary change and serum cholesterol shows

The relationship of mean serum cholesterol and percent of dietary calories from saturated fat in sixteen populations. Each population is one cohort of the seven countries study. (Dietary intake for the four populations in dashed rings was estimated using a less reliable technique).

Figure 5

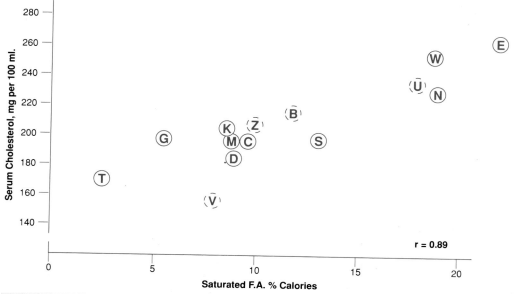

Source: Keys A. (1970). *The Seven Countries study*. Circulation 41 supplement 1, 1-185.

considerable variation over time even without dietary change. It is therefore very difficult to predict how big a change in serum cholesterol would be caused by a change of diet in any particular individual.

While the main effects of dietary fat on serum cholesterol are understood there are many details which are yet to be elucidated. The effect of any particular fat depends in part on the other constituents of the diet in which it is included. It is also important to remember that all the studies cover short periods of weeks or months and the effect of dietary fats over many years may not be identical with their short term effects.

Dietary cholesterol

Early U.S. dietary recommendations laid great emphasis on the reduction of dietary cholesterol while U.K. recommendations paid less attention to this factor. It is possible that the public enthusiasm for reducing dietary cholesterol was increased by a misunderstanding of the increased risk associated with serum cholesterol and a failure to distinguish this from dietary cholesterol. The early studies[11] had suggested that the effect of dietary cholesterol on serum cholesterol was small compared to that of dietary fatty acids. Most of the serum cholesterol is of endogenous origin (produced in the body). Recent studies[15] have confirmed that modest changes in the amounts of cholesterol in most diets have little influence on serum cholesterol. There is however some suggestion that dietary cholesterol might increase risk of coronary heart disease independently of any effect on serum cholesterol[16].

Figure 6

Observed cholesterol (group mean) and cholesterol predicted from diet. Chol = 2.6 S - 1.3 P + 1.5 C + 160

Where S is % from saturated fat in diet (chain length <C18)
Where P is % energy from polyunsaturated fat in diet
Where C is mg cholesterol per 1,000 cals in diet

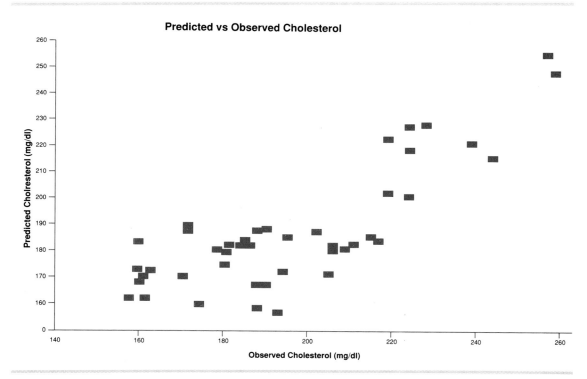

Drawn using data from Keys A., Anderson J.T. & Grande F. (1965). Serum cholesterol response to changes in the diet IV particular saturated fatty acids in the diet. Metabolism 14, 776-787.

Fish oils

Fish oils deserve special mention. Several cohort studies suggest that consumption of fish is protective against heart disease[17]. The most likely reason for this is the fish oils which are rich in eicosapentaenoic acid and other ω polyunsaturated fatty acids. (The ω refers to the position of the first double bond in the fatty acid chain). These fatty acids reduce LDL cholesterol, platelet stickiness and have an anti-inflammatory action[18]. All these effects could protect against atherosclerosis and heart disease.

Other dietary factors

The discussion so far has focused on dietary fats but other nutrients are important. There has been much interest in the effect of alcohol intake on risk of heart disease. Several cohort studies have shown a U shaped relationship between mortality and alcohol consumption with mortality risk lowest in light drinkers, slightly higher in abstainers and higher in heavy drinkers[19]. It has also been noted that in the short term moderate alcohol consumption increased the HDL cholesterol[20] though it is not clear whether the fraction of HDL increased was the fraction supposed to be cardioprotective. These two observations led some people to suggest that moderate alcohol consumption decreased risk of heart disease. The excess mortality in abstainers is difficult to interpret but is explained in part by the fact that people who are ill tend to stop drinking alcohol[21]. The evidence certainly does not justify a statement that abstainers would have a reduced risk if they started to consume some alcohol.

Dietary fibre

Most authorities recommending a decrease in total fat intake have also recommended an increase in dietary fibre. At the very least fibre rich foods in the diet displace other foods especially fat rich foods. In short term experiments some dietary fibres, especially the water soluble fibres may reduce serum cholesterol[22] though the evidence that they will do so in the long term is conflicting. Oat fibre had been suggested to be particularly effective in lowering serum cholesterol but properly controlled studies do not confirm this[23].

Sugar

High sugar intakes have been suspected to increase risk of heart disease. Yudkin and others have pointed out that many of the national correlations between fat intake and heart disease mortality could possibly be explained by a correlation with intake of refined sugar. However attempts to demonstrate the same relationship in case control or cohort studies have with a few exceptions been negative. The evidence was recently reviewed by a COMA[24] who concluded that high sugar intakes were not a risk factor for ischaemic heart disease.

Hypertension and obesity

Raised blood pressure plays an important part in causing heart disease. Several dietary factors affect blood pressure. Sodium and potassium intake are the two most commonly considered but other factors such as calcium and fat may also be involved. The subject will not be discussed further in this chapter.

Obesity is also a risk factor for heart disease. It may increase risk by increasing blood pressure and serum cholesterol since it does not remain as an independent risk factor if the adjustment is made for these two. Controlling body weight is a good way for people to reduce their risk of heart disease. Dietary intake is obviously important in determining body weight and the energy in the diet should be adjusted to maintain body weight around the ideal range.

Mechanisms by which diet could produce heart disease

The discussion so far has implied that diet affects risk of heart disease through its effect on blood lipids and atherosclerosis. This is one possible mechanism but there are many others. Atherogenesis is a complex process of which increased blood lipids are only one small part[25].

Atheroma in the coronary vessels is an important factor is limiting the blood supply to the heart (myocardial ischaemia) but other processes are also involved. Changes in blood fibrinogen, blood platelets and other clotting mechanisms may also contribute to heart disease. Changes in myocardial metabolism could also be important. This leads to the conclusion that there are many mechanisms by which diet could affect risk of heart disease and the relationship between diet and serum cholesterol is only part and possibly only a small part of the story.

Intervention trials

So far we have reviewed an impressive body of evidence that high fat diets and raised serum cholesterol are associated with high risk of heart disease. This does not necessarily mean that the association is causal and that lowering the fat in the diet or reducing the cholsterol in the serum would reduce the risk of heart disease. The fact that the associations are consistent, reasonably strong, biologically plausible and show a graded response all suggest that the association is likely to be causal but for the strongest evidence of causality we must look to controlled intervention trials.

In these trials, individuals are randomly allocated to an intervention group or a control group. The intervention group is advised to modify their diet or given some treatment to lower serum cholesterol. The control group receives minimal or no intervention. The two groups are then followed for a period of years to determine their risk of heart disease. If the risk in the intervention group proves to be lower than that in the control group this is very powerful evidence that the intervention has reduced risk.

Lowering cholesterol intervention studies

Several intervention studies have examined the effect of lowering serum cholesterol on risk of heart disease. Some of these studies were secondary prevention (preventing second infarcts in people who had already had one myocardial infarction). Other studies were primary prevention (preventing heart

Results of randomised controlled trials of cholesterol lowering drugs in prevention of coronary heart disease. Percent reduction in CHD rates (intervention vs control) against percent reduction in serum cholesterol. Each point shows one trial and the vertical lines indicate 95% confidence limits. The sloping line is the best fit and shows that a 10% reduction in cholesterol produces a 15% reduction in CHD (95% confidence limit 9-21%)

Figure 7

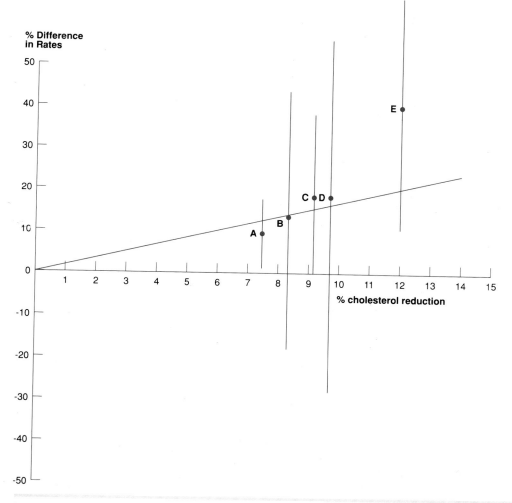

Source: Mann J. & Shaper A.G. (1985). *Chapter 13 – Epidemiology of ischaemic heart disease.* Oxford Textbook of Medicine.

disease in people who had no previous heart disease). Some studies used drugs such as cholestyramine or clofibrate to lower blood cholesterol (Figure 7) while others relied on dietary advice alone (Figure 8). The conclusion of all these studies was clear. Lowering blood cholesterol reduces risk of heart disease both in those who have already had one attack and in those who have not yet suffered heart

Figure 8

Results of randomised controlled trials of diet in prevention of coronary heart disease.
Symbols as described in text to Figure 7. Best fit line shows that a 10% reduction in cholesterol produces a 21% reduction in CHD (95% confidence limit 16-26%).

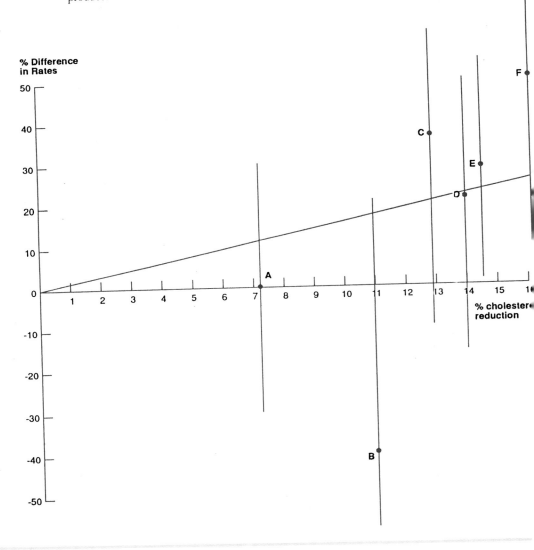

Source: Mann J. & Shaper A.G. (1985). *Chapter 13 – Epidemiology of ischaemic heart disease.*
Oxford Textbook of Medicine.

disease[26]. The greater the reduction in serum cholesterol the greater the reduction in risk. A one percent reduction in cholesterol produces a two percent reduction in risk.

The intervention studies which used diet also show that dietary modification does result in reduction of serum cholesterol. The numbers involved are too small to answer the question whether their effect on risk of heart disease is entirely explained by their effect on serum cholesterol.

The multiple risk factor interventions

The preceding section has considered only those trials which aimed to alter the single risk factor of serum cholesterol. While this makes their analysis much easier there are reasons to think that interventions aimed at several risk factors (such as smoking, blood pressure and serum cholesterol) would be more effective in reducing risk of heart disease than those aimed at single risk factors.

It has to be admitted that these multiple risk factor trials have proved to be less conclusive than was hoped. One trial organised in Oslo showed a clear reduction in risk in the intervention group[27]. The European trial (in which factory workforces rather than individuals were randomly allocated) showed an overall reduction of risk in the intervention group but the effect was rather small and not evident in many of the countries involved[28].

The largest of the multiple risk factor intervention trials was 'MRFIT' in America and this showed only a small and non significant reduction in risk for the intervention group[29]. The explanation for this result was not that the reduction in risk in the intervention group was less than expected but that the control group also showed a large reduction in risk. In part this may be explained by contamination of the control group so that they adopted for themselves many of the life style changes that the intervention group were being encouraged to adopt. While MRFIT was not the final proof of efficacy that it was intended to be, its results are entirely compatible with the view that intervention is worthwhile.

Limitations of the intervention trials

Two limitations of the trials must be noted. First they tended to involve middle-aged men and often middle-aged men at particularly high risk. This concentration on high risk individuals was necessary to increase the power of the trials since there has to be an adequate number of expected outcome events (heart disease deaths or new episodes of heart disease). It seems reasonable to expect that those at lower risk would also benefit from the interventions but this expectation has not been tested.

Second the intervention trials have all looked at fairly short periods of time (the longest was 8 years). The question that we really wish to answer is 'Will adoption of a diet similar to that recommended by NACNE and COMA (i.e. low in saturated fat, high in fibre) by all the population throughout life reduce their risk of heart disease?' The intervention trials have not directly tested this question. The beneficial effects of any change would be expected to be cumulative over time. Therefore the effect of lifelong adherence to dietary interventions would be expected to be far greater than that shown in the trials.

Conclusion

There is a great deal of evidence about the effect of diet on heart disease not all of which seems to point towards the same conclusions. There are many details about the way in which diet affects risk of heart disease that we do not understand. None the less two underlying themes are clear. First, measures which reduce the high levels of cholesterol currently seen in the UK would reduce the risk of heart disease. Second, changing to a diet with a lower percent of energy derived from total fat and from saturated fat in particular, coupled with increased consumption of fibre rich foods and complex carbohydrates would reduce the risk of heart disease. We can confidently give this advice to the general public and to our patients.

References

1   Bingham S. (1984). 'Surveillance of dietary habits of the population with regard to cardiovascular diseases: Premise and methods.' In de Backer G.G., Pedoe H.T. & Duciemetiere P (Eds) *Surveillance of the dietary habits of the population with regard to cardiovascular diseases.* EURONUT Report 2 ISBN 90-70840-04-09.

2   Keys A. (1980). *Seven countries a multivariate analysis of death and coronary heart disease.* Harvard University Press, Cambridge Mass.

3   Shaper A.G. & Mann J.W. (1977). 'Dietary recommendations for the community towards the postponement of coronary heart disease.' *British Medical Journal,* (i), 867-871.

4   Shekelle R.B., Shryock A.M., Paul O., Leper M., Stanler J. Liu S. & Rayner W.J. (1981). 'Diet serum cholesterol and death from coronary heart disease: the Western Electric study.' *New England Journal of Medicine,* 304, 65-70.

5   Dawber T.R. (1980). *The Framingham study: The epidemiology of atherosclerotic disease.* Harvard University Press, Cambridge Mass.

6   Freudenheim J.L., Johnson N.E. & Wardrop R.L. (1989). 'Nutrient misclassification: Bias in the Odds ratio and loss of power in Mantel test for trend.' *International Journal of Epidemiology,* 18, 232-238.

7   Martin M.J., Hulley S.B., Browne W.S., Kuller L.H. and Wentworth D. (1986). 'Serum cholesterol, blood pressure and mortality: Implications from a cohort of 361,622 men.' *Lancet* (ii), 933-936.

8   Durrington P.N. (1989). *Hyperlipaemia: Diagnosis and Management.* Wright, Bristol.

9   Gordon T., Kannell W.B., Castelli W.B. & Dawber T.R. (1981). 'Lipoproteins cardiovascular disease and death. The Framingham study.' *Archives Internal Medicine,* 141, 1128-1131.

10   Pocock S.J., Shaper A.G., Phillips A.N., Walker M. & Whitehead T.P. (1986). 'High density lipoprotein cholesterol is not a risk factor for ischaemic heart disease in British men.' *British Medical Journal,* 292, 515-519.

11   Nichols A.B., Ravenscroft C., Lamphiear D.E. & Ostrander M.D. (1976). 'The independence of serum lipid levels and dietary habits: The Tecumseh study.' *Journal of American Medical Association,* 236, 1948-1953.

12   Keys A., Anderson J.T. & Grande F. (1965). 'Serum cholesterol response to changes in the diet IV Particular saturated fatty acids in the diet.' *Metabolism,* 14, 776-787.

13   Mensink R.P. & Katan M.B. (1989). 'Effect of a diet enriched with monounsaturated or polyunsaturated fatty acids on levels of low density and high density lipoprotein cholesterol in healthy women and men.' *New England Journal of Medicine,* 321, 436-441.

14   Bonanome A. & Grundy S.M. (1988). 'Effects of stearic acid on plasma cholesterol and lipoprotein levels.' *New England Journal of Medicine,* 318, 1244-1248.

15   Eddington J., Geekie M., Carter R., Fisher K., Ball M. and Mann J. (1987). Effect of dietary cholesterol on plasma cholesterol concentrations in subjects

following reduced fat high fibre diets.' *British Medical Journal*, 294, 333-336.

16   Shekelle R.B. & Stamler J. (1989). 'Dietary cholesterol and ischaemic heart disease.' *Lancet*, (i), 1177-1178.

17   Kromhout D., Bosscheiter E.B. & Coulander C.L. (1985). 'The inverse relation between fish consumption and 20-year mortality from coronary heart disease.' *New England Journal of Medicine*, 312, 1205-1209.

18   Leaf A. & Weber P.C. (1988). 'Cardiovascular effects of n-3 fatty acids.' *New England Journal of Medicine*, 318, 549-557.

19   Marmot M.G. (1984). 'Alcohol and Coronary heart disease.' *International Journal of Epidemiology*, 13, 160-167.

20   Thornton J., Symes C. & Heaton K. (1983). 'Moderate alcohol consumption reduces bile cholesterol saturation and raises HDL cholesterol.' *Lancet*, (ii), 819-821.

21   Shaper A.G., Wannamethee G. & Walker M. (1988). 'Alcohol and mortality in British men: explaining the U shaped curve.' *Lancet*, (ii), 1267-1273.

22   Miettinen T.A. (1987). 'Dietary fiber and lipids.' *American Journal of Clinical Nutrition*, 45, Suppl., 1237-1242.

23   Swain J.F., Rowe I.L., Carling C.B. and Sacks F.M. (1990). 'Comparison of the effects of oat bran and low fiber wheat on serum lipoprotein levels and blood pressure.' *New England Journal of Medicine*, 322, 147-152.

24   COMA (1989). 'Dietary Sugars and Human Disease.' *Reports on Health and Social Subjects No. 37.* HMSO, London.

25   Ross R. (1986). 'The pathogenesis of atherosclerosis - an update.' *New England Journal of Medicine*, 314, 488-499.

26   Mann J. & Shaper A.G. (1985). Chapter 13 - 'Epidemiology of ischaemic heart disease.' *Oxford Textbook of Medicine*.

27   Hjermann I., Byre K.V., Holme I. & Leben P. (1981). 'Effect of diet and smoking on the incidence of coronary heart disease: Report from the Oslo study group of randomised trial in healthy men.' *Lancet*, (ii), 1303-1310.

28   WHO European Collaborative Group (1983). 'Multifactorial trial in the prevention of coronary heart disease. 3. Incidence and mortality results.' *European Heart Journal*, 4, 141-147.

29   M.R.F.I.T. Research Group (1982). 'Multiple Risk Factor Intervention Trial: Risk factor changes and mortality results.' *Journal of American Medical Association*, 248, 1465-1477.

Blood Pressure and Heart Disease

D.G. Beevers, Reader in Medicine, Dudley Road Hospital, Birmingham

3

Introduction - Three Risk Factors

The relationships between the three main treatable cardiovascular risk factors, blood pressure, blood lipids and cigarette consumption, are complex. No single risk factor should be considered in isolation because when only one risk factor is present, morbidity and mortality are not particularly high. When two or more risk factors are present, the increasing risk of death is multiplicative or synergistic. This is shown very clearly in the Framingham survey, a long-term follow up of the population of the town of Framingham Massachusetts[1]. A mildly hypertensive man aged 45 years who is a non-smoker with a low serum cholesterol level has a 7 per cent chance of developing cardiovascular disease in the next 18 years. By contrast, a man with the same age and blood pressure, but who smokes cigarettes and has a high serum cholesterol has a 35 per cent probability of cardiovascular disease. If this individual also has glucose intolerance, his probability of developing cardiovascular disease rises to 49%.

It is crucial, therefore, for clinicians, epidemiologists and health care planners to avoid a 'one issue' outlook on coronary prevention related only to their particular sphere of interest.

The Epidemiological Link

The close relationship between a single casual measurement of blood pressure and the risk of cardiovascular and cerebrovascular death has been known since before the second world war. Early analyses of data from Life Insurance Companies and Actuarial Societies demonstrated that the smooth relationship between the height of the blood pressure and death extended down into the 'normal' range. A diastolic blood pressure of 85 mmHg measured on one occasion was associated with a greater risk of death than a diastolic blood pressure of 80 mmHg. The establishment of long-term prospective population cohort studies have confirmed this finding. The Framingham Study (a relatively small project but with very long follow up) and the Whitehall Project (a rather select group of British Civil servants) were notable in this respect. However, these projects are relatively small and now the most reliable data can be obtained from the follow up studies of the male 350,977 screenees for the USA based Multiple Risk Factor Intervention

Trial (MRFIT)[2]. More recently an analysis has been published of the pooled data from all the population studies, thus providing very useful information on the relationship between blood pressure and heart attacks and stroke[3] (Figure 1). These data deny the previous suggestion that there was a tendency for very low blood pressures to be associated with increased cardiovascular risk. With the exception of life threatening diseases associated with low blood pressure (e.g. Addison's disease, diabetic autonomic neuropathy, Shy Drager Syndrome and following a heart attack) it is not possible for a man under the age of 75 years to have too low a blood pressure.

These population based studies were also able to demonstrate an important point with respect to the impact of blood pressure on the health of the population. Severe hypertension, with its very high cardiovascular risk, is relatively rare so the community attributable risk of death due to severe hypertension is small. By contrast, mild hypertension (diastolic blood pressures between 90 and 109 mmHg) are associated with only a relatively modest increase in personal risk of death[4]. Indeed many mild hypertensives have a normal length of life. However, mild hypertension is common (25% of the adult population in the Renfrew Community Study in Scotland). So despite the lower risk, the actual numbers of heart attacks and strokes suffered is large. The community attributable risk of

Figure 1   **Relative risks of stroke and coronary heart disease, estimated from combined results.**
Solid squares represent disease risks in each category relative to risk in the whole study population; sizes of squares are proportional to number of events in each DBP category; and 95% CIs for estimates of relative risk are denoted by vertical lines.

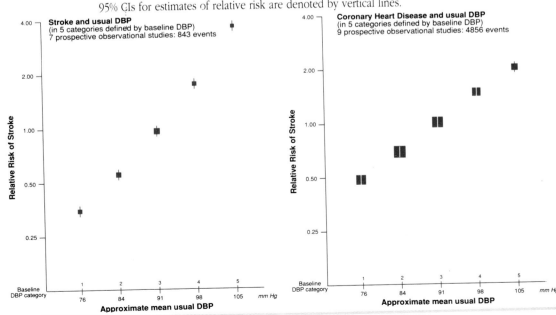

Reproduced from *The Lancet* 1990; 335: 765-74.

death from mild hypertension is very large even though the personal individual risk is low. From a public health point of view, action is needed, therefore, to detect and manage the mild hypertensives in the population. At a clinical level, severe hypertension clearly matters. Malignant phase hypertension (with evidence of retinal haemorrhages, exudates, cotton wool spots and sometimes papilloedema) is very rare (about 5-10 cases per year per 100,000 population) but if left untreated almost all case are dead within 12 months. An untreated diastolic blood pressure of 120 mmHg is associated with a 25% 5 year mortality rate, a figure not dissimilar from that seen in women with breast cancer[5]. These grades of hypertension are not easily assessed in population studies, but clinical follow up data from hospital clinics leaves no doubt of the serious outlook. In the Renfrew study, diastolic blood pressures of 130 mmHg or more were found in 0.5% of the adult male and female population.[4] As discussed in later chapters, failure to detect and reduce this level of hypertension is tantamount to clinical negligence.

Systolic versus diastolic blood pressure

Practically all epidemiological studies have demonstrated that the height of the systolic blood pressure is a better predictor of cardiovascular disease morbidity and mortality than the diastolic pressure. This may partly be because after the age of around 60 years, diastolic pressures cease to rise with age, whereas systolic pressures continue to rise. An example of the power of systolic pressure to detect mortality is provided by the Society of Actuaries data, which show that a man with a blood pressure of 160/85 mmHg has a greater chance of dying than an individual with a blood pressure of 140/100 mmHg, i.e., a higher diastolic pressure but a lower systolic pressure[6].

Notwithstanding the epidemiological evidence favouring systolic pressures, there is as yet little published information on the value of treating high systolic pressures when the diastolic pressure is not raised. Most clinical trials of treating hypertension conducted to date were designed around exclusively diastolic criteria.

Women

For a given level of blood pressure, women have a lower cardiovascular risk than men, even after allowing for differences in cigarette smoking habits and serum cholesterol levels[7]. This may be related to some form of cardioprotective effects of oestrogens. However, it should be remembered that the height of the blood pressure is still a very accurate predictor of death in women.

The elderly

Epidemiological data in the elderly are few. The examinees for the Coope and Warrender trial of drug therapy in people aged 60-75 years show very similar trends to those seen in younger people with the exception that here there was also some excess mortality in subjects with low blood pressures[8].

In the very elderly, over the age of 75 years, this trend appears to continue so that there is a reverse relationship between cardiovascular death rate and blood pressure. Those individuals with the lowest pressures have the worst outlook and those with the higher pressures have a longer life expectancy[9]. The reasons for this paradox are uncertain. Possibly, the individuals with low pressures were once hypertensive and as a consequence of subclinical heart disease, their pressures are now low but their risk remains high by virtue of their having had heart disease. Also it is possible that these very old people represent survivors, their peers with very high blood pressure having died off. Whatever the cause, the routine screening of hypertension cannot be justified in people over the age of 80 years even though around 50% of them have raised pressure by World Health Organisation's criteria (a blood pressure greater than 160/95 mmHg).

The mechanisms of a link between blood pressure and heart disease

High blood pressure leads to the deposition of atheroma particularly in areas of intravascular turbulence. It is possible that the raised pressure itself causes damage to vascular walls which then respond by depositing lipid-rich atheroma. However, high blood pressure may only cause damage when the serum cholesterol levels are either high or at least around average for Western populations. This paradox may explain why two population groups, the Japanese and the Afro-Caribbeans have relatively little coronary heart disease despite the fact that hypertension in these populations is commoner than in the caucasian races. Both groups have lower serum cholesterol levels compared with Europeans.

It seems, therefore, that raised blood pressure alone may not itself cause coronary heart diseases (although it may still cause stroke and heart failure) but that other abnormalities found in hypertensive people are responsible. Hypertensive patients have abnormal blood clotting and have alterations of many local tissue growth factors including endothelin, platelet derived growth factor, endothelium derived relaxing factor, plasma insulin levels and local renin angiotensin systems in vessel walls. There is no doubt that the final common pathway of hypertension is peripheral arteriolar narrowing due to a combination of vasoconstriction and vessel wall thickening.

Additional risk factors

Amongst hypertensive patients, many attempts have been made to identify who will get heart disease and who will not. There does seem to be evidence that the presence of an adverse family history of premature cardiovascular disease is an independent risk factor for the development of heart attack irrespective of the level of blood pressure. In addition, the presence of left ventricular hypertrophy (by ECG criteria) is a powerful predictor of death in its own right. For a given level of blood pressure, an individual with left ventricular hypertrophy has a three fold excess mortality compared with someone with the same level of blood pressure but without left ventricular hypertrophy[10]. The ECG is, in itself, not the optimal method of detecting left ventricular hypertrophy but abnormalities of the ECG when present carry a serious outlook.

It will come as no surprise that for a given level of blood pressure, an individual patient who has already had an episode of coronary or cerebrovascular disease, has a higher risk of death than someone without such a history. Many patients are found to have evidence of a myocardial infarction on ECG even though they have no history of chest pain. These patients also have an adverse clinical outlook.

Casual, basal and ambulatory blood pressure readings

As mentioned earlier, on average, individual patients with mild hypertension have a substantial reduction in life expectancy. However many patients with these levels of blood pressure have a normal life span. Clearly, single casual blood pressure measurements are not ideally predictive. Many blood pressures may, at the time of examination, be raised because the examinee is nervous and unfamiliar with the clinical circumstances of blood pressure measurement ('white coat hypertension'). There has recently been an increased interest in the value of the measurement of more basal blood pressure readings in particular using non invasive 24 hour ambulatory home blood pressure machines[11]. These suggest that the height of the blood pressure during 24 hours whilst away from a clinical environment is more closely related to the thickness of the left ventricular wall than measurements obtained in a clinical out patient clinic setting. There are as yet no longterm prospective studies to validate the use of home blood pressure readings as predictors of death in comparison with clinical readings. Furthermore, ambulatory non invasive automotive blood pressure machines are expensive and often unreliable. There is, however, evidence that blood pressures do settle with repeated measurement. Many patients with raised blood pressure at the first clinic visit will be found to have a normal blood pressure at the third or fourth visit. Whilst individual patients with previous transient mild hypertension cannot be regarded as being without risk, it is inappropriate to give such individuals antihypertensive drug therapy.

The concept of labile hypertension is probably spurious as most blood pressures are variable and in general there is a tendency for higher blood pressure to be more variable than lower ones. People with labile or intermittent hypertension, whose average blood pressures are higher than people with persistently normal blood pressures, cannot be regarded as without cardiovascular risk. In general, there is a tendency for blood pressure levels of individuals to rise with advancing age. Furthermore, there is good evidence that higher blood pressures rise faster than lower blood pressures. The cardiovascular risk of so-called labile hypertensives is probably more closely related to the average blood pressure than to their highest or lowest readings.

The Definition of Hypertension

As has been suggested in the earlier part of this chapter, it is difficult to define hypertension in terms of a single blood pressure reading. A pragmatic definition of hypertension is 'that the level of blood pressure where investigation and treatment do more good than harm'. The epidemiological perspective is rather different. This takes the view that the average blood pressure of the entire Western population is too high and if all people including people with average blood pressure could sustain a small fall in pressure then there would be a major reduction in the epidemic of coronary heart disease.

There is no reason why the dichotomy of approach of epidemiologists (who would like to see a reduction in the average blood pressure of the population) and clinicians (who would like to reduce the blood pressure in people with severe hypertension) should be mutually exclusive.

Figure 2

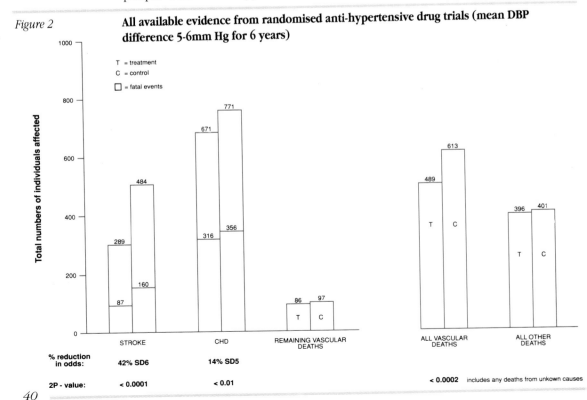

All available evidence from randomised anti-hypertensive drug trials (mean DBP difference 5-6mm Hg for 6 years)

There have been other criteria used for defining hypertension. The World Health Organisation criteria for high blood pressure is if it exceeds 160/95 mmHG. This definition has epidemiological validity by virtue of inclusion of systolic blood pressures. By the WHO criteria, around seven million citizens in England and Wales will be considered to be hypertensive.

The value of treating hypertension

Antihypertensive treatment has been spectacularly successful in preventing strokes. Pooled data from all of the randomised controlled trials have shown that dropping blood pressure by 5 to 6 mmHg brings about a 35-40% reduction in stroke (Figure 2). The data for coronary heart disease are less convincing and a little controversial. The pooled trial data suggests that reducing blood pressure alone did bring about a reduction in coronary heart disease by about 14%. This represents roughly half of the expected effect on heart disease for the achieved fall in blood pressure[12]. The mechanisms for this shortfall are uncertain. However, in any discussion of the relationship between high blood pressure and heart disease, it is now true to say that not only is there a close relationship between blood pressure and heart attacks but also that blood pressure reduction is beneficial.

Conclusion

The height of the blood pressure is an accurate and treatable predictor of premature death from coronary heart disease and stroke. It should not, however, be seen in isolation but should be considered in the light of coexistent risk factors like cigarette smoking and plasma cholesterol levels as well as the presence or absence of left ventricular hypertrophy and the individual's family history. The exact mechanism whereby raised blood pressure causes coronary heart disease is still unknown but at certain levels, drug treatment does reduce this risk. In view of the enormous predictive power of the measurement of blood pressure, all individuals under the age of 75 years should have their blood pressure checked as a routine in primary medical care. Special efforts are necessary to standardise the techniques of blood pressure measurement using the British Hypertension Society[14] criteria or similar criteria. Blood pressures are often measured inaccurately and this may lead either to the false diagnosis of hypertension or the false reassurance of individuals who do have an increased cardiovascular risk. The value and method of detecting, assessing and treating certain levels of hypertension are discussed in detail in chapter 9.

References

1   Kannel W.B. (1974). 'Role of blood pressure in cardiovascular morbidity and mortality.' *Prog Cardiovasc. Dis*, 17, 5-24.

2   Stamler J, Neaton J.D., Wentworth D.M. (1989). 'Blood pressure (systolic and diastolic) and risk of fatal coronary heart disease.' *Hypertension*, 13 (Supplement 1) 2-12.

3   MacMahon S., Peto R., Cutler J., Collins R., Surlie P., Neaton J., Abbott R, Godwin J, Dyer A., Stamler J. (1990). 'Blood pressure, stroke and coronary heart disease. Part 1 - prolonged differences in blood pressure: prospective observational studies corrected for the regression dilution bias.' *Lancet*, 335, 765-74.

4   Hawthorne V.M., Greaves D.A., Beevers D.G. (1974). 'Blood pressure in a Scottish town.' *British Medical Journal*, 3, 600-603.

5   Leishman A.W.D. (1963). 'Merits of reducing blood pressure.' *Lancet*, 1, 1284.

6   Pickering G.W. (1972). 'Hypertension, definitions, natural histories and consequences.' *Journal of the American Medical Association*, 52, 570-583.

7   Silman A.J. (1984). 'Hypertension in women: a separate case for treatment.' *British Medical Journal*, 289, 1021-22.

8   Coope J.S., Warrender T.S., McPherson K. (1988). 'The prognostic significance of blood pressure in the elderly.' *J. Human Hypertens*, 2, 79-88.

9   Lauger R.D., Ganiats T.G., Barrett-Connor E. (1989). 'Paradoxical survival of elderly men with high blood pressure.' *British Medical Journal*, 298, 1356-7.

10   Kannel W.B., Gordon T., Castelli W.P., Margolis J.R. (1970). 'Electrocardiographic left ventricular hypertrophy and risk of coronary heart disease.' *Ann Intern Med*, 72, 813-22.

11   Pickering T.G., Harshfield G.A., Devereux R..B., Laragh J.H. (1985). 'What is the role of ambulatory blood pressure monitoring in the management of hypertensive patients?' *Hypertension*, 7, 171-177.

12   Collins R., Peto R., MacMahon S.W., Hebert P., Fiebach N.H., Eberlein K.A., Godwin J., Qizilbash N., Taylor J.O., Hennekens C.H. (1990). 'Blood pressure, stroke and coronary heart disease. Part 2 - short-term reductions in blood pressure: overview of randomised drug trials in their epidemiological context.' *Lancet*, 335, 827-38.

13   Petrie J.C., O'Brien E.T., Littler W.A., de Swiet M. (1986). 'Recommendations on blood pressure measurement.' British Hypertension Society, *British Medical Journal*, 293, 611-5.

Exercise and Heart Disease

Dorian Dugmore, Director Cardiac Rehabilitation,
'Action Heart', Dudley, West Midlands

4

Introduction

Habitual physical activity is regularly identified as having positive benefits on the heart and circulatory system[1,2]. Such activity is inversely associated with morbidity and mortality from several chronic diseases and in particular, cardiovascular disease, [3].

The relationship between vigorous exercise and the risk of sudden death has long been the subject of controversy[4]. Some investigations report frequent myocardial ischaemia, cardiac arrhythmias and sudden death during vigorous exercise[5], while several epidemiological studies have suggested that habitual vigorous exercise is associated with an overall reduction in the risk of sudden cardiac death[6,7].

The general consensus of opinion reflecting the balance between cardiac benefit versus risk would seem in favour of regular physical activity[8]. This has led to increasing attention being focussed on the role that 'regular exercise' has to play in the prevention of coronary heart disease together with its contribution towards recovery following myocardial infarction and cardiac surgery.

Physical Activity and the Prevention of Heart Disease

Coronary heart disease in the Western World is the foremost cause of death[9]. Although lack of physical activity has been identified as one of the 'risk factors' influencing the increasing incidence of this disease it has often not been accepted as being of major importance[10].

Epidemiological evidence accumulated over the last 30 years would suggest that physical activity has a major part to play in the prevention of cardiovascular disease. Before examining such evidence it is important to quantify what is meant by the term 'exercise' together with key factors influencing its ability to modify recognised coronary risk factors.

According to a recent consensus of current knowledge expressed through the 1988 International Conference on Exercise, Fitness and Health[9], a distinct difference exists between 'exercise' and 'training', the former reflecting the use of leisure time physical activity in order to provide varying degrees of exertion, the latter being a more structured approach involving repetitive bouts of exercise conducted over periods of weeks or months with the intention of developing physical/physiological fitness.

The two terms are often used synonymously, although possessing distinctly different connotations. It would therefore appear necessary to provide a comprehensive description of physical activity over a defined period of time, reflecting the type, frequency, duration and intensity of physical effort if accurate and realistic judgements are to be made as to the effectiveness of a particular 'physical activity pattern'[9].

How much exercise?

At the outset we should be clear that our primary concern is the improvement and maintenance of cardiovascular efficiency. This will involve dynamic physical activity employing the major muscle groups in regular rhythmical contractions, causing a concomitant increase in heart rate, stroke volume and respiration. This is often referred to as aerobic exercise, reflecting an increase in the oxygen cost of physical effort towards a required level of exertion.

The term 'MET'*, representing a unit of energy, helps us to quantify oxygen consumption (VO_2) for a given task or workload, providing a valuable measure of the aerobic cost of selected physical activities (see Table 1).

MARGIN NOTE

One MET is equal to a resting oxygen consumption of 3.5 ml.kg^{-1} min^{-1}. The MET capacity is obtained by dividing oxygen consumption (VO_2) during selected physical activities by the Figure 3.5.

Table 1

Activity	METs
Rest (supine)	1
Dressing and undressing	2
Making beds	3
Cleaning windows	3
Level cycling (9.7 mph)	5
Chopping wood	6.5
Level walking (4 mph)	6.5
Badminton	5.8
Digging	7.5 to 9
Jogging	6 to 7
Level cycling (13 mph)	9
Level running (8 min/mile)	9
Level running (7 min/mile)	12
Squash	15 to 17

From Ashton D & Davies B. Why Exercise? Oxford: Blackwell Ltd, 1986; 125.

It is generally accepted that an intensity of between 50% and 70% of maximum oxygen consumption is needed to make a substantial gain in aerobic fitness. In certain specific circumstances (e.g. a subject who is classified as being in aerobically poor condition; incapable of walking a mile in less than 12 minutes) a work intensity of less than 50% VO_2, may elicit an improvement in cardio-respiratory condition. One should also be aware of the effect of age on the absolute and relative intensity of physical activity; the latter referring to the energy cost of an activity expressed as a percentage of an individual's maximal power output[9], (see table 2).

When prescribing a specific intensity of physical activity in order to improve cardiovascular condition, it is important to realise that although there is very often a linear rise in exercising heart rate (HR) and oxygen consumption (VO_2) in response to increased work efforts, the two are not synonymous (i.e. 50% HR does not equal 50% VO_2)[12] (see table 3).

An important feature in safely improving cardiovascular condition through the use of regular physical activity, is to guide each individual to exercise within their measured or estimated 'aerobic capacity'.

Table 2

	Relative intensity (%)	Absolute intensity (METs)			
		Young	Middle-aged	Old	Very old
Rest		1.0	1.0	1.0	1.0
Light	<35	<4.5	<3.5	<2.5	<1.5
	>35	<6.5	<5.0	<3.5	<2.0
	>50	<9.0	<7.0	<5.0	<2.8
	>70	>9.0	>7.0	>5.0	>2.8
Maximum	100	13	10	7	4

From Bouchard C., Shephard R.J., Stephens T., Sutton J.R., McPherson B.D. (editors). Exercise Fitness and Health: A Consensus of Current Knowledge. Illinois: Human Kinetics Books, 1990.

Table 3

Percent Max HR	Percent Max VO_2
50	28
60	42
70	56
80	70
90	83
100	100

From McArdle W.D., Katch F.I., Katch V.L. Exercise Physiology. Energy, Nutrition and Human Performance (3rd edition). Philadelphia: Lea & Febiger, 1981; 274.

Beyond 70% of an individual's measured oxygen consumption (80% HR) it becomes increasingly unlikely that energy production will be provided in a predominantly aerobic manner (i.e. in the presence of oxygen). Certainly in the early part of a conditioning programme, especially if an individual has been previously sedentary, it would be unwise to go beyond these limits, in order to avoid any excessive strain on the heart and circulatory system.

Cardiovascular fitness experts suggest that the minimum duration of physical activity required to produce significant improvements in cardiovascular condition should be 25-30 minutes per exercise session. At least 3, and preferably 4-5 exercise sessions per week are needed to ensure such improvements.

Equally it is important to guide previously sedentary individuals to build up the length of time they can exercise before increasing the intensity of the physical activity being undertaken. There is little point in increasing the intensity of exercise if you cannot sustain this effort for a long enough period of time in order to gain an improvement in cardiovascular fitness.

The goal of regular physical activity should be to improve the 'aerobic capacity' of the individual. Many physiological and clinical factors influence this improvement, these being well recognised in the literature[9, 10, 11, 12].

Epidemiological evidence

The positive benefits of leisure time physical activity in sedentary populations has become well recognised[3, 9]. An increasing number of the population are modifying their lifestyles to include regular habitual physical activity.

The inter-relationships between exercise, fitness and health and their opposites can be represented by a series of ratios as illustrated below[13].

$$\frac{\text{Active}}{\text{Sedentary}} \qquad \frac{\text{Fit}}{\text{Unfit}} \qquad \frac{\text{Healthy}}{\text{Diseased}} \qquad \frac{\text{Long-lived}}{\text{Short-lived}}$$

The adoption of a lifestyle predominantly above or below the line can often lead to either desired or unfavourable results.

A lifestyle 'above the line' should be the goal for both individual and community health aimed at improving quality of life, longevity and, in particular, improved cardiovascular fitness. The requirements for promoting such positive changes are complex and often not well understood (see chapter 10, The Promotion of Exercise).

Occupational physical activity and CHD

Epidemiological evidence reflects the frequency and distribution of lifestyle elements versus morbidity and mortality patterns[13].

Comprehensive data presented by Morris et al (1953)[14], and Paffenbarger et al (1951-72)[7], contrasted the coronary heart disease (CHD) risks of thousands of sedentary versus active subjects involved in the London Transport Company and San Francisco Longshore Companies respectively.

In both studies, subjects undertaking more vigorous occupational physical activity had significantly less CHD, together with lower risks of fatal heart attacks in comparison with their less active associates working in more sedentary jobs.

Zukel and co-workers conducted a one year study comparing the incidence of heart disease among farmers and non farmers living in the same vicinity[15]. The farmers exhibited lower rates of heart disease in comparison with the non farmers, the farmers recording greater levels of occupational physical activity, together with a lower incidence of smoking. Interestingly this study, although much shorter in duration than those previously mentioned, identified specific levels of physical activity above or below which there was an increased incidence of heart disease. This has interesting connotations suggesting a possible optimum range of physical activity beyond which cardiovascular risk may be increased. There are many other studies illustrated in the literature, indicating an overall lower incidence of CHD in groups that are occupationally physically active in comparison with their more sedentary counterparts[9, 10]. It is necessary to emphasise that a certain threshold of energy expenditure is required to confer any advantage with respect to habitual physical activity and its association with reduced risk of CHD.

Secondly, in many epidemiological studies it has proved difficult to isolate factors which may influence physical activity patterns, due to the additional effect of other contributory factors, e.g. socio-economic status and other lifestyle elements. Accepting such limitations there still appears to be clear evidence supporting the positive role that regular physical activity has to play in reducing the risk of coronary heart disease.

Leisure time physical activity and CHD

Similar evidence has been reported when comparing the incidence of leisure time physical activity and its association with CHD. Morris and co-workers studied the lifestyles and health records of nearly 18,000 British civil servants with sedentary occupations. Those who participated in vigorous leisure time physical activity demonstrated a much lower incidence of CHD in comparison with their fellow workers who were less active in their leisure time.

An equally interesting finding of this research identifies a threshold of physical activity (7.5 kcal.min^{-1}) beyond which aerobic or cardiovascular benefits were more likely to be gained together with a lower risk of CHD.

The Multiple Risk Factor Intervention Trial (MRFIT) demonstrated a consistent gradient of benefit against CHD seen across three activity tertiles, the highest activity tertile conferring the greatest benefit[16]. Scragg and associates found that risks of myocardial infarction and sudden death were progressively reduced in New Zealand men and women (age range 35-64 years) the longer they engaged in vigorous sport and leisure time physical activity[17]. The famous 'Harvard Alumni' study showed that the physical activity habits of the alumni and not their athletic histories as students influenced their middle aged patterns of CHD risk.

The consistent positive relationship between habitual physical activity and a reduced incidence of CHD has been substantiated in many studies readily available in the literature, but too numerous to mention[9]. Although this evidence of cause and effect must be considered circumstantial, it is quite strong and most of it has been accepted as valid and important[9].

A positive relationship would appear to emerge from many studies indicating a more substantial cardio-protective effect of exercise, if energy expenditure is equal to or greater than 2,000 kcal per week[9]. Certainly a gradient response of declining CHD incidence is evident in the research literature with increasing energy expenditure.

In a study of 10,244 middle aged men Blair and associates found that mortality rates declined across physical fitness quintiles by 70% from the least to the most fit men. These trends remained after considering differences among quintiles in age, smoking, blood cholesterol, blood pressure, blood glucose levels and parental history of CHD. Despite the lack of a randomized approach in this study, there is still strong evidence that higher levels of physical fitness led to a delay in all cause mortality, primarily cardiovascular disease and cancer mortality. In a recent study Pekkanen and co-workers reported the influence of vigorous physical activity on the incidence of premature death from any cause among 636 healthy Finnish men aged 45-64 years at entry, who were followed for 20 years (1964-84)[19]. Of the 287 deaths, 106 were attributable to CHD, but the men who had been most active lived 2.1 years longer, in comparison with their less active counterparts, mainly because of their differences in CHD risk.

Certain additional statements can be made following this summary of epidemiological evidence relating to the role that habitual physical activity plays in the prevention of heart disease. Firstly, there is an inverse relationship between vigorous habitual exercise and CHD risk, this being particularly evident in middle age[13]. The previous studies cited suggest that habitual physical activity tends to promote longevity by preventing premature death but is unlikely to extend the natural lifespan of humans.

There is, however, a certain merit in critically evaluating the benefits of regular habitual exercise and its relationship in preventing CHD when considering that appropriate physical activity may 'add life to years' as opposed to just adding years to life.

Certainly, physical activity is a positive influence that tends to benefit health and it counters adverse lifestyle elements that tend to promote negative health and the development of CHD.

Assessment of cardiovascular fitness

In assessing cardiovascular fitness it is important to distinguish between 'performance related fitness' and 'health related fitness'; the latter could equally be entitled 'wellness related fitness'.

Performance related fitness refers to those components of fitness that enable and support optimal work effort or sports performance, while

Health related fitness refers to three components that hold a relationship with health status and the cardiovascular risk factors without necessarily implying excellence of performance in a 'sporting context'[20].

Also as it pertains to exercise and health, a distinction needs to be made between physical fitness reflecting an ability to perform muscular work satisfactorily as opposed to sports related fitness reflecting a need for optimal performance[9]. With respect to the community at large more concern should be directed to physical fitness and the assessment of health related fitness.

At this point a distinction should be made between exercise testing which often implies a strong bias towards 'diagnostic' evaluations for the purpose of clinical interpretation and health related fitness testing that may exhibit similar elements but is essentially aimed at prognosis for the future with a major emphasis on improving physical fitness and reducing CHD risk.

Caution should still be exercised when assessing apparently healthy 'sedentary' individuals and it would be wise to be cleared for testing either by a physician or through a valid medical screening device such as the 'Physical Activity Readiness Questionnaire (PAR, Q)[21].

Using the PAR, Q may help to identify those individuals for whom physical activity might prove inappropriate or who may require medical counselling before proceeding with a physical activity programme.

If serious doubts exist, the 'PAR, X' may be administered which is a questionnaire designed for use by physicians with individuals who are not 'symptom free' and hence not cleared for testing by the 'PAR', Q,[22].

All participants should register their signed informed consent prior to being assessed, indicating their full awareness of test procedures plus risks, together with realising they are able to discontinue the test at any time without detriment.

The assessment of health related fitness normally contains a heavy bias towards testing general endurance (aerobic capacity) due to the previously documented positive relationship between a high level of cardio-respiratory fitness and reduced risk for CHD. The need for the testing of maximum oxygen consumption (Max VO_2) widely employed as an accepted index of cardio-respiratory fitness would not always seem appropriate or necessary, particularly if clearance beyond pre-determined percentage of an individual's capacity is obtained in order to safely initiate a regular exercise programme.

Secondly, it is possible to significantly improve cardio-respiratory fitness without marked improvements in Max VO$_2$. It would therefore appear necessary to utilise other more sensitive measures of improved endurance in order to assess qualitative changes in health related fitness[20].

Predicted tests of cardio-respiratory fitness, based upon the often observed linear relationships between heart rate and oxygen consumption, can be used, whereupon maximum values can be extrapolated from sub maximum results. Such tests possess a 10-15% degree of error[20]. In some instances clinical abnormalities relating to the heart's function may not present themselves until an individual is evaluated beyond 70-80% of their aerobic capacity[23]. If a subject is adminstered a maximal test, and especially if that individual is over 40, it is advisable to include medical personnel in the testing team, together with the constant monitoring of electrocardiographic and blood pressure response to exercise.

Accurate and effective standardisation procedures for the assessment of cardio-respiratory fitness must be adhered to and should include reference to recognised 'contraindications' for testing together with the provision for effective cardio-pulmonary resuscitation[24].

It may well be advisable to consider health related fitness in terms of assessing any individual's endurance capacity (EC), reflecting their ability to sustain an improved percentage of their oxygen consumption as opposed to the 'traditional' measurement of Max VO$_2$. Although the latter is considered a major factor in endurance capacity (EC) the two variables are not closely related[9].

When testing the cardio-respiratory fitness of older sections of the community the measurement of EC, even at lower percentages of peak oxygen consumption, could be a useful procedure which could then relate to their physical performance in every day life (e.g. during brisk walking). Only one third of older men can show a true capacity for reaching their maximum O$_2$ consumption very often due to limitations in peripheral factors (e.g. leg strength) as opposed to central limitations[25].

Sidney and Shepard[26], cite many older individuals as being unsuitable for maximum tests due to health problems. In one study medical screening eliminated 21% of elderly volunteers for a physical training programme involving VO$_2$ Max test[26]. A more pragramatic approach may be to report data at absolute and relative sub maximum energy levels, so that more elderly people can receive cardiovascular fitness assessments with less risk.

The benefits of regular exercise on the heart and CHD risk factors

Research findings have demonstrated than an appropriate level of habitual physical activity, predominantly aerobic in nature (brisk walking, jogging, cycling, swimming) directly affects many of the risk factors associated with CHD[23].

Reductions in body weight, fat, blood pressure, serum lipids and blood sugar have all been reported together with an increased efficiency of the cardiovascular system in response to aerobic endurance activity. A summary of these benefits is presented in table 4. Whether the effects of regular exercise act on the atherosclerotic process directly or indirectly is still a subject for debate[23].

Coronary collaterals have become more predominant in regularly exercised animals following induced non fatal heart attack[27]. Similar evidence still remains inconclusive in humans.

However, greater cardiovascular efficiency through improved myocardial blood flow and subsequent oxygen supply to the heart, together with improved myocardial contractility confer distinct advantages in coping with the demands of everyday living and helping to reduce the risk of heart disease through a more economical and efficient response of the heart to varying intensities of physical activity[10].

Table 4

Increase	Decrease
Coronary collateral vascularization	Serum lipid levels
Vessel size	Triglycerides
Myocardial efficiency	Cholesterol
Efficiency of periphal blood distribution and return	Glucose intolerance
Electron transport capacity	Obesity-adiposity
Fibrinolytic capability	Platelet stickiness
Red blood cell mass and blood volume	Arterial blood pressure
Thyroid function	Heart rate
Growth hormone production	Vulnerability to dysrhythmias
Tolerance to stress	Neurohormonal overreaction
Prudent living habits	'Strain' association with psychic 'stress'
'Joie de vivre'	

From Pollock M..,, Wilmore J..,, Fox S.M.. Health and Fitness Through Physical Activity. New York: John Wiley & Sons 1981;19.

Interestingly, Glenhill[20] refers to those individuals who are genetically endowed with a high VO_2 Max, possibly deriving the associated high stroke volumes and cardiac outputs of their hearts from large ventricular volumes and not from enhanced myocardial contractility. In comparison, he refers to those individuals who exercise vigorously on a regular basis, but with a low VO_2 Max being genetically endowed with smaller ventricular volumes in spite of an enhanced myocardial contractility[20].

More clinical evidence is needed to substantiate these statements, but it raises the question, 'which individual has the lower risk for CHD?' Speculation could suggest that the latter is at lower risk due to a stronger heart and a variety of other exercise related benefits as previously documented (see table 1.4).

Sudden death and exercise

Sudden death (defined as death occurring within 6 hours of the onset of symptoms)[28], receives great attention when associated with physical exercise[28]. Northcote and co-workers reported the circumstances surrounding 60 sudden deaths in the game of squash, concluding that some of these deaths might have been prevented by appropriate counselling of players after prospective medical screening, which they suggest would have detected most of the subjects with overt cardiovascular disease and some of those with sub clinical coronary artery disease.

Cooper and associates refer to the sudden death of Jim Fixx, a famous sportswriter who died while jogging. Such research destroys the 'myth' surrounding 'invulnerability' for those who pursue regular aerobic activities.

However, the risk associated with sensibly prescribed regular exercise is no greater than the expected death rate due to chance, providing the exercise regime is followed sensibly which infers having regular medical examinations and following doctors' advice[28].

Clearly there is less risk involved in predominantly sub maximal, moderate intensity exercise and research clearly indicates that when sudden death does occur and is related to physical activity, underlying symptoms have often been present and ignored to the detriment of the individual concerned[28].

There are risks associated with exercise but most of the victims who suffer collapse and subsequent death could have taken steps to save themselves if they had only been aware of what to do[28]. Previous discussions have emphasised the need to be

a) aware of risk factors, and
b) to act positively towards their reduction.

If such action is coupled with regular 'sensible exercise', then the following quotation from Ashton and Davies becomes very apt.

'Tens of thousands of people die suddenly from cardiac disease each year, and the only relationship exercise has to these deaths is the fact that the victims did not take enough of it.'

The role of exercise in cardiac rehabilitation

Until the mid 1960s many cardiologists prescribed prolonged complete rest following myocardial infarction. This approach was based upon studies of pathologists who established that a 12 week period was needed for total healing of the infarcted tissue and replacement of the infarcted zone by stable scarred tissue[30]. By the end of the 1960s several adverse effects related to prolonged immobilization were identified. These included severe de-conditioning, postural hypotension and venous thrombosis[31]. Subsequently, early mobilization began to replace the traditional longer periods of immobilization, following myocardial infarction[32,33].

Many studies have suggested a relationship between regular physical activity and reduced morbidity and mortality amongst post infarction patients undertaking comprehensive cardiac rehabilitation[34,35,36,37]. Kallio and co-workers[38], in a randomised trial over 3 years found mortality to be significantly less in a group receiving rehabilitation compared with the control group. This intervention was multi-factorial in nature, providing a wide range of psycho-social measures to assist the rehabilitation process.

Other randomised clinical trials investigating the role of exercise and risk factor rehabilitation following infarction have demonstrated a lower mortality in treated patients. Results of these trials have not always been statistically significant. Recognising this problem, Oldridge and co-workers conducted a meta analysis on the combined results of 10 selected randomized clinical trials that included 4,347 patients[39]. A significant reduction of 25% in cardiovascular mortality was reported in patients allocated to a comprehensive cardiac rehabilitation programme when compared with control subjects. Although meta analysis has been subject to some criticism in terms of its statistical accuracy, such reductions offer positive support to the benefits gained by post coronary patients through regular participation in a cardiac rehabilitation programme.

The physiological benefits of regular endurance training upon post myocardial infarction patients are well documented in the literature and summarized by Mathes[40] who identifies adaptations to endurance training even in the seventh decade of life. Froelicher and his associates[41] have demonstrated a decrease in the extent of myocardial ischaemia in patients with angina, with or without myocardial infarction and after cardiac surgery, as a result of regular physical exercise.

Within the United Kingdom research has been conducted on post infarction populations including patients with an initial poor prognosis following early exercise stress testing, demonstrating the effectiveness of regular physical exercise post infarction[42,43,44]. Kavanagh and associates[45] have reported the beneficial effects of training on heart transplant patients. An economic analysis of cardiac rehabilitation has shown a high cost-effectiveness for this form of therapy in non selected MI populations[46]. It should be stressed that exercise alone is not the main determinant in enhancing work resumption both following myocardial infarction or coronary artery bypass surgery. Exercise in combination with attention to psycho-social rehabilitation probably has a key role in improving work resumption and promoting the most effective cardiac rehabilitation[47]. This in turn will help reduce economic losses to the nation resulting from the premature exit of some coronary heart disease sufferers from the labour force[48].

Past studies have claimed that vigorous exercise programmes have positive effects on post infarction patients' mental health. Langosch[49], has questioned the reliability of such studies and suggests it would be more meaningful to integrate exercise into a well designed treatment package. Typically this would contain relevant information, counselling, relaxation training and stress management as a better way of improving patients' psychological and psycho-social functioning.

In summary, Wenger[33] identifies exercise as being helpful in hastening the recovery process after myocardial infarction and cardiac surgery. This process should be started early in the recovery period. Wenger[33] further states that exercise helps to reduce mortality when combined with a multi-factorial programme. The report of the 'British Cardiac Society Working Group on Coronary Disease' (1987) recognises the nature and complexity of the problems associated with the disease in the following quotation.

'Coronary heart disease (CHD) is complex and multi-factorial in origin. Recommendations aimed at its reduction . . . are based on the weight and consistency of evidence, and the likely balance of benefit and harm. They cannot be based on certainty of effectiveness.'[50]

It can now be suggested that the weight and consistency of evidence supporting the effectiveness of cardiac rehabilitation should encourage its implementation on a much wider basis throughout the United Kingdom. In return it is hoped that such measures would help improve the quality of life post infarction and post cardiac surgery together with making positive steps towards the reduction of morbidity and mortality associated with coronary heart disease.

Summary

There would appear to be little doubt that regular habitual physical activity has positive as opposed to detrimental effects on the heart and circulatory system[51].

Increasing care should be taken when administering both exercise assessments and subsequent exercise prescriptions to sedentary middle aged subjects and elderly sections of the population.

Exercise applied to 'high risk' groups (eg cardiac patients) should be carefully monitored and controlled with regular re-evaluations as to the appropriate intensity, frequency and duration of exercise. An increasing need prevails to effectively determine the 'quality control' associated with both physical capacity testing and the administration of subsequent exercise prescriptions. This is particularly necessary with higher risk groups. To offer certified standards which accompany recognised levels of expertise within the field of health related fitness and human performance would be a step in the right direction. Such an approach has already proved effective in other countries[24].

Further prospective as opposed to retrospective epidemiological research may benefit the future reduction of CHD mortality and morbidity statistics. An example of such research undertaken by Salonen and associates demonstrated that both leisure time and occupational physical activity significantly lowered the risk of CHD[52].

References

1   Morris, J.N., Adam, C., Chave, SPW., Sirey, C., Epstein L. (1973) 'Vigorous exercise in leisure time and the incidence of coronary heart disease.' *Lancet*, 334-339.

2   Fixx JF. *The Complete book of running*. (1979) Chatto & Windus, London. 46..

3   Blair S.N.., Kohl H.W., Paffenbarger R.S (Jr)., Clark DG., Cooper K.H., Gibbons L.W. (1989) 'Physical fitness and all-cause mortality,' *Journal of the American Medical Association*, 262, 2395-2401. (3 November).

4   Opie L.H. 'Sudden death and sport.' *Lancet*, (1975) 263-266. (1 February).

5   Thompson P.D. 'Cardiovascular hazards of physical activity.' (1982) Exercise Sports Sci Rev 10, 208-235.

6   Morris J.N., Everitt M.G., Pollard R., Chave S.P.W. (1980) 'Vigorous exercise in leisure time: protection against coronary heart disease.' *Lancet*, 2, 1207-1210.

7   Paffenbarger R.S. (Jr), Hale W.E. (1975) 'Work activity and coronary heart mortality.' *N Eng J Med*, 292, 545-550.

8   Siscovik D.S., Weiss N.S., Fletcher R.H., Lasky T. (1984) 'The incidence of primary cardiac arrest during vigorous exercise.' *New Eng J Med*, 311, 874-877.

9   Bouchard C., Shephard R.J., Stephens T., Sutton J.R., McPherson B.D. (editors). *Exercise fitness and health: a consensus of current knowledge*. Human Kinetics Books, Illinois. (1990).

10 Ashton D., Davies B. *Why exercise?* Blackwell, Oxford. (1986) 60-62.

11 Kavanagh T. (1985) *The healthy heart program*. Key Porter Books, Toronto. 126-127.

12 McArdle W.D., Katch F.I., Katch VL. *Exercise physiology, energy, nutrition and human performance* (3rd edition). Lea & Febiger, Philadelphia. (1981)

13 Paffenbarger R.S. (Jr), Hyde R.T., Wing A.L. (1990) 'Physical activity and physical fitness as determinants of health and longevity.' In *Exercise Fitness and Health* (Bouchard C., Shepard RJ., Stephens T., Sutton JR., McPherson B.D.). Human Kinetics Books, Illinois. 33.

14 Morris J.N., Kagan A., Pattison D.C., Gardner M., Raffle P.A.B. (1966) 'Incidence and prediction of ischaemic heart disease in London busmen.' *Lancet*, (ii), 552-559.

15 Zukel W.J., Lewis W.J., et al. (1959) 'A short term community study of the epidemiology of coronary heart disease.' *Am J Public Health* 49, 1630.

16 Leon A.S., Connett J., Jacobs D.R., Rauramaa R. (1987) 'Leisure time physical activity levels and risk of coronary heart disease and death: the multiple risk factor intervention trial.' *Journal of the American Medical Association* 258, 2388-2395.

17 Scragg R., Stewart A., Jackson R., Beaglehole R. (1987) 'Alcohol and exercise

in myocardial infarction and sudden coronary death in men and women.' *Am J Epidemiol* 126, 77-85.

18 Blair S.N., Kohl H.W., Paffenbarger R.S. (Jr), Clark D.G., Cooper K.H., Gibbons L.W. (1989) 'Physical fitness and all-cause mortality.' *Journal of the American Medical Association* 262, 2395-2401.

19 Pekkanen J., Marti B., Nissinen A., Tuomilehto J. (1987) 'Reduction of premature mortality by high physical activity: A 20 year follow up of middle aged Finnish men.' *Lancet*, (i), 1473-1477.

20 Sutton J.R., McPherson B.D. (1988) 'Assessment of fitness.' In *Exercise, Fitness and Health*. (Glenhill N., Bouchard C., Shephard RJ., Stephens T). Human Kinetics Books, Illinois. 121-126.

21 Chisholm D.M., Collis M.L., Kulak L.L., Davenport W., Gruber N. (1975) 'Physical activity readiness.' *Br Columbia Medical J* 17, 375-378.

22 Shephard R.J., Par, Q., (1988) 'Canada home fitness test and exercise screening alternatives.' *Sports Med* 5, 185-195.

23 Pollock M.L., Wilmore J.H., Fox S.M. (1981) *Health and fitness through physical activity*. John Wiley & Sons, New York. 265-288.

24 American College of Sports Medicine. *Guidelines for exercise testing and prescription* (3rd edition). Lea & Febiger, Philadelphia. (1986) 9-30.

25 Thomas S., Cunningham D., Rechnitzer P., Donner A., Howard J. (1987) 'Protocols and reliability of maximum oxygen uptake in the elderly.' *Can J Sports Sci* 12, 144-151.

26 Sidney K., Shephard R. (1977) 'Maximum and submaximum exercise tests in men and women in the seventh, eight and ninth decades of life.' *J Appl Physiol* 43, 280-287.

27 Eckstein R.W. (1957) 'Effect of exercise and coronary artery narrowing on coronary collateral circulation.' *Circulation Research* 5, 230-235.

28 Cooper K.H. *Running without fear*. Bantam Books, London. (1985) 49.

29 Northcote R.J., Flannigan C., Ballantyne D. (1986) 'Sudden death and vigorous exercise - a study of 60 deaths associated with squash.' *British Heart Journal*. 55, 198-203.

30 Denolin H. 'Physical training in coronary disease.' *European Heart J* (1988) 9, (supplement M) 1.

31 International workshop on physical training and ventricular dysfunction. *European Heart J* (1988) 9, (supplement F) 77-78.

32 Kavanagh T. *The healthy heart program*. Key Porter Books Limited (1985).

33 Wenger N.K. (ed). . (1985) *Exercise and the heart*. In cardiovascular clinics series. FA Davies, Philadelphia. 4-5.

34 Kannel W.B., Gordon T., Sorlie P., et al. (1971) 'Physical activity and coronary vulnerability. The Framingham Study.' *Cardiology Digest* 6, 28.

35 Wilhelmsen L., Sanne H., Elmfeldt D., et al. (1975) 'A controlled trial of physical training after myocardial infarction.' *Prev Med* 4, 491.

36 Shaw L. (1981) 'Effects of a prescribed supervised exercise program on mortality and cardiovascular morbidity in patients after a myocardial

infarction.' *Am J Cardio* 48, 39.

37   Rechnitzer P.A., Cunningham D.A., Andrew G.M., et al. (1983) 'Relation of exercise to the recurrent rate of myocardial infarction in men.' *Cardio* 51, 65.

38   Kallio V., Hamalainen H., Hakkila J., et al. (1979) 'Reduction in sudden deaths by a multifactorial intervention programme after acute myocardial infarction.' *Lancet,* 2, 1091.

39   Oldridge N.B., Guyatt G.H., Fischer M.E., Rimm A.A. Cardiac rehabilitation after myocardial infarction. (1988) 'Combined experience of randomized clinical trials.' *Journal of the American Medical Association* 260, 945-950. (19 August).

40   Mathes P. (1988) 'Indications for contraindications to training in angina pectoris.' *European Heart J* 9, (supplement M) 2-6.

41   Froelicher V., Jensen D., Genter F., et al. (1984) 'A randomized trial of exercise training in patients with coronary heart disease.' *Journal of the American Medical Association* 252, 1291-1294.

42   Carson P., et al. (1984) 'Activity after myocardial infarction.' *BMJ* 288.

43   Dugmore L.D., Tipson RJ., Millward A., Bone M.F. (1986) 'Cardio-respiratory responses to maximal exercise stress testing: a comparison between post myocardial infarction subjects and asymptomatic members of the adult population.' *Sports Sci,* E & FN Spon, London..

44   Dugmore L.D., Bone M.F., Phillips M.H., Tipson R.J. (1990). 'A long term study on the use of exercise training in the rehabilitation of high risk post MI patients.' *Proceedings of World Congress of Cardiology, Manila, Philippines 1990.* C403, 185.

45   Kavanagh T., Yacoub M., Mertens D. (1986) 'Exercise rehabilitation after cardiac transplantation.' *Care of the Critically Ill* 2, 96-98.

46   Perk J., Hedback B. (1988) 'Cost effectiveness of cardiac rehabilitation.' *Proceedings of IV World Congress of Cardiac Rehabilitation, Queensland, Australia, October 1988.*

47   Danchin N., Goespfert PC. 'Exercise training, cardiac rehabilitation and return to work in patients with coronary artery disease.' *European Heart J* (1988) 9, (supplement M) 43-46.

48   *Coronary heart disease - the need for action.* Office of health economics, April 1987.

49   Langosch W. (1988) 'Psychological effects of training in coronary patients: a critical review of the literature.' *European Heart J* 9, (supplement M) 37-42.

50   'Report of British Cardiac Society Working Group on Coronary Disease Prevention.' *British Heart J* February 1987, 188-189.

51   Fentem P.H., Bassey E.J., Turnbull N.B. (1988) *The new case for exercise.* Sports Council and Health Education Authority joint publication. 16-18.

52   Salonen J.T., Slater J.S., Tuomilehto J., Rauramaa R. (1988) 'Leisure time and occupational physical activity: risk of death from ischaemic heart disease.' *Am J Epidemiol* 127, 87-94.

Stress, Personality and Heart Disease   5
Michael Frost, South Birmingham Psychology Service

The idea that stress and personality can cause a heart attack is a popular one and an old one. In the Eighteenth Century, the physician John Hunter declared 'My life is in the hands of any rascal who chooses to annoy or tease me'. He proved his point by suddenly dying after a heated discussion at a meeting of the Board of Governors of St. George's Hospital. Acute emotional distress can produce fatal ventricular arrythmias[1] and the predisposition is increased by high levels of catecholamines[2] which are secreted in response to periods of chronic stress[3]. Was it chronic stress that set up Dr. Hunter and acute stress that finally carried him off or was it his volatile personality? Osler, as long ago as 1910, implicates both. 'The high pressure at which men live, and the habit of working the machine to its maximum capacity are responsible for arterial degeneration, rather than excesses in eating and drinking.' He describes the coronary patient as 'not the delicate, neurotic person . . . but the robust, the vigorous in mind and body, the keen and ambitious man, the indicator of whose engine is always at "full speed ahead" '.[4]

The cardiologists, Friedman and Rosenman[5] also thought that the pace of life was implicated in coronary heart disease (CHD). They found that as the 15th April approached, tax inspectors displayed increased levels of serum cholesterol and accelerated coagulation. They went on to study other professional groups who were habitually time pressured and noticed that a particular pattern of behaviours frequently occured in middle aged men with CHD. They were impatient, irritable, quick to anger, and disposed towards ambition, competition, and aggression. For no particular reason they called it the Type A Behaviour Pattern (TABP) and defined it as:

'A characteristic action-emotion complex which is exhibited by those individuals who are engaged in a relatively chronic struggle to obtain an unlimited number of poorly defined things from their environment in the shortest period of time and if necessary against the opposing efforts of other persons or things in the same environment.'[6]

With the emphasis on behaviour they developed an assessment technique based on a structured interview that is designed to be as irritating as possible. It is held at an awkward time, the person is kept waiting and the interviewer appears to be incompetent. The Type A response is to become irritable and to hurry the interview along by butting in and finishing the interviewer's sentences in a loud, clipped voice. The Type A individuals also describe frustrating incidents with a lot of emotional expression as though they are reliving them in the here and now. The interview is scored more on the observation of this pattern of behaviour (75%) than on the answers to questions (25%)[7]. The Type B individual shows none of these behaviours and is more easy going, relaxed and friendly.

Whilst the Structured Interview is considered to be the gold standard for the assessment of the TABP, it is rather too difficult to adminster to be of general use. The Jenkins Activity Survey[8], a self report, multiple choice questionnaire is a more convenient and a psychometrically acceptable alternative for screening purposes.[9]

Between 1975 and 1981, three major prospective studies showed that the TABP doubles the risk of CHD in a healthy population. (For a review, see Haynes and Matthews.[10]) In 1981 a panel of experts declared that the TABP, whether assessed by the Structured Interview or the Jenkins Activity Survey, was an independent risk factor of the same degree of magnitude as smoking, blood pressure and serum cholesterol[11].

Studies since then have produced more equivocal results. Cross sectional studies and smaller prospective studies of high risk individuals undergoing angiography have failed to establish a link between the TABP and CHD. Several possible reasons have been proffered for this anomaly, that beta blockers suppress the Type A response, that in older populations the Type As who were at risk are dead already, and that the way that the TABP was measured was suspect. However, the complexity of the stress pathway makes it unlikely that any single variable will have an independent effect. Proclaiming the TABP as an independent risk factor for CHD has led to a one factor high risk paradigm which is not sustainable.

In their 1978 study of civil servants Marmot and his colleagues[12] found that the TABP was more common in people in the higher grades and CHD was more common in those in the lower grades. On present evidence the TABP can only be considered an independent risk factor for white, middle class, white collar workers. Yet this group has the best chance of surviving a heart attack and the smallest risk of sudden death. There is an increased threefold risk of CHD for people on low incomes who have had less than eight years education. In the individualistic and competitive Western commercial environment, aspects of the TABP confer an advantage. The faster growing the company, the more Type A personnel one finds. In sharp contrast, the Japanese business culture replaces individual competition with corporate co-operation and social network support. Not only is there a very low incidence of the TABP amongst the high flyers, there is also very little CHD in the total population.

The focus of research needs to address the question of who will develop CHD and under what circumstances? There are three possibilities. The first is that some people are more prone than others. The second is that certain circumstances put everybody at risk. Thirdly, it is possible that certain people under certain conditions are more at risk than others. The last is the interactional viewpoint that takes into account features of the social environment and the individual differences that can moderate the amount of strain that is experienced. It can be represented schematically as:

stressors $\rightleftharpoons$ **moderators** $\longrightarrow$ **symptoms of strain**

Glass[13] defined the TABP as 'a style of overt response to certain forms of stressful situation.' This definition assumes that the TABP is a symptom of strain and places the Type A concept within the framework of the Stress Pathway, which greatly increases its heuristic value. The situations that evoke the TABP are moderately competitive, uncontrollable and require endurance. It is also evoked in response to having little to do, undertaking slow and careful work, and tasks that require a broad focus of attention. Thus one would expect the Type A person to feel relaxed and happy when he has autonomy, is busy and feels in control. Chesney and her colleagues[14] found that Type A workers in the aerospace industry had reduced levels of blood pressure when given autonomy. The situation was reversed for their Type B colleagues who responded with increased blood pressure when faced with the prospect of greater autonomy. On the other hand, relaxed Type B individuals coped better when a University computer shut down for 23 days than time pressured Type A's.[15] Type A people are less likely to use helpful coping strategies when there is a work crisis and tend to respond with helplessness and resentment[16]. These findings argue the benefit of a good person-environment fit.

Although the behavioural characteristics that make up the TABP intuitively hang together it is by no means certain that they reflect a single dimension of personality. Factor analysis of the Jenkins Activity Survey reveals three different dimensions: hard driving competitiveness, job involvement which includes the tendency to work long hours and to accept tasks that are beyond one's personal capacity, and thirdly, speed and impatience. When individuals assessed as Type A by the Structured Interview, are placed in a competitive situation and they feel that it is important to win; they respond with a cardiovascular hyper-reactivity which is not seen in the Jenkins assessed Type A individuals. It is thought that this is because the Jenkins Activity Survey fails to sample anger and hostility, which are emerging as the most significant personality mediators between environmental stressors and the coronary prone symptoms of strain.

In 1983 Barefoot, Dahlstrom and Williams[17] followed up 255 physicians who had completed the Cooke and Medley Hostility Scale[18] when they were medical students some twenty five years previously. They found that those who scored above the median had a six fold increased incidence of coronary heart disease and early death than those who scored below it. Barefoot and colleagues[19] found a similar result in a twenty-five year follow up of law students. The frequency of angina attacks has been found to be related to the extent of self reported anger[20].

By contrast, Kobasa[21] has defined a personality style that protects people from the effects of life event stress. She called it 'Hardiness'. Hardy people are committed to self development, the family, friends, and to work. They believe that they have the ability to influence the important things that happen in life and see change as a challenge and an opportunity for new experiences. The concept of Hardiness is proving to be an important moderator in the experience of stress and the development of illness. It has been demonstrated that Type A executives who are low in Hardiness tend towards higher illness scores than other executives[22]. On the other hand, Nowack[23] showed that Hardy Type A's experience less distress from daily hassles than their less Hardy Type B counterparts.

A commitment to intimacy and personal relationships is an important component of Hardiness which has also been found to protect people from CHD. For example, in an angiographic study Blumenthal et al[24] showed that although the TABP was associated with the number of vessels with 75% or more occlusion, those subjects that had close family relationships and supportive friends were less likely to have atherosclerosis. In Gothenburg, two cohorts of 50 year old men were followed for CHD and it was found that those who participated in activities outside the home had less CHD and lower mortality from all causes than the less socially active men[25]. It is not surprising that high Hostility scores which represent a predisposition towards a cynical mistrust of human nature, are associated with low levels of Hardiness and poor social relationships[26].

Stress is thought to contribute to the development of CHD through the neuroendocrine pathways. The first is the pituitary-adrenocortical (P-AC) system which is aroused when the individual perceives circumstances as being uncertain and uncontrollable. The second is the sympathetic adrenal-medullary (S-AM) axis which is involved in situations that require vigilance and close attention, the fight-flight pattern. Noradrenaline is released when the situation demands vigorous action; and norepinephrine and epinephrine when the situation creates anxiety and inhibits action. Nixon[27] summarises the situation concisely. Effort with distress is associated with increased S-AM and P-AC activity. Distress without effort is accompanied by high P-AC activity and high levels of cortisol. The consequences for the cardiovascular system are an increase in systolic and diastolic blood pressure, increased tissue demands for oxygen, increased heart rate and stroke volume, increased serum uric acid, cholesterol and free fatty acids, plasma glucose, platelet adhesiveness and blood viscosity. It is thought that this combination of response produces arterial damage, predisposes to thrombosis and can have an influence on fatal cardiac arrhythmias.

By contrast, effort without distress results in an increase in testosterone and suppression of P-AC activity. Social support and intimacy is associated with lower levels of serum cholesterol, uric acid, heart rate, and blood pressure.

The British Regional Heart Study found that 25% of the male population had some evidence of CHD[28]. Unfortunately, in a quarter of all cases the only indication of CHD is sudden death. This raises the issue of how stress may exert an effect upon an already compromised myocardium. The general public have no doubt that life events are the major cause of death from a heart attack. Indeed, the extensive work of Holmes and Rahe clearly demonstrates that life changes that place a demand for adaptation beyond the capacity of the individual to cope predict illness in general. Theorell and Rahe[29] found that patients with a first myocardial infarction and no previous clinical symptoms of CHD had experienced twice as many life changes in the previous six months than in the chronologically identical six month periods one and two years earlier. Furthermore, patients who die have experienced a significantly greater number of life changes than those who survive. (See Rahe[30] for a review which includes the Recent Life Changes Questionnaire as an appendix.) Bereavement has the greatest impact. The mortality rate from CHD for the widowed in the year following bereavement is ten times greater than for a matched control[31]. Retirement, which may bring a loss of income, status and purpose in life, increases the risk of coronary mortality by 80%[32].

In the year prior to a heart attack or sudden death a majority of patients will have consulted their general practitioner complaining of tiredness and weakness. They also say that they feel depressed because of the struggle of trying complete tasks that once came easily to them[31]. Bruhn et al[32] call this combination of depression and joyless striving the Sisyphus Pattern after the King of Corinth who was condemned ceaselessly to push a heavy stone up a hill only for it to roll back under its own weight.

The transition from healthy functioning, normal tiredness, and refreshing sleep to the decline into vital exhaustion is well illustrated by Nixon's Human Function Curve[33] (Figure 1). On the up slope, increased arousal results in increased performance and a feeling of healthy tiredness. On the down slope, arousal leads only to exhaustion until at point P, a slight increase is all that is required to bring about a breakdown. The dotted line emphasises how the patient's struggle to close the gap between that which he is capable of and that which he believes he should or needs to achieve brings about his own deterioration.

The propensity to live in a state of exhaustion is a feature of the TABP. For example, on a laboratory treadmill task, Type A's do the same amount of work

Figure 1

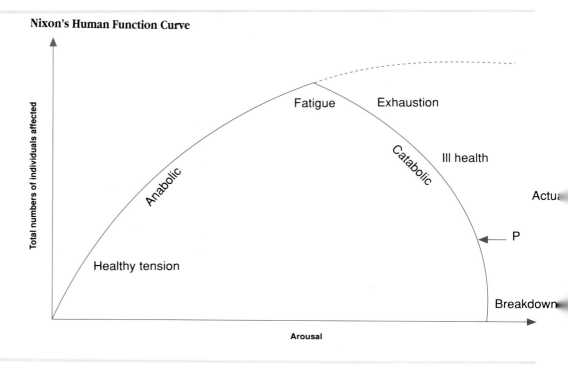

Nixon's Human Function Curve

Total numbers of individuals affected

Anabolic

Fatigue

Exhaustion

Catabolic

Ill health

Actua

Healthy tension

P

Breakdown

Arousal

as Type B's but will not admit to being as tired[34]. Unfortunately, many people who are faced with crushing environmental problems have no option but to keep on going.

It has been estimated that some 26% of men and 21% of women who die of a myocardial infarction do so before they reach hospital[37]. A crucial factor is the time that elapses between experiencing symptoms and seeking help[38]. This is often influenced by the patient defensively denying the severity of the chest pain and attempting to rationalise it as a symptom of something more benign than a heart attack[39].

The main points of this chapter are summarised in the following stress pathway diagram (Figure 2).

Stressor Situations	Moderating Factors	Symptoms of Strain	Coronary Outcome

	Psychosocial	*Physiological*	
Competitive	Education	↑ Catecholamines	CHD
Uncontrollable	Income	↑ Serum Cholestrol	Coronary
Require Endurance	Social Class	↑ Coagulation time	arrythmia
Time pressured	Social Support	↑ Blood pressure	Vital
Slow and careful work	Intimacy	↑ Heart rate	exhaustion
Overburdening		↑ Platelet adhesion	Sudden death
	Personality		
Lack of Autonomy	1) Type A personality	*Emotional*	
Uncertainty	a) Hard driving	Helplessness	
	competitiveness	Resentment	
	b) Job involvement	Anger	
	c) Speed and impatience	Depression	
	d) Hostility		
	2) Hardiness		
	a) Commitment		
	b) Control		
Life Change Events	c) Challenge	*Behavioural*	
Bereavement		TABP	
Retirement	3) Repressed Anger	Tiredness	
		Weakness	
	4) Denial		

65

References

1 Lown B., DeSilva R.A., Reich P. & Murawski B.J. (1980) 'Psychophysiologic factors in sudden cardiac death.' *American Journal of Psychiatry.* 137, 1325-1335.

2 Verrier R.L., DeSilva R.A. & Lown V. (1983) 'Psychological factors in cardiac arrythmias and sudden death.' In Krantz D.S. & Singer J.E. (eds) *Handbook of Psychology and Health.*

3 Frankaenhaeuser M. (1979) 'Psychoneuroendocrine approaches to the study of emotion as related to stress and coping.' In Rowe, H.E. and Dienstbier, R.A. (eds) *Nebraska Symposium on Motivation.* University of Nebraska Press, Lincoln.

4 Osler W. (1910) 'The Lumleian Lectures on angina pectoris.' *Lancet,* 1, 839-844.

5 Friedman M., & Rosenman R. (1959) 'Association of specific overt behavior pattern with blood and cardiovascular findings.' *Journal of the American Association.* 169, 1286-1296.

6 Friedman, M. and Rosenman, R.H. (1974) *Type A Behaviour and your Heart,* Knopf, New York.

7 Rosenman R.H. (1978) 'The interview method of assessment of the coronary prone behaviour pattern.' In Dembroski, T.M., Weiss, S.M., Shields, J.L., Haynes, S.G. and Feinlieb, M. (eds) *Coronary-Prone Behaviour.* Springer-Verlag, New York.

8 *The Jenkins Activity Survey.* The Psychological Corporation Ltd. Harcourt Brace Janovich Publishers, Foots Cray High Street, Sidcup, Kent.

9 Powell L.H. (1987) 'Issues in the measurement of the TABP.' In Kasl S.V., & Cooper C.L. *Stress and Health: Issues in Research Methodology.* Wiley, Chichester.

10 Haynes S.G. and Matthews K.A. (1988) 'The association of Type A behaviour with cardiovascular disease - update and critical review.' In Houston, B.K. and Snyder, C.R. (eds) *Type A Behaviour: Research, Theory and Intervention.* Wiley, New York.

11 Review Panel (1981) 'Coronary prone behaviour and coronary heart disease: A critical review.' *Circulation,* 63, 6, 1199-1215.

12 Marmot M.G., Rose G., Shipley M., and Hamilton P.J.S. (1978) 'Employment grade and coronary heart disease in British civil servants.' *Journal of Epidemiology and Community Health,* 32, 244-249.

13 Glass D.C. (1977) *Behaviour Patterns, Stress and Coronary Disease,* Lawrence Erlbaum Assoc. New Jersey.

14 Chesney M.A., Sevelius G., Black G.W., Ward M.M., Swan G.E., & Rosenman R.H. (1981) 'Work environment, Type A behavior, and coronary heart disease risk factors.' *Journal of Occupational Medicine,* 23, 8, 551-555.

15   Kaplan R.D. and Jones K.W. (1975) 'Effects of workload, role ambiguity and type A personality on anxiety, depression and heart rate.' *Journal of Applied Psychology*, 60, 713-719.

16   Newton T.J. and Keenan A. 'Coping with work related stress.' *Human Relations*, 38(2), 107-126.

17   Barefoot J.C., Dahlstrom W.G. and Williams R.B. (1983). 'Hostility, CHD incidence and total mortality: A twenty-five year follow up study of 255 physicians.' *Psychosomatic Medicine*, 45, 59-63.

18   Cook W. & Medley D. (1954) 'Proposed hostility and pharisaic-virtue scales for the MMPI.' *Journal of Applied Psychology*, 238, 414-418.

19   Barefoot J.C., Williams R.B., Dahlstrom W.G., and Dodge K.A. (1987) 'Predicting mortality from scores on the Cook-Medley Scale: A follow up study of 118 lawyers.' *Paper presented at the Annual Meeting of the American Psychosomatic Society.* Philadelphia.

20   Smith T.W., Follick M.J. and Korr K.S. (1984) 'Anger, neuroticism, Type A behaviour and the experience of angina.' *British Journal of Medical Psychology*, 57, 249-252.

21   Kobasa S.C. (1979) 'Stressful life events, personality and health: an enquiry into hardiness.' *Journal of Personality and Social Psychology*, 37, 1-11.

22   Kobasa S.C., Maddi S.R., and Zola M.A. (1983) 'Type A and hardiness.' *Journal of Behavioural Medicine*, 6, 1, 41-51.

23   Nowack, K.M. (1986) 'Type A, hardiness and psychological distress.' *Journal of Behavioural Medicine.* 9, 6, 537-548.

24   Blumenthal J.A., Burg M.M., Barefoot J., Williams R.B., Haney T., and Zimet G. (1987) 'Social Support, Type A behaviour, and coronary artery disease.' *Psychosomatic Medicine*, 49, 331-340.

25   Welin et al (1985) 'Prospective study of social influences on mortality.' *Lancet*, (i), 915-918.

26   Smith, T.W. and Frohm K.D. (1985) 'What's so unhealthy about hostility? Construct validity and psychosocial correlates of the Cook and Medley Ho Scale.' *Health Psychology.* 4, 503-520.

27   Nixon P.G.F. (1989) 'Human Functions and the Heart.' In Seedhouse D. and Cribb A. (eds) *Changing Ideas in Health Care.* John Wiley and Sons, London.

28   Shaper A.G., Cook D.G., Walker M., Macfarlane P.W. (1984) 'Prevalence of Ischaemic heart disease in middle aged British men.' *British Heart Journal*, 51, 606-11.

29   Theorell T., and Rahe R.H. (1971) Psychosocial factors and myocardial infarction, I. An inpatient study in Sweden. *Journal of Psychosomatic Research*, 15, 25-32.

30   Rahe R.H. (1987) 'Recent life changes, emotions, and behaviours in coronary heart disease.' In Baum, A. and Singer, J.E. (eds) *Handbook of Psychology and Health: Volume V: Stress.* Lawrence Erlbaum Assoc. New Jersey.

31 Rees W.D. and Lutkins S.G. (1967) 'Mortality of bereavement.' *British Medical Journal*, 4, 13.

32 Casscells S.W., Hennekens C.H., Evans D., Rosner B., DeSilva R.A., Lown B., Davies J.E., Jesse M.J. (1980) 'Retirement and coronary mortality.' *Lancet*, 2, 1288.

33 Appels A. (1983) "The year before myocardial infarction.' In Dembroski, T.M., Schmidt, T.H. & Blumchen, G. *Biobehavioural Bases of Coronary Heart Disease*. Karger, Basel.

34 Bruhn J.G., Paredes A., Adsett C.A., Wolf S. (1974) 'Psychological Predictors of sudden death in myocardial infarction.' *Journal of Psychosomatic Research*, 18, 187.

35 Nixon P.G.F. (1976) 'The Human Function Curve.' *The Practitioner*, 217, 765-769 and 935-944.

36 Carver, C.S., Coleman, A.E., and Glass, D.C. (1976) 'The coronary prone behaviour pattern and suppression of fatigue on a treadmill test.' *Journal of Personality and Social Psychology*, 33, 460-466.

37 Pole D.J., McCall M.G., Reader R., and Woodings T. (1977) 'Incidence and mortality of acute myocardial infarction in Perth, Western Australia.' *Journal of Chronic Diseases*, 30, 19-27.

38 Surwit R.S., Williams R.B., & Shapiro D. (1982) *Behavioral Approaches to Cardiovascular Disease*. Academic Press, New York.

39 Olin H.S. and Hackett T.P. (1964) 'The denial of chest pain in 32 patients with acute myocardial infarction.' *Journal of the American Medical Association*, 190, 11, 103-107.

Producing Behavioural Change

Michael Frost, South Birmingham Psychology Service

6

In the last decade, professionals concerned with helping people change have become increasingly eclectic and pragmatic in their approach[1]. With over two hundred theories to choose from, each with its own techniques, choosing the best is not an easy task. Although there is very little evidence to suggest which approach is superior, there are a few common elements that recur with sufficient regularity to merit consideration as guiding principles.

Goldfried[2] suggests that the two most important principles for effecting change are promoting corrective action and providing direct feedback; in other words, using strategies that persuade people to behave in a different way and which give immediately verifiable results. Since there is little point in changing behaviour for its own sake, this presupposes that one is clear about what one is trying to achieve. At its simplest, the process of behaviour change can be expressed as: What did you want? What did you do? and What did you get? The hard part is persuading people to do something different when what they get is not the same as what they want, often for fear that they will get something worse[3].

In an excellent book Peake, Borduin and Archer[4] examine five different schools of psychotherapy in an attempt to discover what therapists do rather than what they say they do. They postulate a 'deep structure' which describes the process of brief therapy regardless of theoretical orientation. Their summary of the common elements of cognitive-behavioural psychotherapies provides a very useful framework for understanding the process of behaviour change. They divide the tasks up into three periods; the beginning, middle and end of therapy.

Beginning

1. Exploring the problem

a)   Make a clear and accurate asssessment of current problems.
b)   Estimate the behaviour and thoughts that maintain the problem.

2. Developing a therapeutic relationship

a)   Create a feeling of hope.
b)   Provide the patient with plenty of opportunity to express his or her feelings.
c)   Communicate an understanding of the patient's need.
d)   Facilitate some immediate improvement.

3. Setting goals

a)   Delineate clear and modest goals.
b)   Develop a contract concerning the parameters of therapy.

Middle

a)   Use directive, goal oriented and empirically based interventions that can be implemented quickly.
b)   Emphasise informational and educational strategies that gradually increase the patient's confidence in his abilities.
c)   If necessary, implement additional strategies.
d)   Attend to relationship and process issues that facilitiate the achievement of goals.
e)   Continuously evaluate progress using scientific methods.

End

a)   Increase the emphasis on generalised skills.
b)   Focus on preventing relapse.
c)   End therapy on a positive note.
d)   Terminate as specified in the therapeutic contract.
e)   Provide follow-ups to assess progress when appropriate.

Exploring the Problem

If one is to develop a lifestyle that protects from coronary heart disease it is necessary to choose healthy rather than unhealthy behaviours. The healthy choice is probably going to be the more unpleasant of the two as it is likely that the alternative has been chosen at sometime in the past as a solution to a difficulty. Watzlawick and his colleagues[5] define a 'difficulty' as an undesirable state of affairs which can either be solved by common sense or can not be solved at all. Feeling awful after a rejection is a difficulty for which, in the short term at least, there is no solution. Learning how to cope with boredom is a matter of common sense. Choosing to smoke as a way of stimulating oneself when bored, or as a means of coping in an emotional crisis, is a solution that very soon becomes a problem. Choosing between the original difficulty and a solution that damages one's health is a choice between a rock and a hard place. This is a conflict that more often than not results in putting off a decision until another, more suitable day. One might have to wait until the summer holidays for a time of emotional tranquility in a stimulating environment but then who can be expected to give up cigarettes when they are duty free?

Making the healthy choice can also be difficult when it conflicts with a major life decision. These are often based upon maladaptive thoughts[6]. For instance the belief that one cannot cope with emotional pain can lead to the decision never to allow oneself to experience it, if it can be avoided. Food and drink can then become important for their comforting and anaesthetic qualities. On the other hand, Orbach[7] describes how conflict can also exist in the choice of the seemingly desirable alternative. Being slim can be associated with selfishness, competitiveness, coldness, having no excuse for the difficulties one faces in life nor means of expressing one's neediness.

Greenwald[8] suggests the following rules for renegotiating an original decision:

1   State clearly what you want to change but keep putting off. Recognise that there is a conflict.
2   Examine the past or original decision that helped to create this conflict.
3   Look at the context of the original decision that helped to create this conflict.
4   What are the alternatives to the original decision? What can be done instead of what you are doing habitually?
5   Choose a new alternative and put it into practice. Resolve the current conflict by using the new alternative.
6   The decision is not made once and for all but on every occasion that the opportunity arises; every invitation to play sport, each offer of a cigarette, every shop window full of cream cakes invites a decision. Reward yourself

every time that you make a decision based on the new alternative and follow it through.

Not all behaviour still serves a function. Smoking may have developed in response to a desire for peer group acceptance. It may now be the only behaviour that hinders it, but it has developed into a habit reinforced by nicotine addiction that the patient just can not break[9].

Developing a therapeutic relationship

The major task in the beginning phase is to increase the patient's confidence in his ability to change. When people believe that they will fail, they do[10]. The relationship between the health care professional and the patient is an important ingredient in creating hope that change is possible and ensuring compliance with requests for action that can bring it about. Goldstein[11] describes the ideal relationship as one of mutual liking, respect and trust. It also helps if the practitioner is seen as an expert and has the ability to communicate knowledge and expertise. There are four essential relationship qualities of the practitioner that have become almost universally accepted. These are accurate empathy, warmth, genuineness and a non judgemental acceptance of the patient[12]. These are qualities that reflect certain skills and attitudes towards the patient such as:

• Attending

Be prepared for the consultation, look through the notes in advance and deal with any other business to avoid interruptions. During the session, be there for the patient, looking at him rather than the clock, the queue in the waiting room or the view from the window. Let him know by your body posture that you are fully paying attention.

• Active Listening

Listen to both verbal and non-verbal statements and continuously assess what the core of the message might be.

• Communicating Understanding

One must not only strive to understand what the patient is saying but also to communicate that understanding. One can do this by periodically paraphrasing and summarising what the patient has said and by reflecting the emotional content of his speech, facial gesture and bodily posture.

• Respect

The patient should be valued as a person acknowledging that he has strengths and skills and a position beyond the helping relationship. Take time to introduce oneself and to learn something about the patient's work and family life. Avoid patronising by respecting his views, his values and particularly his right to confidentiality by refraining from gossip.

For further reading in the interpersonal aspects of behaviour change, the texts by Egan[13], Ley[14] and Meichenbaum and Turk[15] are recommended.

Setting Goals

Negotiate goals with the patient that are personal, specific and attainable. When goals are vague or overambitious, it is difficult to work out strategies to accomplish them and impossible to know when they have been achieved. For instance: 'I want to be fit' could mean 'I want to be able to climb the stairs without getting out of breath' or 'I want to come first in the London Marathon'.

It is essential that the patient believes that the goal is attainable. In some circumstances, it may be necessary to choose a goal that is the very minimum change that can show that change is possible. In the same vein, choose goals that can be achieved sooner rather than later as this enhances the patient's belief that he can succeed[16]. This may mean focusing on immediate behaviours that will bring about a larger, more distant goal. If the goal is to lose a stone in weight, a better target would be what the person eats and when, rather than losing pounds. It is of less importance if the goal is seen as difficult, as a failure can be attributed to lack of effort rather than lack of ability. However, the effort required should be unambiguously stated. It is of no use recommending someone to try their hardest, or to just do their best. 'Trying' licenses 'Failing' as every smoker who says 'I'm trying to give up' as he lights up is witness. Rewards should accrue to success and not to effort.

Once goals have been agreed one can then negotiate strategies to bring them about. Join with the patient in thinking up as many alternatives as possible. At this stage they do not have to be practical; so avoid criticism and accept anything - the wilder the better. It is quantity, not quality that matters. It is easier to tone down a suggestion than it is to work one up. The more ideas one has, the more choices one has, and the greater the chance that there will be a good one. Leapfrog each other by suggesting ideas by association and how an existing idea might be improved by adding on to it (see [17]).

The chances of a strategy working will be much enhanced if it is framed within the basic principles that increase and decrease the frequency of a behaviour pattern occuring.

- The likelihood of behaviour being repeated is increased if it is rewarded. When behaviour results in a pleasant outcome it is said to be positively reinforced. It is negatively reinforced when it brings an undesirable state of affairs to an end.

Many unhealthy behaviours are immediately gratifying and intrinsically pleasurable. By contrast, developing a healthy lifestyle involves effort, deprivation and discomfort, which is undoubtedly an unpleasant state of affairs that can be quickly brought to an end by reverting to old habits. Paradoxically, the very attempt to change provides yet another opportunity to reinforce unhealthy behaviour. Against these odds, it requires a great deal of ingenuity to think up effective rewards for the healthy alternative.

One can begin with listing the reasons for wanting to change and the benefits that are expected as a result. One way of doing this is to ask the patient to imagine that he has achieved his goal and is at a social event; to imagine it in as much detail as possible and then to describe where he is, who he is with, what is happening, what is being said and how he is feeling. For example, a patient who was a smoker, took no exercise and was easily winded imagined that he was playing a flute, with his daughter, on the lawn of a country house during a summer school. This rather surprised him as he did not own a flute and neither could he play. Nevertheless, he decided to bring this very pleasant image to mind whenever he felt the craving for a cigarette. He would also become aware of fresh cool air as it entered his nostrils and would practise diaphragmatic breathing. As soon as he lit up the scene would fade from his mind to be replaced by an awareness of the poisons that he was sucking into his lungs. This was not always effective and a number of other rewards were devised; one of which was a flute fund. He placed a silver coin into it every time that he performed one of his target behaviours. He did this for a while and then decided that he wanted to buy an instrument straight away. It was a beautiful object which he felt should never be contaminated with foul smoky breath. When it was feasible, such as when he used to have his early morning smoke, he practised instead. If he did smoke he would not allow himself to play again until at least three hours later. This is an example of response cost, more of which later. He received much encouragement from his daughter who looked forward to their sessions together and was openly disappointed but understanding and co-operative on the occasions when they did not happen.

This case illustrates a number of points.

- Rewards are personal.
- Rewards in the future must be translated into rewards in the present. The

reward should be as immediate as possible. If it is delayed then some symbol of the reward can be substituted for it and cashed in later.

- There should be a variety of rewards, so that if the patient becomes satiated or bored with one of them, another can be substituted.
- Rewards can be covert, such as self praise or a pleasant thought, as well as overt.
- A highly valued or often performed behaviour can be used as a reward.
- Eliciting pleasurable responses from others can be rewarding.

In the early stages the behaviour needs to be reinforced frequently. Once it has become more firmly established, the external rewards can slowly be faded out. The emphasis on self praise and other covert rewards is maintained until the long term benefits begin to be experienced and the behaviour becomes more intrinsically satisfying.

Negative reinforcement is harder to arrange because it requires the creation of an unpleasant state of affairs in order to remove it. Nevertheless, it can be done. Penick and colleagues[18] instructed obese patients to place the equivalent weight of pork fat in their fridges to that which they wished to lose by dieting. They were allowed to remove it contingent upon weight loss. Occasionally, a negative reinforcer may already exist. For instance, children who receive health education at school are often upset when their parents smoke. In this instance it is impossible to distinguish between a negative reinforcer for not smoking and punishment for doing so.

- Punishment, defined as an unpleasant consequence of behaviour, will reduce the likelihood of that behaviour being repeated. A behaviour will also be punished if it brings a pleasant state of affairs to an end.

Although punishment procedures will suppress behaviour in the short term, they tend to contribute to relapse because the change is attributed to the punishment rather than to one's own efforts. This can be mitigated if the punishment is self administered. For example, an extremely overweight publican learned from screening that he was at high risk for coronary heart disease. He imagined his wife and children finding him dead in the beer cellar. He visualised their grief and the hardship that they would have to bear. After dietary advice, he would bring this scene to mind whenever he was tempted into unhealthy eating or drinking. If he chose healthy foods he would imagine himself in shorts on a warm beach playing football with his son.

- Whenever the frequency of a behaviour is reduced then the behaviour that replaces it must be highly rewarded.

Another form of punishment, known as Response Cost, involves forfeiting something of value, usually cash or some pleasant activity. This commonly occurs in everyday life; a ban for drink driving, a fine for the late return of library books, a suspension for arguing with the referee. Fines on a deposit-refund basis have been used successfully for a variety of problems including both weight loss and smoking[19]. The response cost can also be devised so that it is more appropriate to the behaviour. For example caloric intake above an agreed limit must be balanced by an equivalent amount of exercise. A bar of chocolate, say, will cost a half hour workout.

Choosing from amongst the range of possible solutions that have been generated and negotiating rewards for behaviours that will lead to achievement of stated goals is the beginning of a therapeutic contract. At its simplest, the patient and the practitioner agree who does what, when and why. The contract can be, but need not be formal, as it is the process of negotiation and putting the patient in control of the process of behaviour change that is facilitative. However, making it public will increase the likelihood of compliance. See Kirschenbaum and Flannery[20] for a fuller discussion.

Middle Period

If the work in the beginning period has been done well enough the patient will believe that the tactics, strategies and techniques that have been negotiated have at least a fair chance of bringing about the desired change in behaviour. The problem now is to enhance the belief that he has the ability to carry it through[21]. The most reliable way of achieving this is to do something and to succeed. Early successes will then minimise the impact if a failure occurs later on. This is especially the case if failing can be attributed to special circumstances, unusual situational demands, physical debility or simply lack of effort. It is unwise to rely upon the vagaries of memory when it comes to assessing how well one is doing. Keeping good records not only helps in charting progress; monitoring behaviour is also one of the easiest ways of changing it[22].

The behaviour to be monitored should be positive and provide a strategic advantage. It is better to record the time between the urge to light up and striking a match than merely to record the number of cigarettes smoked. Recording the former facilitates a delay and provides an opportunity for success whilst the latter merely accentuates a failure. It also encourages monitoring whilst the behaviour occurs rather than making a guess at the end of the day. Not only are records more accurate but it has the advantage that monitoring becomes a distractor task. It also provides instant feedback and an immediate reward.

As certain cues are more likely to elicit a response than others, it is useful to record the antecedents as well as the consequences of a behaviour. This is a form of behavioural analysis that is known as ABC which is shown below with a single incident illustrating the craving for a cigarette.

Antecedent	Behaviour	Consequence
7.30 Smell of coffee from the kitchen	Strong craving for a cigarette. Had lemon tea instead of usual cup of coffee and managed to resist urge to smoke	Felt pleased with myself and my wife commented on how nice it was to kiss a non-smoker

Some cues such as mid-morning coffee and the public house place temptation in the path of the smoker which may be hard to resist. Similarly, it would require superhuman willpower to lose weight if one lunches regularly in a Viennese patisserie. Strategies should be developed to help the patient to avoid and resist temptation. Essentially, these involve restricting opportunity and making accessibility more difficult. One can restrict the opportunity to smoke by using the no smoking areas in public places and by engaging in incompatible activities such as swimming. Friends and relatives can help by creating no smoking areas in the home. The opportunity for snacks can be reduced by only having food in the house that requires cooking. Accessibility can be made more difficult by asking a friend to keep the cigarette packet. In one extreme instance a patient cut down on her drinking by leaving her sherry with a neighbour and suffering the embarrassment of having to ring the doorbell, glass in hand. A lock can be put on the fridge and the pantry and the key left with a relative to prevent midnight feasts.

Not everybody that the patient knows will be supportive of his bid to change. Indeed, some may even attempt to sabotage it, particularly if the unhealthy behaviour is part of the group culture. In the early days, it may be possible to avoid them, but one has eventually to learn how to say no. This may require assertiveness training to learn the necessary skills to refuse gracefully and forcefully and to be able to cope with cajolement[23]. Relaxation training, stress innoculation and coping skills can also contribute towards developing new techniques for dealing with life's daily hassles which put one at risk for unhealthy coping styles[24].

Preventing Relapse

The best time to have a relapse is during the period of the contract. Indeed, one can insist upon it[25]. If the patient lapses, then he is following instructions and so retains his sense of self efficacy. If he fails to relapse then he has cracked it already.

Progress in behaviour change is rarely consistent. Not only are lapses to be expected, they also provide an ideal opportunity to examine the circumstances that surround them and to devise different ways of solving the problem.

If patients are prepared for the occasional failure, it is less likely that they will generalise from the specific and turn it into a catastrophe. If the patient should fall prey to self defeating thoughts:

1   Ask him to describe the event that led up to failure in as much detail as possible.

2   Find out what are the self defeating ideas

3   Discuss what evidence there is for the truth of these ideas. Listen carefully for logical errors such as:

- *All or Nothing Thinking:* one is either a complete success or a total failure and there is nothing in between.

- *Overgeneralising:* assuming that because one has failed on this occasion that one is a total failure.

- *Accentuating the negative and ignoring the positive:* picking out the things that went wrong and ignoring the things that went as planned.

- *Minimising:* ignoring past achievments.

- *Shoulds', 'Oughts' and 'Musts':* being caught up in inflexible demands and perfectionism.

- *Emotional reasoning:* assuming that because one feels hopeless the undertaking is equally hopeless.

4   What is the evidence for the falsity of the self defeating idea?

5   What alternative ideas are there?

6   Role play the incident and substitute coping thoughts for the self defeating thoughts.

See Marlatt and Gordon[26] for a full discussion of relapse prevention.

When all else has failed, end on a positive note: For the most part success comes after several aborted attempts and those who have struggled the hardest do better in the long run[27].

References

1   Garfield, S.L.. & Bergin A.E. (1986) *Handbook of Psychotherapy and Behavior Change*, 6-11.

2   Golfried, M.R. (1980) 'Toward the delineation of therapeutic change principles.' *American Psychologist*, 35, 991-999.

3   Watzlawick, P. (1983) *The Situation is Hopeless but not Serious.* Norton, New York.

4   Peake, T.H., Borduin, C.M. & Archer, R.P. (1988) *Brief Psychotherapies: Changing Frames of Mind.* Sage Newbury Park.

5   Watzlawick, P., Weakland, J.H., & Fisch, R. (1974) *Change, Principles of Problem Formation and Resolution.* Norton, New York.

6   Beck, A.T., (1976) *Cognitive Therapy and the Emotional Disorders.* International Universities Press, New York.

7   Orbach, S. (1978) *Fat is a Feminist Issue.* Arrow Books, London.

8   Greenwald, H. (1973) *Direct Decision Therapy* EDITS, San Diego, California.

9   Jarvis, M. (1989) 'Helping Smokers Give up.' In Pearce, S. & Wardle, J. (eds) *The Practice of Behavioural Medicine.* BPS Books & OUP.

10 Condiotte, M.M. & Lichtenstein, E. (1981) 'Self efficacy and relapse in smoking cessation programmes.' *Journal of Consulting & Clinical Psychology*, 49, 648-658.

11 Goldstein, A.P. (1980) Relationship Enhancement Methods in Kanfer, F.H. & Goldstein, A.P. (eds) *Helping People Change: A Textbook of Methods.* (2nd edn) Elmsford, New York. Pergamon Press.

12 Truax, O.B. & Carkhuff, R.R. (1967) *Toward Effective Counselling and Psychotherapy.* Aldine, Chicago.

13 Egan, G. (1990) *The Skilled Helper.* (4th edn) Brookes/Cole, Monterey.

14 Ley, P. (1988) Communicating with Patients - *Improving communication, satisfaction and compliance.* Croom Helm, London.

15 Meichenbaum, D. & Turk, D. (1987) *Facilitating Treatment Adherence: A Practitioners Guidebook.* Plenum Press, New York.

16 Bandura, A. & Schunk, D.H. (1981) 'Cultivating competence, self efficacy and intrinsic interest through proximal self motivation.' *Journal of Personality and Social Psychology*, 41, 586-598.

17 D'Zurilla, T.J. & Goldfried, M.R. (1971) Problem solving and behaviour modification. *Journal of Abnormal Psychology*, 78, (1), 107-126.

18 Penick, S.B., Filton, R., Fox & Stunkard, A.J. (1971) 'Behaviour modification in the treatment of obesity.' *Psychosomatic Medicine*, 33, 49-55.

19 Brownell, K.D., Marlett, G.A. Lichtenstein, E., & Wilson, G.T. (1986) 'Understanding and Preventing Relapse.' *American Psychologist*, 41, 765-782.

20 Kirschenbaum, D.S. & Flannery, R.C. (1984) 'Toward a psychology of behavioural contracting.' *Clinical Psychology Review*, 4, 597-618.

21   Bandura, A. (1977) 'Self Efficacy: Toward a unifying theory of behavioural change.' *Psychological Review*, 48, 191-215.

22   Kanfer, F.H. & Gaelick, L. (1986) 'Self Management methods.' In Kanfer, F.H. & Goldstein, A.P. (eds). *Helping People Change: A Textbook of Methods*, (3rd edn) Elmsford, New York. Pergamon Press.

23   Smith, M.J. (1975) *When I Say No, I Feel Guilty.* Dial Press, New York.

24   Meichenbaum, D. (1985) *Stress Innoculation Training.* Pergamon, New York.

25   Haley, J. (1976) *Problem Solving Therapy.* Jossey Bass, San Francisco.

26   Marlatt, G.A. & Gordon, J.R. (1985) *Relapse Prevention: Maintenance Strategies in the treatment of addictive behaviours.* Guildford Press, New York.

27   Schachter, S. (1982) 'Recidivism and self care of smoking and obesity.' *American Psychologist*, 37, 436-444.

7 Helping People to give up Smoking

Paul Bennett, School of Psychology, University of Wales College of Cardiff.

Giving up smoking is not easy. The yearly success rates for those who have gone through formal smoking cessation programmes are no better than 15-20 percent[1]. Amongst those that have given up without recourse to professional help, less than half give up before the age of 65, and among all age groups only 30 percent of cigarette smokers manage to quit[2].

These and other statistics have led to arguments that formal smoking cessation clinics contribute little to the reduction of smoking levels throughout the population. They have also led to an increasing emphasis on the development of brief and cheap interventions conducted, for example, by General Practitioners or Practice Nurses[3]. These may have lower absolute rates of success (roughly 5% at one year), but because they involve many more people who receive a much briefer intervention they are more cost effective and have the potential for making larger changes in population smoking levels. This chapter will attempt to provide a structured, but relatively simple, approach to helping people stop smoking that may be used in the primary care setting. It is somewhat more sophisticated than the minimal interventions described by Jarvis and colleagues[1,3], and provides a second level of intervention for those patients who would like (and potentially benefit from) a still relatively brief intervention. But first . . . why *do* people smoke?

Why do people smoke?

To help people give up smoking, some understanding of the processes by which people develop and maintain the habit may be useful[4]. Young people often start to smoke as a result of peer pressure, to look 'cool' or to show some image of independence and being adult - most do not even initially enjoy the sensations associated with smoking.

However, for those that persevere, smoking can quickly become both a habit and a powerful psychological tool. The nicotine in cigarettes has powerful mood altering properties. It can both increase awareness and alertness or can help to relax and calm the smoker. These unique properties depend on the speed of inhalation and can be controlled by the smoker, and contribute to a strong psychological dependence on smoking. In addition, nicotine is addictive, and stopping smoking may result in withdrawal symptoms varying from minor muzziness and poor concentration to severe symptoms including headaches, dizziness and shaking. A third maintaining factor is that smoking often becomes associated with a number of situations in which a person has, and continues, to smoke. For example, many smokers automatically have a cigarette when they answer the telephone, or following a meal - simply out of habit.

Thus, people who stop smoking have three particular problems to cope with; the loss of a powerful psychological support, changing a well established habit, and the possible onset of unpleasant withdrawal symptoms. Each may be a formidable hurdle - together they pose an often unsurmountable barrier. To effectively help people give up smoking some account must be taken of each of these elements.

Giving up smoking: a brief overview of methods

There have been many and various techniques to help people give up smoking, all of which utilise more or less sophisticated equipment and techniques[1,5,6]. Perhaps the most radical approaches involve giving mild electric shocks whilst smokers inhale cigarettes, in order to develop a conditioned aversive reaction to smoking. Similar approaches utilise rapid smoking techniques, in which smokers repeatedly inhale their favoured cigarette at short intervals until they are unable to tolerate a further inhalation. Again, the intention is to associate smoking with an unpleasant association. Unpleasant images related to cigarettes or smoking frequently also form part of hypnotic suggestions, although some[7] have suggested that ego-strengthening suggestions may be more powerful in facilitating change.

Other 'positive' approaches involve individual or group counselling. These vary from three day highly focussed courses to longer, but less intensive, courses that meet over a number of weeks. They also vary in terms of how they are run, with those which engender group support rather than relying upon leadership by a professional being more effective[8].

Unfortuntely, none of these approaches may be considered significantly and consistently more or less effective than any others. Thus, there is some strength in the argument that if clients express any preference for the kind of help they would like this may be the best option for them, as they may have greater expectations of success from this than any other approach. Equally, it is worth reinforcing that however 'high tech' or esoteric the intervention this may be no more effective than the counselling or support that can be provided by a practice nurse or a similar professional, or even a friend who can be supportive at

important times. The rest of this chapter will therefore focus on one relatively simple approach, particularly appropriate for one-to-one counselling. It involves a behavioural approach to combat habitual smoking and reduce any psychological dependence, as well as the possible use of nicotine substitutes to help combat any nicotine dependence.

Facilitating change

The decision to quit smoking rarely occurs out of the blue. It typically follows a number of prior stages[9]. The first or pre-contemplative stage, occurs when the individual occasionally and inconsistently thinks about giving up. At some time this may be followed by the contemplation stage. Here the individual is more actively and consistently considering changing their behaviour. For some, but by no means all smokers, the next stage is to take the final step of actually stopping smoking. Finally, and of critical importance for many former smokers, is the maintenance of change. As has already been hinted, for many this may be the 'failure to maintain' stage, taking them back to the beginning of the change process again.

To facilitate change, it is important to understand at what stage in this continuum the client is at, and to adjust any advice or counselling accordingly. The goal at each counselling session should be to move the individual along to the next stage of the continuum. For people at the pre-contemplation stage the most appropriate input may be to ask them to simply consider the health and other costs of smoking and any benefits they may gain from not smoking. For those at the contemplation stage, advice and consideration as to how the person may best set about stopping smoking may be more relevant. This may move them into the planning and quitting phase. Finally, for those who have given up, it is important to consider ways of avoiding relapse. But first, a brief discussion about counselling in general.

While some people may act upon advice from a health professional to give up smoking, many may need appropriate counselling and advice rather than simple reiteration of the health facts about smoking. The majority of people are now aware of at least some of the health risks associated with smoking, and a sizable majority likely to act upon this advice have now done so. This is leaving a pool of people who have tried and failed to give up smoking previously; about half of all smokers have tried (and failed) to stop smoking during the previous year[10].

Effective advice giving or counselling is conducted through a process of negotiation[11]. Whilst some didactic provision of information may at times be necessary and appropriate, it is important to involve the individual in a problem solving partnership. They are the person most aware of the difficulties they face, and what may or may not work for them. Proscriptive counselling, where the client is advised what to do with no regard to their personal circumstances cannot take into account any of these circumstances, and is often doomed to failure. In addition, if a counsellor tells a person what to do, it is likely that the person will be less able to cope with any unexpected problems when the counsellor is not around to help them. Thus, all decisions about how an individual may go about stopping smoking should arise from discussion between client and counsellor. What follows is therefore a *basis* for an intervention aimed at helping someone to stop smoking, not a series of absolutes that must be followed to the letter.

Stage 1: Thinking about giving up

Encouraging people to consider how they would benefit by giving up smoking is probably the only available strategy for those in the pre-contemplation stage. It is also a useful preparation for anyone preparing to give up smoking. It is important that they are motivated to give up smoking - and sufficiently motivated to continue if they are having difficulties in giving up. Thinking through why they want to give up, and why they want to give up *now* may be essential to this process.

One simple method by which people may be brought to think through these issues is to ask them to brainstorm how they would benefit if they were to give up smoking. Although they may focus on the future health risks, it is also worth trying to focus on more immediate benefits, as these may be more powerful determinants of behaviour. These may include saving money, avoiding having to nip out for a 'quick smoke', cleaner air for their partner and house, preventing burn marks on furniture, getting a bit more puff and so on. The list of benefits whilst not endless nevertheless can be quite long. It may be worth suggesting they write these down as a future reminder, to be used if they begin to lose their motivation to stop smoking.

At this stage it may be also worth looking at any reasons why an individual does *not* want to give up, and deal (if possible) with these at an early stage. Otherwise these may prevent their full commitment to stopping smoking. One anxiety often raised at this stage is that if they have smoked for a number of years that there is little point in giving up, as the damage has already been done, or they are too old. As the evidence strongly suggests that health benefits may be gained at whatever age people stop smoking[12], this need not be a stumbling point.

Stage 2: Planning to give up

Planning is the key to success in giving up smoking. This stage has two primary goals: to determine when and why an individual smokes, and then to use this information to apply the most effective techniques in their attempt to quit.

The simplest and most effective way of helping a person to find out when and why they smoke is for them to complete a 'Smoking Diary'. This can be used to record when and why they smoke each cigarette through the day. Do they smoke out of habit, a need for nicotine, as a means of coping with stress, and so on? When and where do they smoke? Do they always smoke after a meal, when they answer the telephone, when they are with particular people? It can also be used to write down how easy or difficult it would be for the person not to smoke that cigarette. This may give some ideas as to which cigarettes the person may miss out as they cut down their smoking (see Figure 1).

Day	Time	Why did I smoke?	Ease of giving up (0-10)
Monday	7.30	First of the day - lovely!	3
	7.45	With breakfast - habit	6
	8.37	Driving to work - boredom in traffic - even had time to fill in my diary	7
	10.30	Coffee break - sat with smoker	5
	12.30	Lunch break - really need this one	4
	12.40	Enjoying a second one - habit really	8

The diary can be as simple as a piece of paper tucked into a cigarette packet. It is also possible to obtain cigarette pack size smoking diaries from a number of voluntary bodies. Ideally these should be filled in before the client smokes each cigarette. This ensures that they do not forget, and also (if they are conscientious) adds a degree of hassle to smoking, and may mean that they don't smoke as many cigarettes. Unless they want to give up smoking immediately, it may be useful for a client to keep a diary for a week or so before beginning to give up. This should provide much useful information to use during the next stage.

Stage 3: Beginning to give up

Two important decisions have to be made at this point. Would the client benefit from using nicotine substitutes, and would they best give up immediately or cut down slowly? The client may have some ideas as to which of these options they would prefer. However, some advice may be appropriate.

Are nicotine substitutes necessary?

There is growing evidence that nicotine substitutes may help a significant number of smokers to stop smoking[1]. This may be for a number of reasons. Firstly, they help prevent or minimise nicotine withdrawal symptoms in heavily dependent smokers. Secondly, they may act as a psychological support. Both may be powerful determinants of eventual success and if a client feels they are necessary to their efforts then this should not be ignored. One simple guide as to whether nicotine substitutes will be of use is simply to determine how important the first cigarette of the day is. If someone feels that this would be the most difficult cigarette to give up, they almost certainly would benefit from nicotine substitutes. A glance at the diary may also provide some clues. If many cigarettes are smoked because the person was 'desperate for a cigarette' this again may indicate a high nicotine dependence.

To cut down, or quit immediately?

Some smokers want to stop smoking immediately. Others wish to gradually cut down, until one day they find that they are no longer smoking. Whilst these approaches may suit some people, there is considerable evidence that those that follow a middle road actually fair better. Most successful quitters gradually cut down to a level of about twelve cigarettes a day (over a period of, say, one or two weeks) and then stop smoking completely. Smoking twelve cigarettes a day is usually sufficient to prevent nicotine withdrawal symptoms, and can allow the person to develop and practice their strategies for dealing with not smoking without the extra strain of dealing with them. However, extending the period of cutting down beyond this time serves only to prolong these symptoms and to increase the risk of their starting to smoke again.

Beginning to cut down

If the client has been using a smoking diary they should have a good idea how many cigarettes they smoke a day and when and why they smoke them. They may also have some ideas as to how they may go about cutting down. One approach is to plan one day in the following one or two weeks when the person will stop smoking completely - their 'QUIT DAY'. They should have a target of smoking about twelve cigarettes each day by this time. Then work out a gradual reduction over the course of this time period. For example, if a client smokes 35 cigarettes each day and plans to quit in 14 days time, they may cut down to 30 per day immediately, 28 per day by three days time, 25 by five days time, 22 a day by the end of the first week, and so on. The Smokers Diary can now be used as a guide to how successful a client is in cutting down, and to help plan when and how to cut down each day.

It is usually best to cut down on the easier cigarettes at the beginning, although by the end of this period it may be necessary to cut out on some of the more difficult cigarettes. Cutting down may be achieved by not smoking at certain times (e.g. following a meal), not smoking in certain places (e.g. the car) and so on. Again the diary may give some clues as to what is best for the individual. Although cutting down is not as difficult as the final step of stopping smoking, this stage can be made easier by using some tactics described below. If time is available, it may be useful to discuss with any client whether they would find such tactics useful and how they would work best for them. If they think of different tactics that would help them, so much the better!

Those who intend to use nicotine replacements may equally benefit from gradually cutting down and beginning to replace some cigarettes with nicotine substitutes before they stop completely. These can be obtained by private prescription and 'over the counter' from pharmacies and each packet includes detailed instructions for their use and details of contra-indications, so these will not be dealt with here. However, it is worth noting that most people take some time getting used to nicotine substitutes - for example, many people initially find their taste unpleasant, although most get used to it if they persevere. It is worth getting over any difficulties that may arise *before* quitting completely.

Tactics to help 'cut down'

1 Avoiding triggers to smoking

Habit cigarettes are often triggered by routine events. A person may habitually smoke when they answer the telephone, when they are watching television, with friends, and so on. One approach to cutting down is to avoid such situations, as they may 'trigger' a strong desire to smoke. The smoking diary may suggest some key 'triggers' for each client. Below are a few suggestions of fairly common ways to avoid triggers to smoking.

At work:

- Sitting in a different part of the canteen or recreation room with non-smokers.
- Not carrying cigarettes around.
- Going for a walk during breaks.

At home:

- If cigarettes are kept in the house, keeping them somewhere inaccessible so it takes some effort to get them.
- Hiding all the ashtrays.
- Asking partners not to mention smoking.

On the move:

- If travelling by bus, travelling in the no smoking area.
- If travelling by car, keeping cigarettes in the boot or taking out the ashtrays.

Socially:

- Visiting friends who do not smoke.
- Sitting in the no smoking area of the cinema or theatre.
- Avoiding 'borrowing' cigarettes or getting involved in 'rounds'.

2 Coping with triggers

Of course, it is often impossible to avoid triggers to smoking. It is therefore worth encouraging clients to think through some tactics for dealing with these situations. One basic, but important skill is simply being able to say 'NO', not 'I am giving up smoking'. It may be worth encouraging clients to practice in front of a mirror - it may seem strange at first, but practice makes perfect. A second tactic that can be used at any time is that of distraction from the urge to smoke. For example, in a pub (a common trigger to smoking), listening carefully to conversations, enjoying the taste of a drink, concentrating on keeping relaxed, and so on may all help control the temptation to smoke.

3 'Enjoying' giving up

Smoking is often a pleasurable activity. Giving up smoking is not about taking the pleasure out of life - but of changing the source of that pleasure. Allowing, or even encouraging clients to give themselves some rewards for their successes can be an important boost while they are cutting down - and during the first days or even weeks after quitting. These may be small, for example watching a favourite video at the end of a successful day, or larger, for example going out for dinner at the end of a successful week. Of course, one important reward is simply the pride of successfully 'giving up'.

4 Involving others

Support from friends is often the key factor in giving up smoking. Clients may be encouraged to ask friends to support them in their efforts, even if this simply means asking them not to offer them a cigarette. Some people may even wish to stop at the same time as a friend and even form a small self-help group. This form of social support may be the all important factor in the success or failure of any attempt to quit.

Stage 4: The 'QUIT DAY' and beyond

Assuming the client has either cut down to their chosen number of cigarettes or decided to stop smoking immediately, the next vital step is actually stopping smoking. At this time some problems already encountered may continue, and others, in particular the onset of withdrawal symptoms, may begin. Surviving this stage, and beyond, requires the continued use of some techniques already practised, and using a few new techniques. But first, the QUIT DAY.

Stopping smoking is an important event and should be treated as such. Thus, the QUIT DAY should equally be seen as an important day. Most smokers choose not to smoke at all on their QUIT DAY - it helps to start a new day with a new habit. But before this, it may be an idea for the client to smoke their last few cigarettes together and very quickly, so the memory of their last cigarettes is unpleasant. Equally, a ritual burning of the last remaining cigarettes may help people feel they have made a positive change.

Some other things may help make the day special and help the client through the first few hours. Some claim that drinking orange juice helps minimise any withdrawal symptoms. Whether this is true is unclear. Nevertheless, there is a good argument for the client to have a variety of *non-fattening* and fresh tasting alternatives such as fruit, fruit juice, sugar-free gum to eat, drink or chew instead of smoking. Simple ideas, such as starting the day with a special breakfast may help distract from the desire for any early cigarettes and mark the day out as special. Equally, going out for a special dinner will mark the day as special - and make it harder to give up later! If time is available, some time spent discussing how the client can best tackle the first few hours and days after stopping smoking will be time well spent.

1 Coping with craving

Craving a cigarette is one of the most often reported side effects of giving up. The acute phase normally lasts for up to two or three weeks, although the first two or three days after quitting are the worst. The urge to smoke comes in short spells, each peak lasting only two or three minutes with periods of relative ease in between. As time goes by the craving becomes less severe, and at longer intervals. One simple strategy to help through this time is that of simply keeping busy - planning time so that there is no time to be bored and thinking about smoking.

It is important to bear in mind also that these cravings can be viewed in a very positive light. They are an indication of the body getting rid of nicotine. Each craving represents one step further along the road to abstinence. Nevertheless, if the cravings are severe, and an individual has difficulty in coping with them, this may indicate that they would benefit from a nicotine replacement, and this possibility should be discussed with them.

2 Avoiding and coping with triggers

If a client has been using a Smoking Diary they should be aware of most of the likely high risk points in the day, where they are likely to be strongly tempted to smoke. In the first few days after stopping smoking these temptations are most likely to occur, and ideally clients should be advised to avoid these triggers for the first few days. If this proves impossible then some thought should be given as to how they will cope with any temptation. One key way of coping with triggers to smoking is that of not carrying cigarettes from the QUIT DAY onwards. Some people feel they have to carry a packet of cigarettes with them, 'just in case'. However, this seems to be putting temptation rather too close. Ideally, the client may not even carry any money so they cannot pop into a tobacconist to buy any cigarettes. After the first few difficult days, and as the client feels able, they can gradually reduce the number of high risk situations they avoid.

3 "If I should slip" – an emergency drill

Many clients do smoke at least one cigarette after their QUIT DAY. It is important that this does not become a catastrophe, and the client continues smoking as they have already 'failed in their attempt'. Thus, it is worth discussing an emergency routine that clients may use if they give in to temptation. It may be worth writing something like this on a card, so they can re-motivate themselves if necessary:

- 'To err is human'. To have one cigarette does not mean that all my hard work has been in vain, or that I have no will power. It also does not mean that I have to continue smoking.
- Stop smoking NOW. Not tomorrow, not next week. Avoid the cop-out response of 'since I smoked today I might as well go ahead and smoke as much as I want and stop smoking tomorrow'. There is always the danger that tomorrow never comes.

To maintain motivation it may also be useful to have on the same card two of the key reasons for the client wanting to stop smoking. These could be taken from the list of reasons for wanting to quit they may have written down earlier in the quitting process.

4 Using nicotine replacements

Initially, those clients electing to use nicotine replacements can use them regularly (within the prescribed limits) through the day. However, by the end of the first two or three weeks it is important to begin gradually cutting down their use. Some clients take some time doing this (some studies report clients still using them up to one year after quitting smoking[12]), but some active encouragement to cut down should be given.

Stage 5: Staying stopped

As has been hinted at earlier, many smokers succeed in giving up smoking for days, weeks, or even months and then begin to smoke again. For this reason it is important to encourage clients to consider not just how they will cope with the first few days after giving up, but also to consider how they will continue to be a non-smoker in the longer term. Even during the first week or so after their first giving up smoking, it is worth encouraging clients to consider how they may best set about avoiding relapsing. A few more tactics may be useful at this stage:

- Avoiding complacency. One of the commonest reasons for starting to smoke again is that people simple 'felt like a cigarette', had 'just one or two' and became hooked on smoking again.

- Being careful of situations in which the client previously smoked. In particular, care is necessary if they previously smoked when drinking. Alcohol is a well-known destroyer of good resolutions.

- Telling people if they offer you a cigarette that you don't smoke, not that you've given up. It sounds more positive and discourages them from offering you cigarettes that you may find difficult to turn down.

- Being prepared to cope with craving. Some ex-smokers report that they have occasional strong urges to smoke. These do not last very long, and no one is really sure why they occur, but clients may need to be forewarned.

Some final considerations

This chapter has touched upon some of the key issues that may need consideration as clients pass through the various stages of stopping smoking. It cannot be all encompassing and other issues and problems, and ideas of how to solve them, will occur during any counselling of people as they stop smoking. Nevertheless, it provides a basic framework around which the client and helper may together work towards the optimum way for an individual to stop smoking.

How much time should be spent with each client as they give up smoking? This is an impossible question to answer and must be a compromise between the time (and commitment) available from the counsellor and the needs of the client. For some clients one meeting may suffice, for others a series of meetings (of say, 20 minutes) may be necessary. To optimise the time spent in such meetings it is important that at the end of each meeting an informal contract is made in which the client agrees a behavioural goal (i.e. cut down to 12 per day; quit on the day of the next meeting, etc.) to be achieved by the next meeting. If this goal is not achieved, then the intervention should be revised or the meetings stopped. Such agreements thus provide a monitor of progress and indicate quite clearly whether there remains any value to their continuing. Finally, it may be worth being available at the end of a telephone for 5 minutes each day so that clients may contact you for a very brief chat should they need it - you never know, this may be the most important few minutes of the entire intervention!

References

1 Jarvis M. (1989 'Helping smokers give up'. In S. Pearce & J. Wardle (eds). *The practice of behavioural medicine*. British Psychological Society/Oxford University Press, Oxford.

2 Jarvis M.J. & Jackson P.H. (1988) 'Cigar and pipe smoking in Britain: implications for smoking prevalence and cessation.'. *Br J Add* 83, 323-330.

3 Russell M.A.H., Wilson C., Taylor C. & Baker C.D. (1979) 'Effect of general practitioners' advice against smoking.' *Br Med J*, 2, 231-235.

4 Ashton H. & Stepney R. (1982) *Smoking, psychology and pharmacology*. Tavistock, London.

5 Raw M. 'Smoking cessation strategies.' In W.E. Miller and N. Heather (eds) *Treating addictive behaviors. Processes of change*. Plenum, New York.

6 Leventhal H. & Cleary P.D. (1986) 'The smoking problem: A review of the research and theory in behavioral risk modification.' *Psych Bull*, 88, 370-405.

7 Hartland J. (1984) *Medical and dental hypnosis and its clinical applications*. Balliere Tindall, London.

8 Hajek P., Belcher M. & Stepleton J. (1985) 'Enhancing the impact of groups: an evaluation of two group formats for smokers.' *Brit J. Clin Psych*, 24, 289-294.

9 Prochaska J.O. & Di Clemente C.C. Toward a comprehensive model of change.' In W.E. Miller & N. Heather (eds) *ibid* (see 5).

10 Directorate of the Welsh Heart Programme. (1986) *Pulse of Wales. Preliminary report of the Welsh Heart Health Survey 1985*. Heartbeat Wales, Cardiff.

11 Meanes D. & Thorne B. (1988) *Person-centred counselling in action*. Sage, London.

12 Royal College of Physicians of London. (1986) *Health or smoking? Follow-up report of the Royal College of Physicians*. Churchill Livingstone, London.

13 Fagestrom K.O. (1982) 'A comparison of psychological and pharmacological treatment in smoking cesssation.' *J Behav Med*, 5, 255-264.

8

The Control of Cholesterol by Dietary Means

Michael Clapham, Lecturer, Robert Gordon's Institute of Technology, Aberdeen

Introduction

As previously explained in chapter 2 there is evidence that lowering blood cholesterol reduces the risk of heart disease both in those who have already had one heart attack and in those who have not yet suffered clinical heart disease. The greater the reduction in serum cholesterol the greater is the reduction in risk. In fact the National Institute of Health in America reviewed this statement and at a consensus conference on lowering blood cholesterol to prevent disease concluded that for every 1% reduction in serum cholesterol one may expect to see a 2% reduction in coronary risk[1].

The question then asked is 'What should we eat to reduce serum cholesterol levels?'

The dietary treatment of hyperlipidaemia

The cornerstone of therapy for patients with hyperlipidaemia is diet. This is true regardless of the type of hyperlipidaemia. Even if drugs are required to lower lipid levels, diet therapy is always needed to achieve maximum benefit from the drug therapy. It is also good practice to try dietary modification initially because some patients can be unusually responsive to dietary modification despite their degree of raised lipids.

In chapter 2 various components of the diet and their effects on blood lipid levels were discussed. These factors are

Dietary Cholesterol
Saturated Fat
Polyunsaturated Fat
Monounsaturated Fat
Dietary Fibre
Sugar
Alcohol

Many dietary factors affect blood lipid levels. Attention to all of them will achieve the greatest serum cholesterol reduction, but the emphasis needs to be varied to suit the individual patient and the type of lipid disorder being treated.

The following are sensible dietary changes for most patients.

1 Attainment of ideal body weight.
2 Reduction in the consumption of saturated fatty acids, which may be partially compensated for by an increase in polyunsaturated and monounsaturated fatty acids.
3 Increase in fibre rich carbohydrate, particularly soluble fibre.
4 Reduction in alcohol intake by overweight patients and those with hypertriglyceridaemia (raised levels of serum trigylcerides).
5 Dietary cholesterol of 300 mg per day or less.

In recent years, important reports concerning diet and cardiovascular disease have been published.

a) The official British recommendations from COMA (Committee on Medical Aspects of Food Policy)[2] in 1984 which recommended the need for individuals to reduce total fat to 35% or less of their total energy consumption, also recommended to increase the polyunsaturate to saturate (P/S) ratio to approximately 0.45, with no more than 15% of food energy coming from saturated fatty acids.

b) NACNE (National Advisory Council of Nutrition Education)[3] recommended that fat be reduced to 30% or less of total energy, with saturated fatty acids contributing no more than 10% to total energy intake. No recommendation was made regarding unsaturated fatty acids. It should be borne in mind however that these recommendations were not specific to the prevention of heart disease.

c) The 1991 COMA report has proposed a fat consumption of not more than 33% of total energy. Within this, saturated fat should provide 10%[4].

From previously published studies it is possible to predict the effect on the mean serum cholesterol levels of the population which compliance to these recommendations would produce. For example, following the COMA 1984 recommendations one would expect serum cholesterol to be reduced on average by approximately 12%. Following the NACNE recommendations, the serum cholesterol would on average be reduced by 15%. To achieve even better reductions in serum cholesterol the following diet which takes into consideration all the previously discussed factors will have the greatest effect on serum cholesterol (Figure 1).

Figure 1   **Summary of the optimal nutrient composition of a lipid lowering diet[4]**

Total energy	Should be tailored to individual requirements. Weight loss in the obese helps to normalise lipid levels in most conditions.
Fat: <30% energy	Saturated fat should provide 10 per cent or less of total energy - the rest should be from mono or polyunsaturated fatty acids. The ratio of polyunsaturated to saturated fats should be about 0.8 to 1.
Carbohydrate: 50-60% of energy	Unprocessed fibre-rich carbohydrate should predominate. Ideally 20g fibre should be provided for every 1000 kcals consumed. Pectins and other gel-forming fibres (e.g. those derived from various cooked beans) are useful for lowering low density lipoproteins (LDL).
Protein: 10-15% of energy	Vegetable proteins derived from legumes (e.g soya) may help to lower LDL.
Sugar	Should be severely restricted in the obese or if triglycerides are raised.
Alcohol	Should be severely restricted in the obese or if triglycerides are raised. A sensible maximum for others is 12 units per week.
Cholesterol	Less than 300 mg per day should be consumed.

To turn these recommendations into sensible advice on dietary change, a little more knowledge is needed.

Fats

Oils are merely fats which are liquid at room temperature.
Oils and fats come in three different types:

a)   Saturated

b)   Polyunsaturated

c)   Monosaturated

a)   Saturated Fats

Saturated fats tend to increase the level of cholesterol in our blood. They are found mainly as animal fats in beef, lamb, pork, suet, lard and dripping and dairy products such as milk, cheese and butter. Coconut and palm oil are saturated vegetable fats. It is thus not true that all vegetable fats and oils are acceptable in a lipid-lowering diet. Saturated vegetable oils are used extensively in the manufacture of cakes and biscuits. Vegetable oils can also be 'hydrogenated' to make them saturated. Hydrogenated vegetable fat for example is used in the manufacture of margarine, where liquid oils are 'hydrogenated' to make them hard enough to spread.

b)   Polyunsaturated Fats

These are found in vegetable oils such as sunflower, corn and soya oil, in special soft margarines labelled 'high in polyunsaturates' in nuts and all oily fish such as herring, mackerel, pilchards and trout. They have a cholesterol-lowering effect.

c)   Monosaturated Fats

These are found in olive oil, peanuts, peanut oil and rapeseed oil. They also have a cholesterol-lowering effect, and have the added benefit of not reducing high-density lipoprotein (HDL) levels. Their overall beneficial effect on blood lipids may thus be greater than that of polyunsaturated fats.

At present, the average U.K. diet contains approximately 42 per cent of calories from fat. Saturated fat contributes approximately 17 per cent of calories (National Food Survey 1988)[6]. Hence, in order to comply with the COMA 1991 dietary recommendations, a reduction in total calories from fat of 9 per cent and calories from saturated fat of 7 per cent is necessary.

One way to achieve this dietary change is firstly to look at the sources of fat in the UK diet and in particular, sources of saturated fat. This fat comes from four main sources. Approximately 20 per cent comes from milk, 25 per cent from meat and meat products, 25 per cent from butter and margarine and 10 per cent from cooking fats. These are thus the categories of food to concentrate on when promoting dietary change.

For example, a person consuming one pint of full cream milk per day who changes to one pint of skimmed milk per day reduces the fat consumed by 21g per day or by 7.8 kg per year (Table 1). In addition to the reduced consumption of dietary fat, calorie consumption is reduced by 66,000 Kcals per year. As one kilogram of adipose tissue contains approximately 7,730 Kcals, this would produce a weight reduction of 8.5kg in one year, if a compensating increase in calories were not made elsewhere.

Table 1

Difference in fat consumption changing from 1 pint of full cream milk to 1 pint of skimmed milk per day

Food Item	Fat g Day	Fat g Consumed Per Week	Fat g Consumed Per Year	K cals Per Year
1 Pint Whole Milk	22g	154	8030g	134,758
1 Pint Skimmed Milk	0.6	4.2	219g	68,415
Yearly Reduction of		149.8	7811g	66,343

Similarly, if 100g of butter is consumed per week, changing to 100g of low fat spread would reduce fat consumption from 4.4 kg to 2.2 kg and calories would be reduced by 18,200 Kcals per year (See Table 2).

Table 2

Difference in fat consumption changing from 100g of butter per week to 100g of low fat spread

Food Item	Fat g Week	Fat g Per Year	K cals Per Year
100g Butter	82	4264	38,480
100g Low Fat Spread	39	2028	20,280
Yearly Reduction of		2236	18,200

Which type of spread or oil should be used?

'Low fat' spreads

These spreads usually have half the fat and therefore half the calories of butter or margarine. Generally the fat present is predominantly polyunsaturates, but brands vary and patients should be advised to check the label (See Table 3).

Table 3

Comparison of fat, calories and saturated fat content of butter, polyunsaturated spread, and a low fat spread

	Total Fat	Saturated Fat	Calories
Butter	81%	52%	740 kcal
Polyunsaturated Margarine	80%	14%	730 kcal
Low Fat Spread	39%	10.5%	390 kcal

Margarines

Margarines can be made from a single oil or a blend of oils. To solidify the oil into margarine it is hydrogenated as previously discussed. The degree of solidity depends upon the level of hydrogenation. The more complete the hydrogenation the harder the spread and the more saturated the fat. In polyunsaturated margarines a single polyunsaturated oil is used and hydrogenated minimally. Some vegetable margarines are made from blends of naturally saturated vegetable oils such as palm oil and coconut oil. It is therefore very important to discuss actual brands and types of margarine used, with patients. Low fat spreads labelled 'high in polyunsaturates' are generally advised.

Cooking oils

Many cooking oils are made from blends of cheap naturally saturated oils and must be avoided. Pure single oils are advised, for example sunflower oil, corn oil, olive oil and rapeseed oil (See Table 4)

Table 4   *Composition of oils, margarines and fats*

Food	Saturated %	Mono unsaturated %	Poly unsaturated %
Coconut oil	91	7	2
Butter	60	32	3
Palm oil	47	44	9
Lard	44	44	9
Beef dripping	43	50	4
Margarine, hard (vegetable only)	39	49	12
Margarine, hard (mixed oils)	39	45	16
Margarine, soft (vegetable)	33	44	23
Margarine (polyunsaturates)	24	21	55
Margarine, soft (mixed oils)	31	47	20
Ground nut oil	19	50	30
Corn oil	17	30	52
Soya bean oil	15	25	59
Olive oil	15	73	12
Sunflower seed oil	14	33	52
Safflower seed oil	11	13	75
Rape seed oil	6	67	26

Reference Paul A.A. & Southgate D.A.T. (1978), McCance and Widdowson's The Composition of Foods 4th edn, London, HMSO.

Switching foods from high fat sources to lower fat sources can have a considerable effect on the proportions of calories derived from fat. Taking this a stage further, a simple list of practical ways to reduce saturated fat in the diet can be constructed.

Practical ways of reducing fat and saturated fat in the diet

- Use skimmed milk instead of full cream milk (it is advisable not to give skimmed and semi-skimmed milk to babies or children under 5).
- Substitute polyunsaturated margarine for butter and spread thinly. A low fat spread contains half the fat of margarines.
- Grill, bake or steam foods rather than fry them. To fry, use a little polyunsaturated or monounsaturated oil.
- Choose lean cuts of meat and smaller portions; trim off any fat.

- Eat chicken, turkey or fish more often; remove poultry skin, it is full of fat.

- Eat sausages, beefburgers and savoury pies only occasionally.

- Cheddar type cheeses are high in fat; try a lower fat variety and eat less.

- Try low fat yoghurt and skimmed milk cheeses in place of cream, mayonnaise and salad cream, or use a small quanity of olive oil as a dressing.

- Do not add fat or oil in cooking; for casseroles, brown the meat first and skim off the fat.

- Crisps, biscuits and nuts are rich in hidden fat, and should be eaten only occasionally.

Generally speaking it is best not to try to make all the above changes to the diet at once, but to make a list of planned changes, tick the things which are already being done, put a cross next to the things which are not, and then perhaps change one thing a week so that the diet becomes gradually healthier. Most people find it better to change the easy items first, leaving the difficult dietary modifications until last.

Figure 2

Approximate fat content of various cheeses

High Fat	Medium Fat	Low Fat
Contains approx 35-40 per cent fat	Contains approx 20 per cent fat	Contains than 5 per cent fat
Cream cheese	Brie	Cottage cheese
Cheshire	Baby bel	low fat soft cheese
Cheddar	Camembert	
Danish blue	Edam	
Lymeswold	Gouda	
Leicester	Gruyere	
Stilton	Mozzarella	
Double Gloucester	Parmesan	
	Low fat cheddar	

Fish

Fish deserves a special mention as oily fish is a rich source of polyunsaturated fats. One of the fatty acids which makes up the fat content of oily fish is eicosapentanoic acid. There is evidence this fatty acid reduces LDL cholesterol, platelet stickiness and has an anti inflammatory action[7]. These effects could therefore be protective against heart disease.

Dietary fibre

Most dietary recommendations advise an increase in dietary fibre, basically for two reasons. Firstly fibre rich foods in the diet are often eaten in place of fatty foods. Secondly a certain kind of fibre known as soluble fibre may reduce serum cholesterol by binding to cholesterol and bile acids (which contain cholesterol) in the gut. Hence less cholesterol is absorbed and blood cholesterol may be reduced.

To increase the amount of soluble fibre in the diet the following foods are to be encouraged: oats, oat bran, all types of peas and beans, and fruit rich in pectins such as apples[8].

Fibre also has a role to play in those patients who need to lose weight, as fibre-rich foods are filling, without providing too many calories. The following list contains some tips on how to eat more fibre.

Tips on how to eat more fibre

As before the best way to use this list is to just change one item a week and slowly increase the fibre in your diet, making the easy dietary modifications first.

- Try using more peas, beans and lentils. You can replace some or all of the meat in stews or casseroles with beans. This will also save money.
- Eat more potatoes, pasta, rice - very filling and low in fat!
- Eat breakfast cereals - go for wholegrain varieties and avoid sugar coated types. Porridge is a good source of soluble fibre.
- Wholemeal bread is best but all bread is good as it fills you up without adding to your fat consumption, if little spread is used.
- Try to eat at least one piece of fruit a day and get a good variety of vegetables.

Sugar

Sugar does not directly increase serum cholesterol levels, but being overweight may do. Adding sugar to foods makes it easier to eat more calories which can lead to overweight. Sugar contains only calories and very little nutrition in terms of vitamins and minerals. The following list contains some tips on how to reduce sugar consumption.

Tips to reduce sugar in the diet

- Check the label of foods. Sugar can be listed as sugar, sucrose, glucose, dextrose, fructose, maltose, syrup, raw sugar, brown sugar, cane sugar, honey, muscovado or molasses.

- Choose low calorie soft drinks, or unsweetened fruit juice.
- Use tinned fruit in natural juice rather than syrup.
- Go easy on cakes and biscuits. These also contain fat.
- Try drinking tea or coffee without sugar, or use an artificial sweetener.
- Breakfast cereals - choose those which are not sugar coated (check the label).

Overweight

Obesity is a risk factor for heart disease, as it effects adversely the serum levels of cholesterol and lipoproteins. The high intake of total calories in obesity may cause hypertriglyceridaemia. High levels of triglycerides in the blood stimulate the production of cholesterol as this is required for the transportation of trigylcerides around the blood stream; as a result some obese patients develop raised levels of serum cholesterol[10,11]. Even when LDL cholesterol is not elevated the lipoproteins present in obese patients are abnormal[11] and may be unusually atherogenic. Obesity also lowers the HDL level[12] and this may also contribute to increased risk of CHD.

To assess if someone is overweight, the body mass index (BMI) can be used. This index is calculated as the person's weight in kilograms divided by their height squared in metres. A BMI greater than 25 indicates that someone is overweight, and an index of 30 or more that they are seriously obese.

How to lose weight

It is not easy to lose weight. It is important not to put patients on crash diets, but to adjust them if possible to a healthy lifestyle.

The best way to lose weight is to reduce fat and sugar in the diet and to increase exercise. The strategies for reducing fat and sugar in the diet have been previously discussed in this chapter. Aim for an average weight reduction of 1 to 2 lb (0.5-1kg) each week. Follow-up of patients trying to lose weight is very important, to maintain their motivation. Here a slimming group or club can provide much encouragement and support.

Dietary compliance

Just as patients cannot always be relied upon to complete a course of drug therapy, patients vary enormously in their ability and willingness to follow a diet.

Advice must be tailored to suit personality type, budget, cooking skills and aptitude. The dietary treatment should not just stop with one session of instructions. It is important that the dietary changes are evaluated and reinforced.

Most patients eating a traditional UK diet, who comply with the lipid lowering diet, should achieve a reduction of approximately 15 per cent in their serum cholesterol. This may be greater if weight loss is also achieved were appropriate, but there is a great deal of individual variation in response. The precise diagnosis is an important factor in determining response.

Patients with familial hypercholesterolaemia usually respond less well to diet than those with common hyperlipidaemia or familial combined or remnant hyperlipidaemia. As a general rule drug therapy should not be considered until maximum response to dietary change has been achieved. Once the diet has been adopted it may take several months before the results are seen.

In those who do not respond to diet, it is advisable for a dietitian to reassess their dietary intake to determine the degree of dietary compliance. If dietary compliance is poor the patient can be remotivated or the diet modified if necessary. If dietary compliance is good alternative therapies may be required.

Conclusions

Dietary advice should be tailored to the individual. It is better to make one or two significant dietary changes which are adhered to permanently, than several complicated sets of instructions which are abandoned as impractical after a few weeks. The diet recommended for hyperlipidaemia is appropriate for the general population and as such is suitable for the whole family. The exception to the rule is children under 5 years. If dietary modification is needed for this group advice should be sought from a dietitian.

References

1   Consensus Conference (1985). Lowering blood cholesterol to prevent heart disease. *J.A.M.A.*, 253, 2080-2090.

2   COMA (1984) 'Diet and Cardiovascular Disease.' *Reports on Health and social subjects No 28*. HMSO, London.

3   NACNE (1983) *Proposals for nutritional guidelines for health education in Britain*. London Health Education Council.

4   COMA (1991) Dietary reference values for food energy and nutrients for the United Kingdom. *Reports on Health and Social Subjects no 41*, HMSO, London.

5   Ball M., Mann J. (1988) *Lipids and Heart Disease, A Practical Approach*. Oxford Medical Publications.

6   *National Food Survey* (1988). HMSO, London.

7   Leaf A., Weber P.C. (1988). 'Cardiovascular effects of N-3 fatty acids.' *New England Journal of Medicine*, 318, 549-557,

8   Miettinen T.A. (1987). 'Dietary fibre and lipids.' *American Journal of Clinical Nutrition*, 45, Supplement 1237-1242.

9   Paul A.A, & Southgate D.A.T. (1978): *McCance and Widdowson's The Composition of foods*, 4th edn. HMSO, London.

10 Grundy S.M., Mok H.Y.I., Zech L. (1979) 'Transport of very low density lipoprotein triglycerides in varying degrees of obesity and hypertriglyceridaemia.' *J. Clinical Invest*, 63, 1274.

11 Kesaniemi Y.A., Grundy S.M. (1983). 'Increased low density lipoprotein production associated with obesity.' *Arteriosclerosis*, 3, 170.

12 Wolf R.N., Grundy S.M. (1983). 'Influence of weight reduction on plasma lipoproteins in obese patients.' *Arteriosclerosis*, 3, 160.

9

The Control of Hypertension

D.G. Beevers, Reader in Medicine, Dudley Road Hospital, Birmingham

The Value of Reducing Blood Pressure

Antihypertensive drug therapy first became available in the late 1950s. Early drugs were, however, extremely difficult to tolerate and their use was reserved only for patients with very severe or malignant hypertension. Despite the side effects, the results of treatment were spectacular. Malignant hypertension with its 80% one year mortality was converted to a disease with a 50% ten year survival rate.

The first well tolerated antihypertensive drugs were the thiazide diuretics and methyldopa. Their value in the treatment of non malignant hypertension was proven in 1964. A trial conducted in Chelmsford, England showed an impressive reduction in stroke incidence, a reduction of heart failure and of the development of malignant phase hypertension. The data on coronary heart disease were, however, less convincing. During the late 1970s, three major trials of the treatment of mild grades of hypertension were published. These were all able to confirm that antihypertensive treatment prevents stroke but the data on coronary heart disease were less impressive. The USA based Hypertension Detection Follow Up Programme[1] did show some evidence of coronary prevention as did the Australian National High Blood Pressure Study[2]. The British MRC trial of mild hypertension[3] showed unconvincing evidence of coronary prevention except possibly amongst patients who were randomised to receive a beta blocker as opposed to a thiazide diuretic.

A recent meta-analysis or overview of the pooled data from all of the randomised trials of mild hypertension however strongly suggest that the treatment of hypertension brings about an approximately 14% reduction in the incidence of coronary heart disease as discussed in a previous chapter[4]. This amounts to about half of that which would have been expected for the amount of reduction of blood pressure achieved in these trials.

The reasons for the shortfall in coronary prevention are uncertain. Many of the trials used thiazide diuretics which are known to cause a 1-2% rise in plasma cholesterol levels. Such a rise in plasma cholesterol might be expected to cause a 3-6% rise in Coronary Heart disease which would only, in part, offset the benefits of blood pressure reduction. It is possible that other coronary risk factors including some relatively under recognised factors like clotting indices may also explain why antihypertensive treatment has not been as effective in coronary prevention as had been hoped. It should be stressed that the prevention of stroke by antihypertensive treatment is very successful.

The elderly

For a given level of blood pressure, older people have a much higher risk of developing coronary heart disease and stroke. There was some doubt about the value of treating hypertension in the elderly but this was resolved by the publication of two major trials of mild hypertension in patients over the age of 60 years. These trials were able to confirm a halving of the incidence of stroke as a result of antihypertensive treatment. One of the trials (which used thiazide diuretics as first line therapy) also showed some evidence of coronary prevention[5]. The other trial (which employed a beta blocker as first line therapy) showed no effect on coronary disease[6]. At the current state of knowledge, antihypertensive treatment, therefore, can be justified in patients up to the age of approximately 75 years. Above that age, antihypertensive treatment may not be of any value and there are no trials that have the power to test out the hypothesis.

Isolated systolic hypertension

With advancing age, isolated systolic hypertension becomes increasingly common. The criteria for this diagnosis are a diastolic blood pressure of below 95 mmHg associated with a systolic blood pressure greater than 180 mmHg. The recently published Systolic Hypertension in the Elderly Program (SHEP) has shown impressive benefits in terms of both stroke and coronary prevention in isolated systolic hypertensives[7]. It is notable that this was achieved using thiazide diuretics as first-line therapy. A similar European study (SYST-EUR) using calcium channel blockade is still underway.

All the trials listed above concentrated on the reduction of blood pressure alone. A more global approach has only been tested in one survey. The American Multiple Risk Factor Intervention Trial (MRFIT), which investigated blood pressure reduction, cholesterol lowering and smoking advice, did not initially demonstrate any benefits but the more recent data of the ten year follow up of MRFIT participants does show good evidence of coronary prevention[8].

Hypertension following cardiovascular complications

There are reliable data that show that in ambulant patients with moderate to severe hypertension who have recovered from a stroke, antihypertensive treatment causes a reduction in a second stroke. However, treating hypertension immediately after a stroke is hazardous because it may be associated with a reduction of cerebral perfusion. The value of treating milder grades of hypertension following stroke is, however, uncertain.

There is no information available on the value of treating hypertension following a myocardial infarction. However, the use of beta blockers in infarct survivors has been shown to reduce the re-infarction rate, independent of whether the blood pressure is raised or not. This is probably related to the anti-arrhythmic effects of beta blockers rather than blood pressure lowering effect.

The clinical management of hypertension

All individuals, whether detected in screening programmes in general practice, or attending blood pressure clinics, with diastolic blood pressures exceeding 90 mmHg should be fully assessed for evidence of other cardiovascular risk factors, particularly hyperlipidaemia and cigarette smoking. A suggested scheme for detecting and managing hypertension in general practice is provided in fig. 1. Amongst mild hypertensive patients, blood pressures frequently settle on rechecking and, therefore, antihypertensive treatment should not be instituted until after the fourth visit to the clinic or health centre[9]. A decision to institute antihypertensive therapy will, however, be influenced by the presence of left ventricular hypertrophy, an adverse family history, concurrent glucose intolerance or renal impairment. For this reason, all patients with any elevation of blood pressure should undergo urine testing, an ECG and full biochemical profile with a blood glucose estimation.

Non pharmacological blood pressure reduction

High alcohol intake, obesity and a high sodium intake are all known to be associated with high blood pressure. There is good evidence that moderation of alcohol intake is associated with a fall in blood pressure[10]. Patients should be advised that they should reduce their intake to no more than 21 standard units of alcohol for a man and no more than 14 standard units of alcohol for a woman, where one unit of alcohol is equivalent to half a pint of beer, a small glass of wine or a single measure of spirit. A reduction in alcohol intake can be associated with a reduction in the need for antihypertensive drug therapy and may avoid it altogether in some patients.

Similarly, weight reduction can lead to a useful fall in blood pressure[11]. The diastolic blood pressure will fall by approximately one to two mmHg for each kg of weight loss. Both weight reduction and alcohol restriction may be difficult to

Suggested scheme for the protection and follow up of hypertension in general practice   *Figure 1*

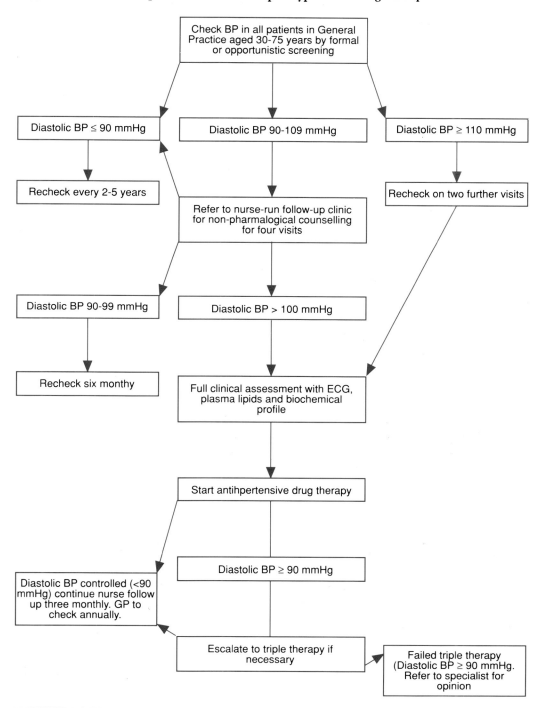

Check BP in all patients in General Practice aged 30-75 years by formal or opportunistic screening

Diastolic BP ≤ 90 mmHg

Diastolic BP 90-109 mmHg

Diastolic BP ≥ 110 mmHg

Recheck every 2-5 years

Refer to nurse-run follow-up clinic for non-pharmalogical counselling for four visits

Recheck on two further visits

Diastolic BP 90-99 mmHg

Diastolic BP > 100 mmHg

Recheck six monthy

Full clinical assessment with ECG, plasma lipids and biochemical profile

Start antihpertensive drug therapy

Diastolic BP ≥ 90 mmHg

Diastolic BP controlled (<90 mmHg) continue nurse follow up three monthly. GP to check annually.

Escalate to triple therapy if necessary

Failed triple therapy (Diastolic BP ≥ 90 mmHg. Refer to specialist for opinion)

achieve but the patient can be reminded that he will benefit by avoiding drug therapy if he complies with recommendations.

The value of restricting salt intake is slightly controversial. Randomised controlled trials suggest that some, but not all patients, with elevated blood pressures do sustain a fall in blood pressure if they reduce their salt intake from 150 down to 80 mmols per day[12]. This can be achieved by avoiding salty foods and avoiding adding salt to food at the table.

The value of potassium supplementation, either by tablets or by dietary means is uncertain and cannot be recommended at the current state of knowledge. However, many patients have a low potassium intake associated with a low intake of fruit and vegetables and they can be advised that both these foods are beneficial and not harmful.

Epidemiological and clinical evidence that environmental or emotional stress is related to high blood pressure are controversial and often unreliable. Patients with high blood pressure have been included in randomised controlled trials of stress management with variable results. Whilst patients might therefore be counselled about avoiding very stressful situations, the routine employment of stress management in the management of mild hypertension cannot be recommended.

When to start drug therapy

If after the fourth visit and despite counselling about sodium, weight and alcohol, the diastolic blood pressure remains at 100 mmHg or more, then antihypertensive drug therapy is mandatory in all patients up to the age of 75.

Lower levels of blood pressure (90-100 mmHg) might also be treated with antihypertensive drugs if there are other adverse risk factors present. Unfortunately most patients have to remain on antihypertensive treatment until the age of 75. Some whose blood pressure is well controlled on single tablet therapy only may be able to stop but they still require careful supervision if this strategy is embarked upon[13]. They will, therefore, continue to be attending some form of blood pressure clinic. At this stage patients need careful counselling to ensure that they are complying with the various non-pharmacological measures. It is then important to explain that drug therapy is necessary and that the results of treatment of hypertension are very encouraging, leading to a prolongation of useful life. An optimistic line with well organised follow up is likely to produce better results than a haphazard or over casual approach.

First line therapy

The most commonly used first line drugs in the United Kingdom are the thiazide diuretics and the beta blockers. These drugs are now, however, being challenged by the newer Angiotension Converting Enzyme (ACE) inhibitors, calcium channel blockers and long acting alpha blockers.

Thiazide diuretics

Whilst many clinicians are turning against thiazide diuretics, they still do have a role particularly in older hypertensives. The most commonly used thiazide is bendrofluazide but this should not be given in a dose of more than 2.5 mg per day. Above this level, biochemical side effects including glucose intolerance, hyperlipidaemia, hyperuricaemia and clinical side effects including erectile impotence are more common. Patients, who before treatment, have borderline glucose intolerance or slightly raised cholesterol levels should not receive thiazides as they may make things worse. It is not normal practice to give potassium supplements or potassium retaining agents in conjunction with thiazide diuretics. In a low dose, hyperkalaemia is uncommon but serum potassium should be measured between three and six months after starting therapy.

Beta blockers

There is a wide choice of beta blockers in most countries. The most commonly used beta blocker now in Britain and North America is atenolol. The reasons for this is that it is cardioselective and hydrophilic. Hydrophilic beta blockers cause less cerebral side effects of tiredness, exhaustion and vivid dreams.

Beta blockers are absolutely contraindicated in people with heart failure, heart block, asthma or peripheral vascular disease but they are specifically indicated in patients who have already suffered a myocardial infarction. The correct starting dose of Atenolol is 50 mg daily.

ACE inhibitors

The angiotension converting enzyme (ACE) inhibitors are probably the most well tolerated antihypertensive drugs although they have the disadvantage that they may cause a dry and irritating cough in about 10 percent of patients. They are potentially hazardous in people with undiagnosed renovascular disease. This is a common problem in elderly arteriosclerotic hypertensives who also smoke cigarettes. ACE blockers should, therefore, be instituted in very low doses in older people. Lisinopril and Enalapril can be given once daily and most patients feel entirely well on them. ACE inhibitors are also effective in patients with severe heart failure where they have been shown to prolong life. Hypertensive patients with heart failure, therefore, should routinely receive ACE blockers unless there are other contraindications. These drugs are probably the agents of first choice in hypertensives who also have diabetes mellitus.

Calcium channel blockers

The calcium channel blockers of the dihydropyridine group (e.g. nifedipine) are very safe although they can occasionally cause some myocardial depression. The main side effects of the dihydropyridines are flushing, headaches and ankle swelling which obviates their use in about 15% of patients. In general, this class of drug is very safe and the recent marketing of amlodipine, a once daily calcium channel blocker, is possibly going to be an important advance. The calcium channel blocker, verapamil, and to a lesser extent diltiazem, certainly do cause myocardial depression so they should almost never be used in conjunction with beta blockers.

Alpha blockers

The two new long acting alpha blockers, doxazocin and terazocin, have the added advantage of causing a small reduction in plasma cholesterol levels. Alpha blockers have not been popular as first line therapy in the United Kingdom but it is possible that new developments in this field will make the group more popular.

The last three classes of drugs listed above (ACE inhibitors, calcium channel blockers and alpha blockers) have not formerly been tested to see whether they have advantages over beta blockers and thiazides in the prevention of heart attack and stroke but there is no reason to suppose that they will not bring about the same benefits. These three groups of drugs cannot as yet be recommended as routine first line therapy but they are very acceptable as first line therapy where other drugs are contraindicated. In view of the problems with beta blockers and thiazides in relation to airways disease, heart failure, reduced peripheral perfusion, loss of exercise capacity, hyperlipidaemia, gout, diabetes, and erectile impotence, there is a good case for using the newer first line drugs more liberally. They are, however, expensive although the increasing number of competitors being marketed by different drug companies may bring about a reduction in price.

Double therapy

If a routine dose of a single hypertensive drug has been shown after four weeks to be ineffective, then it is usual to add another drug rather to increase the dose. In general, any class of drug can be added to another class with a genuine additive effect. The popular combinations are beta blockers with thiazide diuretics, ACE blockers with thiazide diuretics and the combination of ACE blockers with calcium channel blockers. However, other combinations are also effective.

Triple therapy

Triple therapy is necessary in approximately 5% of hypertensive patients. Where blood pressure is, however, proving resistant, special efforts should be made to ensure that the patient is complying with his medication and that there are no underlying renal or adrenal causes for the high blood pressure. Underlying causes of high blood pressure are unlikely to be present if the serum potassium, blood urea and serum creatinine levels are entirely normal and there is no proteinuria. Patients with episodic hypertension should be investigated to exclude phaeochromocytoma.

Triple therapy regimes usually comprise any three of the five classes of drugs listed above. Particular popular triple therapy regimes are a beta blocker, a thiazide diuretic and a calcium channel blocker as well as an ACE inhibitor, a thiazide diuretic and a calcium channel blocker.

Who to refer for specialist opinion

All but about 5-10% of patients can be managed exclusively in general practice. A small minority of patients need referring to specialist centres for detailed investigation usually because baseline investigations suggest the possibility of an underlying cause for the hypertension. In addition, patients with resistant hypertension who have failed on triple therapy should be referred for specialist opinion.

Within the context of general practice, nurse run hypertension clinics have been shown to be very effective in bringing about a reduction in blood pressure and patient compliance[14]. It is strongly recommended that all GP groups should have special hypertension (and other risk factor) screening and follow-up clinics and that hypertensive patients should normally be seen by a specially trained nurse; the doctor need only see the patient about once per year as long as the nurse has received appropriate instruction on the methods of managing patients.

The detection and management of hypertension within the context of general practice provides a major challenge. An average general practitioner in the United Kingdom probably has approximately 250 patients on his list with diastolic blood pressure of greater than 90 mmHg. Of these approximately half should be receiving antihypertensive drugs. The practicalities of screening, treating and following up such patients require a multidisciplinary approach from both primary health care nurses and doctors. In addition, local health authority facilitators and relevant local specialists in cardiovascular disease have a role to play. Clinicians should remind themselves that the treatment they are giving can halve the chances of a patient developing stroke and have a small but useful impact on coronary heart disease.

References

1   Hypertension Detection and Follow-Up Programme Cooperative Group. (1979) 'Five year findings of the Hypertension Detection and Follow up Program I. Reduction in mortality in persons with high blood pressure, including mild hypertension.' *JAMA*, 242, 2562-2571.

2   Australian National Blood Pressure Measurement Committee. (1980) The Australian therapeutic trial in mild hypertension.' *Lancet*, (i), 1261-1267.

3   Medical Research Council Working Party. 'MRC trial of treatment of mild hypertension: principal results.' *British Medical Journal*, (1985) 291, 97-104.

4   Collins R., Peto R., MacMahon S., Hebert P., Fiebach N.H., Eberlein K.A., Godwin J., Qizilbash V., Taylor J.O., Hennekens C.H. (1990) Blood pressure, stroke and coronary heart disease - Part 2, Short term reductions in blood pressure: overview of randomised drug trials in their epidemiological context.' *Lancet*, 335, 827-838.

5   Amery A., Birkenhager W., Brixko P. et al. (1985) Mortality and morbidity results from the European Working Party on High Blood Pressure in the Elderly trial. *Lancet*, 1, 1349-1354.

6   Coope J., Warrender T.S. (1986) 'Randomised trial of treatment of hypertension in the elderly in primary care.' *British Medical Journal*, 293, 1145-1151.

7   SHEP Cooperative Research Group. (1991) Prevention of stroke by anti hypertensive drug treatment in older persons with isolated systolic hypersensive. JAMA 265 3255-3264.

8   Multiple Risk Factor Intervention Trial Research Group. (1990) 'Mortality rates after 10.5 years for participants in the Multiple Risk Factor Intervention Trial.' *JAMA*, 263, 1795-1801.

9   Watson R.D.S., Lumb R., Young M.A., Stallard T.J., Davies P., Littler W.A. (1987) 'Variation in cuff blood pressures in untreated outpatients with mild hypertension - implications for initiating antihypertensive treatment.' *J. Hypertension*, 5, 207-211.

10 Potter J.F., Beevers D.G. (1984) 'Pressor effect of alcohol in hypertension.' *Lancet*, (i) 119-122.

11 Staessen J., Fagard R., Amery A. (1988) 'The relationship between body weight and blood pressure.' *J. Human Hypertens*, 2, 207-217.

12 MacGregor G.A., Markandu N.D., Best F.E. et al. (1982) 'Double-blind randomised cross-over trial of moderate sodium restriction in essential hypertension.' *Lancet*, (i) 351-355.

13 Hudson, M.F., (1982) 'How often can antihypertensive treatment be discontinued?' *J. Human Hypertens*, 2, 65-69.

14 Kenkre J., Drury V.W.M., Lancashire R.J. (1985) 'Nurse Management of Hypertension Clinics in general practice assisted by a computer.' *Family Practice*, 12, 17-22.

10   The Promotion of Exercise

W. Tuxworth, School of Sport and Exercise Science,
University of Birmingham

Progress has provided the so-called 'developed' nations with a different pattern of illness and dying from their fellow human beings in less priviliged countries. In the West, old age is now a frequent cause of death with more people achieving a 'maximum' life span (which in itself has not been substantially increased). However, premature death is still the rule rather than the exception, due to the steep rise in degenerative diseases, which now dominate the statistics of morbidity and mortality. These have been dubbed 'the diseases of affluence'.

The biggest single scourge within the degenerative group is cardiovascular disease, followed closely by cancers. For cardiovascular disease it is now well recognised that low physical activity is a potent risk factor. This potency lies not so much in the strength of the risk factor, (lack of exercise being of similar weighting to high serum cholesterol, hypertension and smoking), but in its much greater prevalance. (Figure 1).

As dietary education and practice improve and tobacco consumption is reduced, so the importance of lack of exercise as a risk factor will become relatively even greater. Nor are the four risk factors referred to entirely independent. Indeed, taking up regular exercise may improve the lipid profile, reduce moderate degrees of hypertension, and affect other health-related behaviour, in particular helping the cessation of smoking.

Medical opinion endorses the importance of regular exercise to good cardiovascular health, despite the mechanism of protection not being fully understood.

However, inactivity also leads to physiological changes which include poor cardiovascular function, weakness of muscles and reduced bone strength. An individual finds that after a period of prolonged inactivity he or she cannot work as hard or for so long; a greater effort is required than previously and there is an increased sense of effort for any given task. Because levels of habitual physical activity among the general population are low this disability, attributable to an inactive lifestyle, is an unnecessary but not uncommon cause of incapacity. The Toronto Conference concluded that 'Exercise training in the fifth and sixth decades of life may alleviate this decline, but more importantly will induce a functional gain, equivalent to as much as 10 to 15 years of ageing in many individuals[1].

Prevalence of four coronary risk factors in the population of the United States

Figure 1

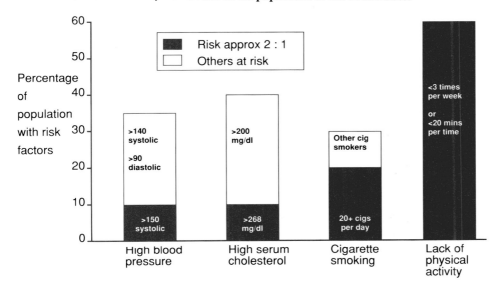

The relative importance of the lack of physical activity as a risk factor for disease and as a cause of incapacity and loss of functional ability is emphasised by the comparatively low levels of habitual physical activity among the adult population. For example, data collected by the Centers for Disease Control, Atlanta showed that approximately 60% of Americans do not perform physical activity with the regularity likely to offer protection against coronary heart disease (the criterion they use is a threshold of three or four times a week for at least 20 minutes)[2].

Figure 1, which compares the four main CHD risk factors, demonstrates why health education to encourage exercise should be a priority. The other three risk factors have a much lower incidence than the risk due to physical inactivity among the American population.

Information about the level of physical activity of the British population is sparse. In a pilot survey to develop the methodology for the national fitness survey (carried out in the West Midlands in 1988) results were similar to those found in Canadian and American studies. For example, the pilot survey results showed that:

• Only 6% of adults took part in regular weekly vigorous exercise.

- Around 30% engaged in some vigorous activity, but not regularly.
- Among people aged 60 and over more than 50% did little activity of any kind.

The health value of exercise is even more readily acknowledged by the general public. Typically, a random sample within a normal population will produce an affirmative response from at least 80% of those asked the question 'Do you think exercise is important for good health?' By contrast, a survey of activity among the same individuals will usually reveal that only some 15 to 25% take any regular exercise of consequence. This huge gap which we find between belief (in the value of exercise) and behaviour (in taking any), is a good starting point for our discussion of the promotion of exercise.

There is certainly no lack of endeavour in this field. Regional and district health authorities have active health promotion teams, who see healthy exercise as one of their principal vehicles of intervention, and many authorities have formulated their own exercise policies and campaign strategies[3,4]. At national level, the Health Education Authority is committed to the promotion of exercise, principally through the 'Look after your Heart' campaign[4], and jointly with the Sports Council and the Department of Health in commissioning the first major investigation.[5]. This study of the physical activity, fitness and health of the nation is intended to improve the knowledge base for exercise counselling. At international level, such enterprises also exist, for example the 'Eurofit' projects initiated by the Council of Europe's Committee for the Development of Sport, and the Council's 'Sport for All' movement[7] which has positive health as well as the enjoyment of leisure among its objectives. The extensive exercise promotion campaign run by Canada Fitness is an interesting example of a national venture supported by government. Considerable success is claimed for this campaign in achieving the increase in participation reported over the years from 1976-88, the last eight of which are the period covered by the Campbell Survey[8].

How may exercise be promoted?

Given that it is desirable to encourage most people to take more exercise than they do at present, what are the avenues for bringing this about? There are three principal areas of lifestyle where physical activity may occur: 1) occupational activity; 2) leisure time activity, i.e. sport and games, and 3) incidental activity, including general mobility ('getting about') but also reflecting disposition to exertion.

Occupational physical activity has declined almost completely over the last half century in the developed countries, and it would now be quite difficult to find a population on which to carry out a study similar to Jerry Morris's pioneering work with bus drivers and conductors just 40 years ago[9]. Studies of the association between habitual exercise and morbidity now focus on the physical activity of leisure[10,11]. We cannot expect to promote exercise at the workplace by some sort of Luddite revolution, but the workplace may still provide more opportunities than it does at present for incidental exertion, especially the encouragement of walking and cycling to work (parking, changing and showering facilities)[12]. The recent growth of 'in-house' exercise schemes, within large corporations is an encouraging development, but such a provision needs to be very carefully designed and professionally resourced if it is to serve those who need it most.

Leisure is the obvious context for the promotion of physical activity. There has in some respects been a dramatic recent growth in the provision of access to active leisure. For example, the number of leisure centres in Britain has more than doubled in the last few years. Assuming that they are well attended, the question remains as to what extent this is by new recruits to exercise or by people who previously took exercise elsewhere. Recent studies still show a low percentage of physically active adults in the community[13]. We do know from statistics produced by the Sports Council that most sports are flourishing in terms of participation[14]. This must be a healthy sign, though a sceptic might suggest that perhaps more people are taking part in sport in an organized fashion who previously were participating more informally. Real facts about population activity levels are very elusive, and we hope that the approach of the Allied Dunbar National Fitness Survey through its questionnaire inventory of all recollectable physical activity will help clarify participation rates, whether casual or in the context of some sports body.

A recent phenomenon is the rapid growth of classes in 'keep-fit' type activities such as 'aerobics', 'pop mobility', and health club gymnasium-based exercises. It would seem that many people are driven by a perceived need for exercise, whether for health or to improve their appearance. The social appeal of exercising in a group is however a strong contribution to the success of these classes and probably for many people strongly complements or even overrides the medical or cosmetic incentive. Most of these activities are now well taught and supervised, and present a pleasurable means of health related exertion. The main content of a typical exercise programme is based on aerobic or 'heart and lungs' work rather than emphasising local muscle groups. Although popular enthusiasm for such classes has now persisted for over 20 years, we must be alert to the possibility that some aspects at least may be characteristic of a fashionable and therefore transient mode of social behaviour. Such a view is supported by the influence that the clothing for 'fitness' activity and for sport generally has exerted over everyday wear. Is the whole movement perhaps vulnerable to the caprice of 'popularity'? Some far-sighted commercial groups in the fitness industry are beginning to look to the broader horizons of exercise counselling for lifestyle change, including the taking up of activities of intrinsic value, rather than confining their prescription to exercise machines or fitness classes.

At this stage, in claiming that a more fulfilling and lasting benefit may be afforded to an individual by a sport, game or pursuit, we begin to identify the root cause of low participation in active leisure. The problem begins with the experiences offered to the growing child. Studies in several countries have shown that the principal decline in physical activity occurs during adolescence[15,16], even during the years of attendance at school, and that the activity status of the late teenager tends to determine adult activity. There are exceptions to this generality, particularly in recent years where people in middle age take up exercise because of health reasons and may be considerably more active in their middle years than they were in early adolescence. We know from Paffenbarger's 'Alumni' study[11] that it is more important to long-term cardiovascular health to exercise continuously throughout the middle years than to have had an athletic youth. The point remains that at the time where the maturing child should be presented with every opportunity for developing a lasting interest in a variety of physical activities, this does not effectively occur. It is easy to blame the physical education profession, but the accusation is unjust. Valiant attempts are made by physical educators in schools to present a large range of appropriate activities, including many which will last throughout adult life and suit the context of family leisure. But time and resources, particularly the former, are very limited. The time allotted to physical education has declined in most British schools and in many participation is made optional in later years. In primary schools the situation has recently been shown to be appalling in that hardly any vigorous activity was observed even during physical education lessons[16]. Physical education is rarely taught by specialists in primary schools and the amount and quality of instruction usually depend fortuitously on the ability and interest of the class teacher.

The situation is compounded by the nature of modern day childrens' leisure time activity. Rather than general play at an informal 'fun' level, instead a minority of children, potential elite performers, are involved in specialised, intensive training and practice, while somewhat more attend organized clubs, but the majority are hardly involved in active leisure at all. With average childrens' television watching time in excess of three hours a day, it is not difficult to see that, together with time for homework, eating, travel to and from school, very little time remains for active play. So it seems that, in the lives of many children, the school physical education periods, insubstantial as they are as a portion of that child's waking life, are the only significant occasions for physical exercise. Teaching does not always mean active doing, and although most physical education teachers will attempt to introduce as much vigorous activity into their classes as possible, in the knowledge that children in the main may have little other opportunity or inclination to exert themselves, many aspects of teaching physical activity require demonstration, explanations and other features which occupy time without providing exercise. It has also been seen by many teachers, quite properly, as incumbent on them to teach children about their bodies and the relationship of lifestyle and behaviour to health. Very often such teaching may only occur within the physical education syllabus. In all, the physical education teacher has an impossible task to perform given existing resources, a situation which has been highlighted by the recent report of the Secondary Heads Association[17]. In reality it is the whole community which is responsible for ensuring that children have an appropriately active lifestyle. Hence, the first and most important measure in improving the physical activity level of the nation is to give much more emphasis to the importance of physical education at school, and the need, within school, for other disciplines to contribute to health education. Most important of all, the whole community, especially parents, should recognise childrens' need for activity. Ultimately, the best way to build a physically active nation is through activity which people enjoy for its own sake. Of course such activity affords many other valuable cultural benefits beyond the maintenance or acquisition of good health, but that is not the subject of this chapter, except in that these benefits are more powerful stimuli to participation than the avoidance of ill-health.

Accepting that the major thrust in the promotion of exercise should be within the eduction and upbringing of children and adolescents, what can be done for those (unfortunately, it would seem, the majority of adults) who have passed through this phase of life without benefitting from either good positive advice or direct experience of pleasurable activity? The health message seems well enough accepted, but as mentioned before, behaviour does not conform with belief. What then are the constraints on behaviour? First of all, physical exertion is relatively more uncomfortable for those who are least accustomed to it. This discomfort is accentuated by the natural disinclination of people generally to undertake anything which is not familiar to them. There is also embarrassment at not doing things well, at presenting or revealing a body shape or physique to others which does not conform to present-day cosmetic standards, and a cultural notion that the consequences of exertion - sweating, breathlessness, redness of the skin - are socially unattractive, even repugnant and alarming. These cultural attitudes have reached an extreme point in our society where many people, perhaps even most, feel that they should not provoke the symptoms of exertion such as getting hot and sweaty without changing into special clothing to do so. Whereas it may be an ideal situation that exercise should involve the change of clothing followed by a shower and a rest in a peaceful social environment, effective exercise promotion should include encouraging people to be more exertion-seeking in their general lives. All those involved in exercise promotion in the community have talked glibly about persuading people to walk rather than take the car, to climb stairs rather than using the lift and so on. Such advice is frustrated by the cultural attitudes just mentioned. Habitually sedentary people will also be accustomed to wearing clothing which keeps them adequately warm at very low levels of exertion and which in consequence causes them to rapidly overheat if they do take exercise. Other more obvious constraints are make-up, expensive hairstyles and movement-inhibiting clothing, particularly footwear. The possibilities for re-education in this enormously complex cultural area need the closest study and it has to be recognised that it is unlikely that a substantial erosion of attitudes will be achieved, at least in the short term. Perhaps one of the most fruitful lines will be the encouragement of the existing trend for lighter, more casual clothing for everyday wear, supported perhaps by the notion that moderate exertion in an appropriately clothed person will produce desirable levels of body warmth rather than overheating and discomfort. It would help too if, for example, the distorting and inhibitive footwear so often inflicted by fashion and peer-group pressure on women and girls were the subject of informed condemnation by health professionals.

To turn to the broader area of how our built environment, both urban and workplace, may contribute to imposing a greater level of physical activity upon our population, an obvious candidate for consideration is the increased creation of pedestrian areas. Many people will gladly use their own muscle power to get about if they can do so with convenience, comfort and overall safety. But we are so used to associating progress and luxury with the avoidance of exertion that very often the active option, where available, is distinctly unattractive. Grim subways and dingy stairwells in office buildings and hotels are the environment of the determined urban walker and stair climber. The cyclist has a worse deal in Britain than in most other European countries. There are very few effective urban cycling schemes, hardly any protected cycling routes in any of our major cities, and even the road surfaces are hazardous because of their poor maintenance. This inhibits the use of cycling for travel to and from work and shopping, which in turn reduces the perceived need for adequate parking facilities for cycles in towns and at places of work. We should look to the experience and example of town planners in major cities in other European countries to investigate the possibility of making Britain once again a cycling nation. Studies of aerobic fitness in cycling populations would be very informative.

Stemming from the foregoing, it can be seen that promotion of exercise makes a happy bedfellow with environmental concern; it is in fact a very 'green' endeavour. A real reduction in the use of the car for private transport, particularly within cities, could result from the measures advocated in the last paragraph. The use of leisure time for active pursuits, particularly emphasising those involving walking and cycling, would favour the conservation and protection of rural areas in the long term, despite the management problems that might initially occur.

Although the health value of exercise has been well accepted by the general public, there is still a need for much better and more detailed information. On the negative side, many people, particularly squash players, have been alarmed by the reports of deaths during vigorous exercise which although infrequent receive vivid coverage. The risk of exercise itself needs to be much better understood so that it may be explained to the individual who sees something of a paradox in taking exercise for the sake of health which in itself may increase the acute risk of a cardiovascular incident.

The other area of poor information, even misinformation, is that regarding the required dosage of exercise for health benefit. In almost every publication, whether it be popular fitness book or review in a professional journal, one finds reference to dosages loosely derived from the American College of Sports Medicine's recommendation[19] concerning the desirable frequency, intensity and duration of exercise for health. The recommendations have led to a generalized view that exercise to benefit cardiovascular health must take place at least three times a week, must on each occasion last for 20 to 40 minutes, and that it must take the heart rate up to or beyond certain threshold levels. Research evidence is scanty to support this view; not, perhaps, that such a prescription may well represent for an average middle-aged man an optimum regime, but that it is the *minimum* effective dosage. For the sedentary person, it is discouraging and in many cases totally inhibiting to be told that such a frequency and duration are the minimum requirements. Clearly, a common reaction is to say, 'Well if that's it, I can't manage that so I won't bother at all!' That a lower frequency is ineffective is very challengeable, and even more so is the inadequacy of shorter durations. Are we really wishing to say to the previously sedentary person that a 1 hour walk once a week is of no cardiovascular benefit, likewise a 10 minute cycle ride several times a week? The comprehensive message, and it is a simple one, that needs to be delivered is that virtually any increase over the previous habit level of exercise will bring about an improvement in fitness. At a later stage then perhaps frequencies, durations and intensities of the order proposed by the American College of Sports Medicine may be discussed as target objectives.

The common suggestion that pulse rate should be self monitored to ensure the adequacy of training intensity and even to prevent excessive exertion, is for most individuals impracticable and unrealistic. Monitoring during exercise itself is impossible without instrumentation, and unreliable even with all but the most expensive devices, while stopping suddenly to take the pulse at intervals is difficult, inaccurate and physiologically questionable. The concept of effective and safe training heart rate 'zones' is, however, sound. What people need is guidance in recognising when their bodies are working at the required level. Perception of exertion is the key to self-monitoring. One of the principal challenges to the health educator is to help the sedentary individual recognise and understand the normal healthy sensations and symptoms of vigorous exercise which he may at present be disposed to perceive as the onset of health-threatening exhaustion. Where facilities and resources exist this can be done by monitoring heart rate on a cycle ergometer (or treadmill) and teaching the individual to equate their own sensations with the measured response. Using the Borg Scale[20] they can then be directed to exertion in the 12-14 range as optimal, somewhat higher perhaps for those already in training. But usually such resources do not exist and effective counselling as in all aspects of health promotion will depend on the tact, imagination, understanding and ingenuity of the health professional.

References

1   *Exercise, fitness and health, a Consensus of Current Knowledge.* eds Bouchard C., Shephard R.J., Stephens T., Sutton J.R., McPherson B.D., Human Kinetics Books, Champaign, Illinois, USA. (1990).

2   *Morbidity and Mortality Weekly Report.* Centers for Disease Control. (July 1987).

3   *Exercise Policy for Coventry.* Coventry Health Authority, (1988).

4   *Finding the Key to Fitness. A Community Handbook for Fitness & Health.* West Midlands Regional Health Authority. (1988).

5   *Beating Heart Disease in the 1990's, a strategy for 1990-1995.* Health Education Authority, London. (1990).

6   *Project Description, Allied Dunbar National Fitness Survey.* Published by Allied Dunbar on behalf of the Department of Health, Health Education Authority and the Sports Council. (1990).

7   Marchand J. (1990) *Sport for All in Europe.* Council of Europe, HMSO, London.

8   Stephens T., Craig C.L. (1990) *The Well-Being of Canadians: Highlights of the 1988 Campbell's Survey.* Canada Fitness and Lifestyle Research Institute, Ottawa.

9   Morris J.N., Heady J.A., Raffle P.A.N., Roberts C.G. and Parks J.W. (1953) 'Coronary heart disease and physical activity of work.' *Lancet,* (ii), 1053-1057.

10 Morris J.N., Everitt M.G., Pollard R. and Chave S.P.W. 'Vigorous Exercise in Leisure Time; protection against coronary heart disease.' *Lancet,* (1980) (ii), 1207-1210.

11 Paffenbarger R.S. Jr, Hyde R.T., Wing A.L. and Steinmetz C.H. (1984) 'A natural history of athleticism and cardiovascular health.' *Journal of the American Medical Association,* 252, 491-495.

12 Muir Gray J.A., Young A., Ennis J.R. (1983) 'Promotion of Exercise at Work.' *British Medical Journal,* 286; 1958-159.

13 *Office of Population Censuses and Surveys General Household Survey 1986.* HMSO, London. (1989).

14 *Sport in the Community - Into the 90's Strategy for Sport. 1989-93.* The Sports Council, London (1988).

15 Butcher J., Hall M.A. (1983) *Adolescent girls' participation in physical activity.* Edmonton: Planning services, Alberta Education.

16 Engstrom L.M. (1986) 'The progress of socialisation into keep-fit activities.' *Scand J Sports Sci,* 8, 89-97.

17 Sleap M. and Warburton P. (1990) *Physical activity patterns of primary school children: Interim Report.* Look after your heart 'Happy Heart Project'. Health Education Authority, London

18 *A report on survey concerning sport in secondary schools. SHA.* (1990).

19 ACSM. (1978) 'Position statement on the recommended quantity and quality of exercise for developing and maintaining fitness in health adults.' *Med Sci Sports Exc,* 10, vii-x..

20   Borg G.A.V. (1982) 'Psychological bases of perceived exertion.' *Med Sci Sports Exc*, 14, 377-384.

Stress Management

11

Michael Frost, South Birmingham Psychology Service

Dr Peter Nixon, Consultant Cardiologist at Charing Cross Hospital, noticed that after a heart attack some of his patients began to lead healthier and happier lives and that ten years later, they were 'physically more active and more efficient in the business of living and making a living than they were before the breakdown.'[1] He calls them gifted patients. One of these was Rex Edwards who wrote of his experience:

> *I know for a certainty that I will never have another heart attack, unless in some way it is brought about by me, either by allowing my physical condition to degenerate, my mind and body to become overtired and overtaxed, or by permitting a too personal and subjective reaction to some situation of stress. This conviction has relieved my mind of its most potent weapon for destruction: worry ... Stage two on my road back to health was the ability at last to learn to 'box clever' - that is to deal with all stressful conditions, whatever their nature, intelligently and constructively or else calmly to refuse to have anything to do with them. This implies a degree of mental awareness and self control which is difficult to cultivate, but which , with perseverance, will always come. Instead of reacting to a situation - one reacts with reason. In matters involving personalities one comes to understand other people better, to see more of them as it were. Situations which contain the seeds of hostility undergo a subtle and significant change: in fact life itself takes on altogether more significance.*[2]

The research evidence supports the anecdotal. In a recent review, Bennett and Carroll[3] concluded that learning how to cope with stress can significantly reduce levels of blood pressure, serum cholesterol, and the type A behaviour pattern. These risk factors are independent and multiplicative in their effect. Any one doubles the risk of developing coronary heart disease (CHD), two quadruple it and three produces an eight fold increased risk. A single intervention that can moderate all three, and whose only side effect is an increased enjoyment in living, is of considerable clinical importance.

Although there has been very little research into the effectiveness of stress management techniques in reducing the incidence of CHD, the early findings are positive and promising. Ninety nine people, with two or more risk factors for

CHD, underwent stress management training with Patel and her colleagues[4]. Only one developed CHD during the next four years compared with six, one of whom died in a matched control group that received only health education advice. The Recurrent Coronary Prevention Programme[5] (RCPP), which focused upon modifying the coronary prone Type A Behaviour Pattern, reduced the cardiac recurrence rate to 12.9% over a four and a half year period compared with 21.2% for patients treated with a more medically orientated rehabilitation programme. Nevertheless, this latter group had its exceptional patients. Overall, those patients who reported the most behavioural change had the least recurrence of CHD.

Even though a wide variety of psychological techniques is used in stress management training, stress management programmes are remarkably consistent in their structure. They differ in what they include rather than what they leave out. Patel's programme is one of the simplest. It consists of eight weekly sessions of an hour each and centres upon the essentials of relaxation training with some stress education including a film 'Stresses and Strains' by Walt Disney. (For a fuller outline of the programme see Appendix VII in Hart[6]). It is of particular value in the treatment of patients with hypertension who do not show marked features of the coronary prone personality, such as time urgency and hostility[7]. The RCPP which was designed to address these problems uses a remarkably comprehensive range of techniques which have been described by Powell and Friedman.[8]

The optimum design of a stress management programme depends mostly upon the assessed needs of the patient, and ideally, should also incorporate a system for evaluation and programme development. There are many stress checklists, profiles and questionnaires available. Since they tend to focus on only one aspect or other of the Stress Pathway, such as life events, type A behaviour, or subjective signs of strain, their usefulness is limited. Some programmes solve the problem by using a battery of tests. Another solution is to use the Derogatis Stress Profile[9] (DSP), in both assessment and evaluation. It is a 77 item questionnaire which has been directly derived from Lazarus's Interactional Theory of stress[10] and which samples dimensions appropriate to CHD (Figure 1).

The ideal number of people for a stress management group is eight to twelve. There is no clear guidance about how long a programme should last but six to eight sessions is fairly typical. The RCCP, which has been the most extravagant programme to date, offered weekly sessions for two months, biweekly for two months and then once a month for the remainder of the study, totalling 29 sessions in all. Whatever its advantages[11], with a 42.7% drop out rate[5] a programme of this length runs into the problem of diminishing returns.

Group membership adds an extra dimension to stress management training[12]. It provides an opportunity for developing close, supportive relationships. It confronts people with the negative consequences of their defensive coping styles and allows them to experiment with more appropriate behaviour in the

The Structure of the Derogatis Stress Profile *Figure 1*

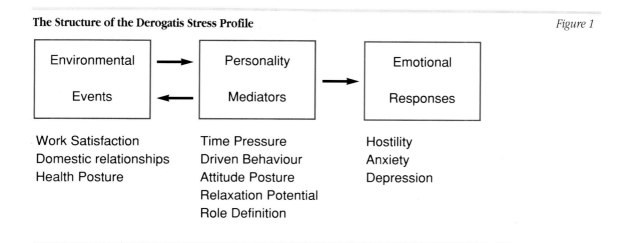

Environmental Events	Personality Mediators	Emotional Responses
Work Satisfaction	Time Pressure	Hostility
Domestic relationships	Driven Behaviour	Anxiety
Health Posture	Attitude Posture	Depression
	Relaxation Potential	
	Role Definition	

safety of the group. Thus the people who benefited most from the RCCP were those with high levels of hostility who alienate themselves from others, and as a consequence have low levels of social support.[13] Unfortunately, they are also the most likely to drop out, so that careful attention needs to be given to the dynamics of the group.

It is good practice to begin each session with a 'warm up' exercise[14] and to end it with a debriefing. In the first session the group members might be invited to introduce themselves and to say something about the significance of their names; why they were chosen or what they mean. Then they might take turns in describing a period in their lives when they felt completely free of stress.

The first step in learning how to cope with stress is learning what it is and being able to recognise when one is suffering from it. The first part of this can be addressed with a talk on the nature of stress and its association with health and CHD. The second requires that people have the opportunity to identify their own personal pattern of response to stress. A symptom checklist can be used to raise awareness and because it can not be exhaustive, to generate discussion (Figure 2).

Figure 2. Checklist of stressful symptoms

Physical Symptoms	**Rating of Frequency**

Muscular tension ....

Muscular aches and pains ....

Tension headache ....

Palpitations ....

Changes in appetite ....

Indigestion ....

Constipation or diarrhoea ....

Breathlessness ....

Dizziness ....

Tiredness ....

Feeling weak ....

Insomnia ....

Behavioural Signs

Smoking ....

Drinking more than usual ....

Poor concentration ....

Putting things off ....

Inability to finish things ....

Reduced level of skill ....

Avoiding people ....

Stress related thoughts

Intrusive, unwanted thoughts ....

Worrying obsessively ....

Inability to make a decision ....

Self critical ....

Critical to others ....

Lapses of memory ....

Emotional Symptoms

Irritability ....

Anger or resentment ....

Loss of temper ....

Anxiety ....

Feeling weepy ....

Feeling helpless ....

Loss of sense of humour ....

Feeling guilty ....

An exercise derived from Gestalt[15] therapy and modified by Nelson-Jones[16] can help to develop a more immediate awareness of the signs of strain. It is also useful as a means of identifying the difference between thinking and sensory awareness, learning to stay in the present, and the realisation that one often has a choice in whether to suffer discomfort or not. For example, as one becomes aware of muscular tension, so the choice between tension and relaxation presents itself. The members of the group take turns to be in the 'hot seat' whilst the leader talks them through the exercise.

Gestalt Awareness Exercise

1   Close your eyes and listen carefully. Then say: "Now I am aware of hearing ………" and complete the sentence. Notice the difference between listening to thoughts and the sound of the outside world.

2   Open your eyes and become aware of what you can see. In a similar fashion, complete the sentence: "Now I am aware of seeing ………"

3   Now become aware of the physical sensations in your body at the point of contact with the outside world. The pressure of the chair, the warmth of the sun, the texture and weight of your clothes.

4   Become aware of the sensations in your body such as the muscular tensions, your heart beat and pulse, the sensation of warmth in your stomach.

5   Now allow your awareness to drift from one sense to another. As you become aware of sensations, say "Now I am aware of choosing to ………" and make a choice between holding on to a sensation or modifying it. (e.g. Now I am aware of choosing to take off my jacket and tie rather than suffer with the heat).

Not only do people respond to stress in different ways, they also vary in the situations that they experience as stressful. Maintaining a Stress Awareness Diary is a good way of monitoring daily hassles and the accompanying signs of strain.

Stress Awareness Diary

Time	Situation	Symptom of Strain
8.05	Stuck in traffic at roadworks	Pounding the steering wheel. Thinking that I am going to be late. Shout at the temporary signals to hurry up.

Time	Situation	Symptom of Strain
8.15	Someone carves me up at the roundabout and makes a rude gesture	Angry, Gritting teeth
8.20	Arrive at work find that first client has cancelled	Headache. Frustration Feel short of breath

There are three options for dealing with the stress that accompanies the hassles of daily living. The first is to remove the cause, the second is to reframe the way that it is perceived, and the third is to modify the response. Since it is impossible to be relaxed and under stress simultaneously[17] and because relaxation facilitates problem solving both in thought and deed, it is most appropriate to begin at the end of the stress pathway and review the techniques for modifying the stress response.

Progressive Relaxation[18] teaches the distinction between muscular tension and relaxation by first creating tension in a muscle group and then suddenly releasing it. For example, by making a fist and clenching it tighter and tighter, becoming aware of the tension that is being created in the hand and forearm and then letting it go. Notice the difference between tension and relaxation. Whilst tensing up there is a tendency to hold one's breath as the costal muscles will also tense in sympathy. This can be obviated by breathing in as one tenses the muscle group and breathing out as one lets go. This procedure is known as 'Cue Controlled Relaxation' and is to be preferred over the basic progressive relaxation technique.

Correct breathing habits are an important part of stress management, particularly as an antidote to hyperventilation during periods of acute stress, and upper chest breathing as a result of chronic abdominal tension. Hyperventilating lowers the concentration of carbon dioxide in the blood, which can result in myocardial vasoconstriction, that in turn can result in a pain that mimics angina. Costal breathing reduces the amount of available oxygen, placing an increased demand upon cardiovascular activity. In Eastern cultures breathing exercises have long been integral in learning to quieten the body and the mind.[19] Stress management training borrows heavily from these techniques. The basic exercise is Breathing Awareness to slow and deepen the breath which facilitates diaphragmatic rather than costal breathing. People often find active breathing exercises difficult and become breathless or giddy. The group leader can talk through the following exercise, which is very gentle, relies upon imagery and just letting things happen.[20]

1   Lie flat on the floor with legs straight and slightly apart with arms at the sides and not touching the body with palms uppermost.

2   Breathe regularly and place your hand at the point which moves the most as you breathe. (If this is on the upper chest, point out that the body is not making the best use of the air).

3   Now place your left hand on your upper chest and your right hand upon your abdomen. Imagine that your stomach is a balloon which inflates as you inhale, lifting your right hand. As you breathe out it deflates and your hand lowers. All the while your other hand remains still.

4   Do not force things. Just be aware of the movement of your hands and the rhythm of your breathing. Allow your right hand to rise and fall as your left hand remains still. Imagine that your right hand is a boat rising and falling on a gentle sea and your left is in the stillness of the harbour.

The breathing exercises naturally lead into a group of techniques for inducing states of deep mental and physical relaxation which include visualisation techniques[21], meditation[22], self hypnosis[23] and autogenic training[24]. It is useful to teach a range of techniques since individuals will find some more attractive and more effective than others. Some are also more appropriate for certain situations than others. For instance, autogenic techniques can be practised in a traffic jam and self hypnosis can be used as an aid to concentration. With practice these techniques become second nature. Until then it is necessary to keep a record of daily practice sessions and a diary recording the use and effectiveness of relaxation during moments of stress.

      The relaxation exercises will have demonstrated how some thoughts bring about feelings of peace whilst others create tension and arousal. There are three aspects of cognition that can moderate the experience of stress. The first of these is passive thinking which occurs as a stream of consciousness. This inner dialogue also contains active thoughts which differ from the passive by serving a practical or executive function, such as - 'I am going to make a cup of tea. Now where did I leave the kettle?' A passive thought merely states that something is the case, such as 'I am cold and miserable and fed up' or 'I am never going to be good enough to do this job properly.' Self doubting, anxiety provoking thoughts which are uncritically accepted are an independent source of stress and become the stuff of worry, unpleasant emotional states and self fulfilling prophecy. They can be interrupted by silently commanding oneself to stop, by tweaking an elastic band worn on the wrist or by visualising a red traffic light. Another thought can then be substituted by using the Gestalt awareness technique and focusing upon some other aspect of the situation - 'The snow on the trees is absolutely stunning.' Or the significance of the situation can be reframed[25] - 'I am learning from my mistakes all the time.'

The second is the manner in which experiences are interpreted. In the words of Epictetus: 'Man is not disturbed by events, but by the view he takes of them.' The role of disabling interpretations is briefly discussed elsewhere in this volume (Producing Behavioural Change) and is described at length by Beck et al[26] and by Ellis[27].

Both automatic thoughts and the interpretation of experience are supported by a set of beliefs and attitudes that are an aspect of an individual's personality. For example, the person who scores highly on the 'Driven Behaviour Scale' of the DSP is someone who feels that they should always be involved in something constructive and not waste time on trivia. Their motto might be 'If something is worth doing it is worth doing well.' Someone who scores low on this scale would probably believe that if something is worth doing, it is worth doing badly. A high scorer on 'Attitude posture' believes that they are only as good as their achievements. Their motto might be 'If at first you don't succeed, try, try and try again'. A low scorer would be more likely to think 'try again by all means but if you fail try something different'.

Stress inoculation[28] training within the safety of the group provides an opportunity to experiment with different ways of thinking about and approaching stressful situations.

An Outline of Stress Inoculation

1   Describe the difficult situation using the present tense.

    What thoughts do you have in this situation?

    In single words, describe your feelings.

    Describe how you would typically behave.

2   What result do you want out of this situation?

    What is the worst thing that could happen?

    What good things might come about as a consequence of the worst happening?

3   What do you have to do to meet the demands of the situation?

    Work out a plan.

    Avoid negative statements - be rational.

    Relax.

4   Role play the situation using the new plan.

     Focus on what you have to do, not on what you feel.

     The feelings are what you expected them to be.

     Take slow deep breaths - relax.

5   Feedback from the Group.

     Reinforce the good things.

     Modify the plan as necessary.

Closely allied to stress inoculation are the techniques for developing assertiveness. The popular view of the unassertive character is the person who finds it difficult to express strong feeling and as a result never gets what he wants. Equally problematic is the hostile and aggressive person who is never taken advantage of but whom nobody wants to know. By contrast, the assertive person can stand up for himself and yet be considerate of other people's feelings. As hostility is associated with heart attacks and anger with angina, particular attention should be paid to its creative use in developing assertiveness.[29,30]

In the space available, it has been possible to describe only a limited number of stress management techniques. There are a great number of stress management texts and resources currently available; many of indifferent quality. There are three which would make a very useful contribution to the design of a stress management programme. The most comprehensive and the most practical is Davis, Eshelman and McKay.[31] Patel's[32] contribution in its theoretical passages is more directly relevant to CHD and Wallace and Bundy[33] direct their attention to the needs of patients who suffer with angina.

References

1   Nixon P.G.F (1989) Human Functions and the Heart. in Seedhouse D. and Cribb A. (eds) *Changing Ideas in Health Care.* John Wiley and Sons, London.

2   Edwards R. (1964) *Coronary Case.* Faber, London.

3   Bennett P. and Carroll D. (1990) 'Stress management approaches to the prevention of coronary heart disease.' *British Journal of Clinical Psychology,* 29,1-12.

4   Patel C., Marmot M.G., Terry D.J., Carruthers M., Hunt B., Patel M. (1985) Trial of relaxation in reducing coronary risk: four year follow up. *British Medical Journal,* 290, 1103-1106.

5   Friedman M., Thoreson D.E., Gill J.J., Ulmer D., Powell L.H., Price V.A., Brown B., Thompson L., Rabin D., Breal W.S., Bourg E., Levy R., & Dixon T. (1986) Alteration of Type A behaviour and its effect on cardiac recurrences in post myocardial infarction patients: Summary results of the recurrent coronary prevention project. *American Heart Journal,* 112,4,653-665.

6   Hart J.T. (1987) *hypertension Second Edition* Appendix VII pp. 241-242. Churchill Livingstone.

7   Johnston D. and Steptoe A. (1989) 'Hypertension'. In Pearce S. and Wardle J. (eds) *The Practice of Behavioural Medicine.* The British Psychological Society in association with Oxford Science Publications.

8   Powell L.H. and Friedman M. (1986) 'Alteration of Type A behaviour in coronary patients.' In Christie M. and Mellett P.G. (eds) *The Psychosomatic Approach,* Wiley.

9   Derogatis L.R. (1984) *The Derogatis Stress Profile (DSP): A summary report.* Clinical Psychometric Research, 1228 Wine Spring Lane, Baltimore, Maryland 21204.

10 Lazarus R.S. (1966) *Psychological Stress and the Coping Process,* McGraw Hill, New York.

11 Price V.A. (1988) 'Research and clinical issues in treating type A behaviour.' In Houston B.K. and Snyder C.R. (eds) *Type A Behaviour Pattern: Research, Theory and Intervention.* Wiley.

12 Yalom, I..D. (1970) *The Theory and Practice of Group Psychotherapy.* Basic Books, New York.

13 Powell L.H., Thoreson C.E., & Friedman M. (1985) 'Modification of the Type A Behaviour pattern after myocardial infarction.' In Hofmann (ed) *Primary and Secondary Prevention of Coronary Heart Disease.* Springer-Verlag, Berlin.

14 Brandes D. & Phillips H. (1978) *The Gamesters Handbook.* Hutchinson.

15 Perls F., Hefferline R. H., Goodman P. (1973) *Gestalt Therapy: Excitement and Growth in the Human Personality.* Penguin Books, Harmondsworth.

16 Nelson-Jones R. (1988) 'Choice Therapy'. *Counselling Psychology Quarterly,* 1,1,43-55.

17 Wolpe J. (1969) *The Practice of Behaviour Therapy*. Pergamon Press, New York.

18 Jacobson E. (1976) *You Must Relax*. Souvenir Press, London.

19 Levey J. (1987) *The Fine Arts of Relaxation, Concentration and Meditation: Ancient Skills for Modern Minds*. Wisdom Publications, London.

20 Poppen R. (1988) *Behavioural Relaxation Training and Assessment*. Pergamon Press, New York.

21 Fanning P. (1988) *Visualisation for Change*. New Harbinger Publications, Oakland.

22 Harp D. (1987) *The Three Minute Meditator*. Mind's eye press, San Francisco.

23 LeCron L. (1970) *Self Hypnosis*. New American Library, New York.

24 Schultz J.H. and Luthe W. (1969) *Autogenic Training Volume 1*. Grune and Stratton, New York.

25 Bandler R., and Grinder J. (1982) *Reframing*. Real People Press, Utah.

26 Beck A.T., Rush A.J., Shaw B.F., and Emery G. (1979) *Cognitive Therapy of Depression*. Guildford, New York.

27 Ellis A. (1984) 'Rational Emotive Therapy'. In Corsini R.J. (ed) *Current Psychotherapies*, 3rd edn. F.E. Peacock. Itasca, Illinois.

28 Meichenbaum D. and Jaremko M. (1983) *Stress Reduction and Prevention*. Plenum, New York.

29 Novaco R.W. (1979) 'The cognitive regulation of anger and stress.' In Kendall P. and Hallon S. (eds) *Cognitive Behavioural Interventions: Theory and Procedures*. Academic Press, New York.

30 Bach G. and Goldberg H. (1974) *Creative Aggression*. Doubleday, New York.

31 Davis M., Eshelman E.R. and McKay M. (1988) *The Relaxation and Stress Reduction Workbook*, 3rd edn. New Harbinger Publications, Oakland.

32 Patel C. (1989) *The Complete Guide to Stress Management*. Macdonald Optima, London.

33 Wallace L. and Bundy C. (1990) *Coping with Angina*. Thorsons, Wellingborough.

III
Involving People Outside
the N.H.S.

12 The Environmental Health Department

N.B. Lawrence, Environmental Services Department,
Birmingham City Council

Introduction

The nature of the Environmental Health Officer's role in coronary heart disease Prevention is not immediately clear. The Environmental Health Officer's diverse range of duties; food hygiene, occupational health and safety, slum clearance and housing renovation, pollution and pest control, that all embracing term 'nuisances', and, more recently, health promotion, look more like a list of local authority services than a job description! Environmental Health Officers have always attempted to improve 'individual' health by securing 'environmental' improvements in these diverse fields. The principle that 'prevention is better than cure' still holds as true today as it did in the prevention of infectious diseases during the nineteenth and early twentieth centuries. In recent years therefore Environmental Health Officers have applied the same approach to the prevention of so-called 'lifestyle' illnesses such as Coronary Heart Disease.

Many people already have a basic awareness of the causes of coronary heart disease, but even the strongest will can be sapped by an average day of fried canteen meals, smoky workplaces and public houses, and the inexorable influence of TV advertising. Pursuing a low fat, high fibre, non-smoking, sensible drinking and aerobic life style is rarely the easy 'choice'. Providing an 'environment' which encourages the adoption of healthy lifestyles is a complex but essential requisite in securing any significant reduction in Coronary Heart Disease.

A new 'Public Health Movement', committed to achieving improvements in the services and superstructure which can determine the healthy 'choices' at an individual's disposal, is still in its infancy. Nevertheless, many Local Authorities have registered a commitment to health promotion, in its widest sense. The World Health Organisation's 'Health for All by the Year 2000' campaign has helped to accelerate this process by identifying targets which are intended to improve the population's health, and reduce inequalities.

Developing coronary heart disease prevention policies

The Environmental Health Department is traditionally responsible for 'leading' on health issues within the Local Authority. Of the 402 local authorities in England, Wales and Northern Ireland, 228 employ Environmental Health Officers who co-ordinate Health Promotion activities. By 1988, 127 local authorities were committed to achieving the 'Health For All' targets whilst 128 local authorities were actively considering doing so.[1]

As a major employer and an influential force on community and industrial development, local authorities can play a significant role in a wide range of health issues. The final decision about what a Local Authority does is taken by the elected members (Councillors). Their support can lend legitimacy to health-related proposals. Many local authorities operate a 'corporate' decision making process which allows policies proposed by one Department to be adopted and disseminated by others. Bermingham City Council Environmental Health Committee, for example supported a smoking policy which resulted in every city council workplace discussing, voting upon, and in most cases introducing, no smoking areas. Smoking advertisements were subsequently banned from City Council hoardings. Tobacco sponsorship has been refused for the Birmingham Super Prix roadrace and even the smoking habits of prospective foster parents are now taken into account by the Social Services Department.

The relationship between Health Authorities and Local Authority Environmental Health Departments can also be important in strengthening and disseminating health-related proposals or policies. This is easiest to achieve where the local authority shares the same geographical boundaries as the Health Authority. Life is not always so simple! Birmingham City Council's boundaries include four health authorities and form only a small part of the 20 health authorities within the Regional Health Authority. Despite this, successful joint initiatives have been organised. Nationally, only 18 local authorities have *no* formal links with Health Authorities and 21 local authorities operate jointly financed health promotion activity[2].

Although it is important to persuade local authorities and health authorities to adopt health-related policies, it is the professionals 'on the ground' that can ensure their success. The 'network' which often exists between district nurses, environmental health officers and social workers can achieve a great deal for 'problem' clients. In the same way health promotion and primary care staff from the health authorities, environmental health officers, teachers and other local authority based professionals make a powerful team. It isn't just that 'many hands make light work', working together means more ideas, opportunities and often a great deal of enthusiasm as well.

Implementing coronary heart disease preventive policies

To succeed, any Coronary Heart Disease prevention policy pursued by an over-worked and under-resourced public sector organisation, must compete effectively with the social pressures which are already 'selling' an often far from healthy lifestyle.

Providing information about coronary heart disease is an essential part of such a strategy. Environmental Health Departments often target the distribution of health promotion material around high profile 'events', such as 'No Smoking Day', 'Drinkwise Day', 'Low Fat Fortnight' etcetera. Many of these events are organised nationally by the Health Education Authority, usually with the support of pressure groups or commercial sponsorship. They allow participating organisations, however large or small, to become involved, without wasting unnecessary time and effort in creating their own materials and ideas.

Local campaigns can also be linked by 'umbrella' organisations, such as the 'Look After Your Heart!', 'Health For All' or 'Healthy Cities' Campaigns. If a local Committee can succeed in gaining the support of local authorities, health authorities, and voluntary agencies, their pooled resources and combined mailing systems can access most community facilities including schools, libraries, leisure centres, health centres, G.P. surgeries and clinics.

These Campaigns are not centrally funded to any large extent. The national 'Look After Your Heart!' Campaign will pay local grants for some time limited initiatives but most participating groups are expected to resource their own activities. Multi-agency organisations such as local 'Look After Your Heart!' campaigns are more likely to succeed in bidding for commercial sponsorship, health authority or urban programme funding, than would be the case if each constituent organisation sought funding separately.

A great deal of free publicity can also be obtained from the media. Local daily newspapers tend to concentrate on media stunts, (public displays, launches etc.), personal interest stories or health related advertising features. Many of the weekly advertising newspapers are more than willing to carry regular features if they are provided in a readable style, and on time!

However imaginative and consistent a message may be, there is , of course, no guarantee that the public will take any notice! It is all too easy to eat a bar of chocolate, or a bag of chips, because nothing else is available. Examining the contributory factors for coronary heart disease reveals a number of other areas where the environmental health officer can make a positive contribution.

Diet

The 'low fat, high fibre' message is not a difficult one to communicate and is a proven commercial success. Wholemeal bread sandwiches do sell better than white bread; baked potatoes will be chosen instead of chips as will low fat milk drinks if they are offered and displayed in an attractive manner. Shops which have recognised this deserve praise whilst those that haven't which often includes subsidised work canteens and 'take aways', need encouragement to improve their menus. Many Environmental Health Departments operate the national 'Heartbeat Award' scheme to do this. The scheme is jointly administered by the Institution of Environmental Health Officers and by the Health Education Authority. At a local level the 'Heartbeat Award', may be run by Environmental Health Officers, Health Promotion Officers and the Health Authority Dietitians (if the Local Authority does not have its own). Any catering premises, whether eat-in or take away, are eligible for the award if they maintain good standards of food hygiene, provide no smoking areas, and offer a variety of healthy food choices. This does not mean 'unhealthy' food cannot be offered but the alternatives must always be available and displayed prominently. Businesses receiving the award will get a certificate and sticker which can be displayed on their premises and used in advertising material. Ninety five local authorities were running the Heartbeat Award Scheme by 1988 and a further 27 were considering doing so. By 1990, 820 awards had been awarded nationally.

Smoking

Smoking tobacco represents the single largest preventable cause of coronary heart disease. Environmental Health Officers have played an active role in the campaign to reduce tobacco use. By 1988, 156 local authorities engaged in anti-smoking activity, 86 operated a smoking policy and 87 were intending to do so.[4]

Early in 1989 the European Commission produced a draft directive proposing that European member states pass legislation restricting smoking within all public and work places.[5] The British Government opposed this vociferously but sympathetic support from other member states and the lead already taken by the United States[6] almost certainly means that it will eventually be implemented in the UK. The draft directive also seeks to establish the legal principle that the right of the non-smoker to health overrides any 'right' smokers have to smoke.

It has only been socially acceptable to smoke in public since the first world war, but this alone has probably been the major factor in promoting smoking amongst young people.

'Allowing unrestricted smoking denies you freedom of choice and your right to unpolluted air.[7]'

The current trend away from social acceptance of smoking can be seen most clearly in the proliferation of 'smoke-free' workplaces. It is likely that over the next few years Environmental Health Departments will be forced to take legal proceedings to require the implementation of a 'no-smoking' policy within one of the non-factory workplaces where the local authority have responsibility for the enforcement of Health and Safety at Work legislation.

Industrial tribunals have already recognised the legitimacy of smoking policies when the workforce involved are consulted, given adequate notice, and provided with some form of support e.g. access to smokers cessation classes etc[8]. Cynics might suggest that the eagerness shown by many employers in introducing smoking policies arises from the lower absenteeism rates amongst non-smokers and the consequential reduction in fire risks, redecoration costs and stock damage. However, 'grass roots' support from much of the work force is also a significant factor. The consultation procedure in introducing the workplace smoking policy is often the first involvement many workers have had in determining policy affecting their working environment and can provide an important basis for further health promotion work.

Much of the media attention given to the European Community Draft Directive has been focused on proposals to restrict smoking within indoor places used by the public for the provision of services. This would include shops, places of entertainment, sports facilities, libraries, health centres, modes of transport, and so on. The risks of inhaling environmental tobacco smoke have now been formally recognised by the Government[9]. This fact, coupled with the worrying increase in smoking amongst teenage girls,[10] lends little justification to the Government decision not to impose at least partial smoking restriction within public places or at least restriction in premises frequented by young people. Successive surveys have demonstrated the public support for banning smoking in public places.

'Non smokers now comprise two thirds of the adult population in the UK and are therefore a force to be reckoned with.'[11]

Birmingham City Council has launched a campaign to restrict smoking in all public places by the year 2000. By providing publicity and advice it is hoping to demonstrate to businesses the 'commercial sense' of introducing smoke-free areas without having to resort to legal proceedings, although this possibility has not been excluded.

Environmental Health Officers, along with Trading Standards Officers, and occasionally, the police, can be empowered to prosecute shopkeepers for the illegal tobacco sales to children under the age of 16 in contravention of the Protection of Children (Tobacco) Act 1986. The pressure group 'Parents Against Tobacco' is now seeking more widespread enforcement of this legislation. They estimate 50% of shops which sell tobacco break the legislation on a regular basis, although in the U.K. during 1988 there were only 29 prosecutions and 23 convictions. There are, however, serious problems in the enforcement of this legislation. Prosecutions have been secured by Officers using children to carry out 'test' purchases of tobacco. This practice gave rise to the claim that the children were being used as 'agent provocateurs'. The most practical way of avoiding this situation is by members of the public coming forward as witnesses.

Exercise and stress

The importance of these inter-related factors in the prevention of coronary heart disease are often 'forgotten' by both Environmental Health Officers and employers. Environmental Health Officers frequently have contacts which can be useful for negotiating concessionary rates with local authority Leisure Services Departments or in organising 'Look After Yourself!' or other 'Keep Fit' groups. The holistic approach adopted by 'Look After Yourself!' offers much to workplace based coronary heart disease prevention. In Birmingham, the Environmental Health Department has trained staff to run these courses. These will initially be run within the local authority, but courses are also planned in private workplaces and community facilities.

Individual-based approaches to exercise and stress such as these fail to take into account environmental factors such as high stress/low physical exertion or monotonous work routines. Unfortunately, British courts would be unlikely to accept that poor job satisfaction, unrealistic management demands, a failure to improve repetitive work routines or provide access to exercise facilities represented an occupational hazard. This is not universally the case, Health and Safety Inspectors in the Netherlands, for example, are far more likely to concentrate on the 'quality' of working.[12]

References

1   Ashton L. (1989) *Summary of Health Promotion Activities, England, Wales and Northern Ireland.* Health Education Authority, pp. 24-25.

2   Ashton L. (1989) ibid pp. 26-28.

3   Ashton L. (1989) ibid p. 32.

4   Ashton L. (1989) pp. 31-32.

5   Commission of the European Communities Draft Council Recommendation on Banning Smoking in Public Places, December 1988

6   Anon; (1988) *Restrictions on Smoking - Legislation in Europe, Canada, Australia and USA.* Action on Smoking and Health (ASH).

7   Anon; (1987) *Non Smoking Provision in Public Places: A Checklist for Action.* Action on Smoking and Health (ASH).

8   Jenkins and McEwan et al. (1988) *Smoking Policies at Work.* Health Education Authority, Appendix B.

9   Independent Scientific Committee on Smoking and Health (The Frogatt Report (1988) HMSO, London.

10 Goddard E. *Smoking amongst Secondary School Children in England* (1989) HMSO, London.

11 Anon; (1987) *Non Smoking Provision in Public Places a Checklist for Action.* Action on Smoking and Health (ASH), p1.

12 Campbell S. (1986) *Labour Inspection in the European Community.* Health and Safety Commission pp. 62-65.

The Local Education Authority

Joe Harvey, Education Department, Birmingham City Council

13

A Local Education Authority (LEA) has two major roles, one as a 'provider' of the resources, skills and policies which deliver education, and the other as an 'employer' of many thousands of staff.

The LEA as an employer

As an employer the attitudes that it takes when instituting a pastoral care programme will be as important to its staff as a similar programme would be to children in schools. Though it is not the intention to spend time on an area covered in other chapters of this book, workplace policies to support healthy lifestyles are essential if the LEA is to retain credibility and sustain a consistent approach to promoting positive good health.

Staff should thus have access to and support from a smoking policy which bans smoking in education department meetings, education department buildings including all schools, and runs cessation classes to support its staff.

An alcohol policy should ensure adequate supplies of non-alcoholic drinks at education department functions, education on the problems of alcohol abuse and confidential counselling for staff with an alcohol problem.

A stress management policy should give all staff access to written advice and confidential independent counselling on recognising and managing stress in the workplace.

There are clearly large benefits in being a health promoting employer as managers in business and commerce are increasingly showing they understand. There are equally real dangers facing governing bodies and LEA's from the increasing likelihood of litigation from teachers from the damage caused by passive smoking in staff rooms. But the greatest beneficiary of sound adult lifestyle programmes however are the major customer, the children themselves! If LEA employees have a raised awareness of the importance of their own health to them, this will greatly enhance their willingness to see that health education in the school curriculum is of fundamental importance for their pupils' future health. It will also help to build a supportive and sympathetic school environment where wise food choices can be made, smoking is unpopular, and positive attitudes to lifestyle are fashionable.

The LEA as a provider

There is nothing sadder nor more self-indulgent than the sight of highly intelligent otherwise thoughtful professional men and women wasting time and energy on personal or inter-departmental rivalry. This is especially the case when they have a common client and a common cause. Far too often petty jealousy factionalises local services in their provision of health support for schools and young people. In every local authority in the country there is a wealth of good work being done and resources waiting to be tapped. Far too often individuals and organisations choose to work alone. There are a number of observable syndromes which typify their logic.

The Ostrich Syndrome

used to good effect by education departments and district health authorities who (whenever threatened by collaborative work) bury their heads in the sand neatly not noticing the existence of all other living creatures and therefore avoiding the inconvenience of learning to live together.

The Guard-dog Syndrome

by rushing aggressively to each corner of its territory and barking fiercely this highly trained professional indicates total ownership of all its surveys; unhappily it seems not to notice that the fence which keeps others out of its small world, shuts it out of theirs.

The Paranoid Parrot Syndrome

this exotic bird is often seen squawking loudly, flapping a lot and moving about its cage at terrific speed in order to attract attention to itself - beautiful to look at but useful for decorative purposes only - try to avoid too many on your payroll.

(You might amuse yourselves by making up some more of your own - there are plenty of role models about!)

Partnership

Unless you are one of the above creatures, or a close relation, it will have occurred to you that there is more than enough work to go around. In any local authority catchment no one department has all the skill, training, resources and money. No education department can come close to providing a comprehensive health education service to its schools, colleges and youth clubs on its own. But if it looks to a partnership of provision the results can be quite dramatic. The Local Education Department has the responsibility for initiating and maintaining a network approach and a quick check list of major contributors must include:

- Advisory Staff in Health Related Areas (e.g. Physical Education, Home Economics, Science)
- Community Education
- District Health Authorities' Health Promotion Units
- Education Department - Health Education Staff
- Environmental Services
- Recreation and Community Services

Probably the best approach is then to create a small working group (ten people or less) ensuring that members have the authority to speak for their organisations.

A pro-active group such as this, with each member capable of committing his/her department to programme delivery gives a potential resource base of quite staggering proportions.

All decisions on city or county wide priorities should be jointly planned then jointly implemented remembering that:

- no-one enjoys being asked to help after all the decisions have been taken.
- information about all discrete programmes should be shared so where appropriate they can be mutually supported.
- the programme unit must always be seen to be compatible with the overall city/county strategy.

There are massive spin-offs for both the department and its customers, the young people, by working this way. Advantages include:

- The avoidance of duplication;
- The avoidance of omission;
- The sharing of valuable skills and materials;
- The enjoyment of central and local resource/training bases;
- Co-operation on major city programmes/promotion;
- Better use of personnel;
- The strengthening of the ability to bid successfully for funds;
- The strengthening of the ability to bring about strategic change;
- The avoidance of continual re-invention of the wheel and the re-invention of the flat tyre!

In a world of seemingly endless re-organisation and change, the need to continually attract funding may be important. Though there are many occasions when specific individual bids can be successful, there are many others where national and local government organisations will look more kindly on funding a collaborative project. They may and often do argue that an investment in a multi-agency project will end up 'reaching the parts that other grants cannot reach', thus achieving a more pervasive effect and giving them a better return for their cash.

Strategic change

If we were to take the three major areas of concern for Coronary Heart Disease prevention as smoking, nutrition and exercise, the following policies would appear to be ripe for introduction.

Smoking

1   A ban on all smoking in schools and a change from 'non-smoking' to carefully defined 'smoking' areas in College.
2   Smoking cessation support for post-sixteen students.
3   Developing a pro-active anti-smoking message via primary care staff to key into school curriculum work.

Nutrition

Radical changes in the provision of foodstuffs in schools to present a policy consistent with present nutrition education should be developed including

1   The re-writing of schools' catering specifications so that the childrens' health rather than maintenance of the status quo was the central concern.

2   Similar re-appraisal of tuck shop provision.

3   The provision of a programme of nutrition in-service training for school teaching staff.

4   The provision of food handling course for all school catering staff with a healthy eating element included.

5   The construction of a multidisciplinary school 'food policy group'.

Exercise

The following seem ripe for introduction.

1   Activity programmes for all primary school children supported by a comprehensive in-service training policy for staff responsible for Physical Education.

2   An increased programme of physical activity for secondary pupils with a deliberate policy of developing recreative activities linked to the wider community.

3   Extended physical recreation activity programmes during school holidays for children of all ages.

4   Recognition and payment for teachers taking extra-curricular clubs and teams.

The politics of change

The political and administrative drive needed to bring about change is best not attempted alone. However, for many in a bureaucracy the 'status quo' is their security; change is threatening and challenges basic credibility. The combined authority of professional expertise is a wonderful weapon when wielded intelligently. For example if we wanted a re-examination of school meals specification the team might be:

- Community dietitian
- Home Economics Advisor
- Health Education Advisor
- District Health Promotion Officer
- Environmental Health Officer
- Paediatrician
- Consultant in Public Health Medicine
- Director of Education Catering

Individually each could be ignored; together they are not so easily swept aside.

Most changes be they social, educational or environmental are brought about by small 'p' political action. In order to make progress we must ensure that those with a will to focus on promoting the health of young people work together with conviction. A lack of active co-operation among professionals in health authority and local authority departments is clearly self-indulgent and inevitably results in an ineffective and inconsistent use of the resource base for support available to schools and young peoples health education programmes.

In a publication from the Royal Society of Medicine in 1988*, Dr Richard Hobbs emphasised that we really must concentrate on the children in our society

'It would be grossly irresponsible to condemn another generation to our present mortality statistics before taking action'

He was talking about diet and CHD but his words apply equally well to the whole range of major issues on which joint planning and joint action are essential if we are to avoid his just censure for inactivity.

* Dietary Fat and Heart Disease: Progress since COMA. Royal Society of Medicine, Round Table Series 13.

14

Local Industry

David Davis, Group Personnel Manager,
UK Sandvik Group of Companies

The patient was from a local factory and was clearly agitated. 'Doctor', she said, 'At my annual medical at work my cholesterol level was 11.2 and I'm worried sick!' Heaven preserve us, he thought, from those with a little dangerous knowledge. 'You mustn't worry my dear,' he said, keeping his voice calm and authoritative. 'Was your blood sample just a thumb prick fed into a mobile analyser?' 'Yes' she answered, reassured by his manner. 'Ah,' he said sceptically. Then her face dropped again. 'But my blood pressure is 160 over 95!'

Later, after a full examination and discussion on diet and life style the doctor arranged for the patient to return for another cholesterol test. The subsequent hospital report confirmed an abnormally high blood cholesterol level of 9.5 mmol/litre. Further tests showed a significantly underactive thyroid which could have contributed to the condition. Drugs were prescribed to compensate for the thyroid deficiency and to control the high blood pressure. Counselling was also given to reinforce the advice she had received from her company medical officer to reduce her intake of saturated fats and to increase the content of dietary fibre in her meals.

The patient now has a blood cholesterol level in the upper range of normal and is quietly confident that the situation is under control. And a local G.P. has had cause to reflect on changes in society which are providing extra diagnostic and preventative medicine services to assist him in combating heart disease and in meeting the general health needs of his patients in the community.

A sea-change is occurring throughout the larger and more progressive companies in industry and commerce. Preventative medicine through the medium of annual screening medicals at work is increasingly proving the perfect complement to the hard-pressed general practitioner coping with the curative side. In no area can this partnership be more important than in the diagnosis, treatment and prevention of coronary heart disease which kills over 160,000 people per year in England and Wales.

The screening medicals we make available to our employees are wholly voluntary. They cover lung function (measured by peak flow meter or Vitalograph), blood pressure, sight and hearing tests, heart sounds, and eyes, ears, throat and abdomen and skin examination, urine sample analysis, and breast examination for women. A blood cholesterol test is conducted on the spot with a Reflotron mobile analyser. Chest X-rays or electro-cardiogram readings are arranged if necessary. The examinations are conducted in the company medical centre by doctors and nurses of the Midlands Occupational Health Service. Results of each examination and the medical records on each employee are confidential to the examining doctor and nurse and the company neither seeks nor is allowed access to those records. Only where a condition is work related and raises questions of the company's liabilities under statute is the company approached by the doctor concerned.

The illustration we began with of the patient with her doctor is a true incident which exemplifies what has become a common occurrence since the company embarked on its programme to combat coronary heart disease. Through screening medicals a number of cases of active and incipient diabetes have been detected as well as many cases of hypertension, high blood cholesterol levels and other treatable conditions. The practice by the examining doctor in all cases is to refer employees to their own general practitioners after obtaining their permission to send a medical report. Counselling has also been given on diet, smoking habits, the consumption of alcohol and weight and stress reduction together with encouragement to take up regular appropriate physical exercise. The success of the screening medicals is universally accepted by employees who perceive them as a valuable benefit.

In embarking on our coronary heart disease prevention programme we had to face a number of questions which will be familiar to workers in the medical field. How much could we take for granted that our employees knew about the working of the human heart and the cardiovascular and circulatory system? If we embarked on a programme to impart information, what level should we aim at? Did employees want clinical measurement in blood analysis? Would they prefer reassuring 'within normal limits' or 'at the upper end of average' assessments and would they understand the gravity and need for remedial action of 'significantly above the normal'? Was it necessary to describe the meaning of readings on the dyastolic and systolic scales of blood pressure? Of what relevance would a measurement of blood cholesterol in mmol per litre or milligrammes per decilitre be to the lay person? Was it wise to give medical data to patients who might be wracked with anxiety about figures which on the face of it were abnormal, but were nonetheless insignificant clinically?

In the event, encouraged by some of the literature distributed by the Health Education Authority in their Look After Your Heart Campaign which appeared to be aimed at the intelligent layman, we embarked on an education programme through a series of articles in our company magazine. We described in easily understandable terms the cardiovascular system and how the walls of arteries deteriorated and the arterial pathways become blocked by the build up of fatty deposits. We explained the implications of high blood pressure, diabetes, poor diet, inherited factors, heavy smoking, obesity, lack of exercise and stress in the development of coronary heart disease. Branching out a little further we defined angina and explained the effects of beta-blockers, anti-coagulants and glyceryl trinitrate. Charts were published on both blood cholesterol levels and height/ weight ratios indicating risk gradings associated with readings above or below the norm. The response from employees was very positive. Requests for copies of the articles began arriving from outside the company, and favourable comment was received from Sandvik subsidiaries around the world. Our fears that we might be supplying medical information and comment (all checked by our Medical Officer) at too great a depth proved unfounded, further confirmation arriving with the articles having special mention in a highly commended grading in a House Journal of the Year Award. It had become clear to us that quite detailed information on heart disease had a ready readership.

Finally, to obtain more accurate information on the wishes of our employees concerning the contents of their medical reports and what was an acceptable time lag before receiving them, we circulated a questionnaire. About a third of respondents wanted measurements of blood cholesterol, blood glucose and other haematological measurements or medical conditions provided that they were shown against the acceptable range of measurements for the normal healthy person. If employees could see that their own measurements were within the acceptable range they would feel no cause for concern. But where measurements deviated significantly from the norm an explanation would be expected together with a referral to their own general practitioner for further diagnosis and any necessary treatment. In this way the employees could have an understanding of quite sophisticated clinical measurements particularly with regard to blood analysis, in an intelliglble way. It seems that the layman is increasingly seeking specific clinical measurements in diagnosis provided they they are related in magnitude to a scale around the average or norm.

The second most frequently mentioned need revealed by the questionnaire was for faster communication of the medical reports themselves. Delay in obtaining the results following a medical examination can introduce unacceptable and often unnecessary anxieties in the patient. Where possible our medical officer communicates them immediately. For this reason the use of a Reflotron giving instant blood analysis is in most cases preferable to the delay in obtaining results from a hospital laboratory. It is also becoming clear to us in this computer age of instant service and answers to queries, that patients will soon be wanting a medical diagnosis equally fast.

In one of our magazine articles we attempted an interesting experiment to draw attention to the main factors associated with heart diseases by means of a self-scoring test questionnaire. It was created with the help of Dr. J. Fletcher, the

Director of Occupational Medicine, Midlands Occupational Health Service (Figure 1). People enjoy testing themselves on a scoring basis. The questionnaire is also educational as it indicates what is medically desirable, or acceptable, from the weighted scores attributed to the various factors associated with heart disease. It can be used at two levels of accuracy. If a user knows his or her cholesterol or blood glucose level then this can be utilised in obtaining the overall total risk score. But even if these measurements are not known the questionnaire is so designed that a total risk score can still be obtained, albeit with less accuracy. A likely result may then occur that the individual will be encouraged to find out what his or her cholesterol and glucose levels are, particularly if their scores for other factors in the questionnaire are indicating a possible coronary heart disease risk.

No campaign to try and reduce coronary heart disease would be complete without determined efforts to improve people's diets. It is well known that we are a nation that eats too much fat and, more significantly, too much saturated fat normally present in animal fats and dairy products. This is to be tackled in our next phase of the campaign in conjunction with our local Environmental Health Department. Our caterers will seek to achieve the Heartbeat Award for those caterers who are taking an active part in the fight against Coronary Heart Disease, as part of the Health Education Authority's Look After Your Heart Campaign. Already the heightened awareness on health matters created by our campaign has enabled us to place a total ban on smoking in the company restaurant with the ready compliance of employees. 'Thank You for NOT Smoking' notices proliferate in the Company.

Another area still to be tackled is the encouragment to participate in regular physical exercise. This may prove to be more difficult than initially appears. To reach the optimum target of 45 minutes of reasonably vigorous exercise (e.g. warm-up exercises followed by jogging) three times per week presents problems of encroaching on employees' free time away from the company. Experience at the Exercise Rehabilitation Association for heart patients at Russells Hall Hospital, Dudley, has shown us that regular exercise of this kind must be done collectively as a group to reinforce commitment. Even heart patients won't participate in what is to them life saving exercise without the discipline of attending the hospital. They need to share the experience with others similarly motivated to obtain reinforcement. It must also be pleasurable from a social point of view: keeping fit must be fun. The company's role in this may have to be a passive one: we will concentrate on explaining the benefits of regular physical exercise on the heart and blood vessels and its effect on general health and well being.

It has been said that the 1990s will mark the development of a new era of a caring and sharing Britain. Society is certainly becoming more vocal on such matters as pollution and the widespread waste of the planet's natural resources and their damaging effect on future generations. Industry is already awakening

Are you at risk from heart disease?

The SANDVIK Self-Scoring Test Questionnaire

The higher your score, the higher the risk!

Enter your score

1. **Sex.** Are you male or female?

   Male - 1
   Female - 0

   [ ]

2. **Family history.** How many blood relatives have died through coronary heart problems?

   One to 2
   Two to 4
   Three to 6
   Four to 8

   [ ]

3. **How many cigarettes do you smoke per day?**

   0 - 0
   1 to 10 - 1
   11 to 20 - 3
   21 to 40 - 4
   More than 40 - 7

   [ ]

4. **How does your weight score on the height/weight chart below?**

   Underweight or Acceptable - 0
   Overweight - 2
   Grossly overweight - 3

   [ ]

5. **Cholestrol**
   What is your cholestrol level?* (in mmol/litre)

   *If you don't know your cholestrol level, score 0. But it leaves a question mark over your ultimate risk.

   Less than 4.5 mmol/l - 0
   4.5 to 5.5 - 2
   5.6 to 7.0 - 4
   7.1 to 9.0 - 6
   More than 9.0 - 8

   [ ]

6. **Blood Glucose**
   If you don't know your blood glucose level - score 0.
   If you are a diabetic and your diabetes is controlled - score 1
   If your diabetes is uncontrolled - score 5

   Less than 6.0 - 0
   6.0 - 8.0 - 1
   More than 8.0 - 5

   [ ]

7. **Blood pressure. What is your normal blood pressure?**
   Systolic: Usually the first and higher of the two presssures, e.g. **120** over 80

   Less than 140 - 0
   140 to 159 - 1
   61 to 200 - 2

   [ ]

   Diastolic: Usually the second and lowest of the two pressures, e.g. 140 over **90**

   Less than 90 - 0
   91 to 110 - 1
   111 to 120 - 2
   More than 120 - 4

   [ ]

TOTAL RISK SCORE [ ]

Check your height to weight reading

MEN

WOMEN

Draw a line across from your height and up from your weight - and check how you measure up. The more you are to the right of the diagram, the more 'at risk' you are likely to be when it comes to heart disease.

What does your total score tell you ?

Risk of coronary Heart disease

Total risk score	Risk
Less than 6	Low risk
6 to 9	Moderate risk
10 to 15	Elevated risk
More than 15	High risk

What to do if your score is 10 or above

If you have an *elevated* or *high risk* score you should be doing something about either your excessive weight, diet smoking habits, lack of exercise or high blood pressure. Always remember that there is no substitute for qualified medical advice where high blood pressure or high cholestrol is diagnosed.

ACKNOWLEDGEMENT

Sandvik is grateful to Dr. J. Fletcher, Director of Occupational Medicine, Midlands Occupational Health Service, 83 Birmingham Road, West Bromwich, West Midlands B70 6PX for a portion of the measuring data from his computerised Heart Disease Screening Programme

Produced for employees of Sandvik, manufacturers of cutting tools, cemented carbide and stainless steel products and hand tools, but made available to the public in the SANDVIK SUPPORT TO THE COMMUNITY programme.

Sandvik Limited · Manor Way · Halesowen · West Midlands B62 8QZ. Tel. 021-550 4700 to the powerful effect on sales of the consumer concerned to protect the environment. Companies are now sharpening their social consequences. They are recognising that they must respond more not only to their statutory health and safety obligations but also to the general health needs of their employees. In the area of preventative medicine, and particularly with regard to the reduction in coronary heart disease, they can play a crucial role. By educational and medical screening programmes they can complement the efforts of local medical practitioners and hospital consultants. Furthermore, the beneficial effects of such programmes are likely to impact on the other members of employee's families and the wider community. It is after all only good commercial common sense. Looking after the health of employees can result in improved employee relations, reduced sickness absence, a good recruitment image and lower employee turnover. It demonstrates what has always been recognised by the more enlightened companies: that a company's greatest asset is its employees.

15 The Food Industry

Richard Parish, Humberside College of Health

The food industry has attracted considerable criticism over recent years concerning the alleged damage that it is doing to the nation's health. The entire process, from production and manufacturing through to retailing and marketing, has been subjected to blistering attacks by the health sector and, at times, the media. This scathing condemnation is not entirely without reason. The United Kingdom tops the league table for many diet related diseases, and it was during the early nineteen eighties that health professionals started to use high profile media tactics to bring the diet issue to the centre stage of the public debate.

There is little doubt that the interest shown by television, radio and the printed press resulted in a more informed public. However, knowledge alone would not necessarily bring about the desired changes to the British diet. Ready access to those foods which would be likely to constitute a healthier diet was increasingly seen as being just as important, perhaps more so, than merely concentrating on public education. The emergence of Heartbeat Wales in 1985, the UK demonstration project for cardiovascular disease prevention and heart health promotion, lent credance to this approach, and the need to work closely with the food industry in order to bring about a real shift in the British diet[1]. There was a growing recognition that an improvement in nutritional knowledge would not bring about a change in dietary behaviour without also ensuring that the requisite foods were readily available at the places where people shop and eat, and at a price they could afford.

There is little doubt that the scene was set in the United Kingdom by the publication of two reports, NACNE[2] in 1983 and the COMA Report[3] of 1984. These set out dietary guidelines for the nation and mirrored the recommendations of other industrialised countries. Not only did they help fuel the media debate, which in itself helped create a climate of opinion conducive to change, they also demonstrated a growing interest in the food and health issue on the part of government and its agencies. More recently, the Department of Health has published the most comprehensive dietary recommendations ever available in Britain[4] and translated these into an easy to understand reference guide for health professionals[5].

The food industry's response to the growing public, political and professional awareness about diet and health has been complex and somewhat fragmented.

The drive to improve the availability of 'healthier' foods has, without doubt, been led by the retail sector. In particular, the large supermarket chains, initially Tesco in 1985, recognised the potential marketing advantages associated with the mass media coverage and public interest generated during the second half of the nineteen eighties. Similarly, several of the national trade organisations responded favourably to the NACNE and COMA reports.

Notably, the Meat and Livestock Commission developed a specific strategy for improving the availability of fat reduced red meat through local butchers' shops. Essentially, the strategy throughout the food retailing industry has been to increasingly provide alternative healthy options - low fat, reduced sugar, no added salt, high fibre - without reducing the existing product range. The 'added value' associated with the more healthy alternative, however, has frequently resulted in a higher price, thereby acting as a disincentive to purchase.

The high street shops and supermarket chains were not alone in meeting the challenge of healthy eating posed by popular magazines, television and radio. Caterers also recognised the advantages of following on the back of the media bandwagon. The two largest independent catering companies, Sutcliffe and Gardner Merchant, both introduced healthy eating schemes during the mid 1980s. In a booklet produced for their customers, Sutcliffe demonstrated the significant influence the food industry can have over the nutritional health of the nation.

'Staff caterers can exert a powerful influnce on the eating patterns of their (often) captive customers and they have a responsibility to comply with modern nutritional thinking and to encourage the public to eat accordingly.'

In short, people are constrained by the choices offered by retail shops and catering outlets. Public education is of limited value, therefore, if the food industry does not also ensure that customers are able to translate their new found nutritional knowledge into purchasing behaviour.

The need to address food supply as well as dietary knowledge was explicitly recognised by the World Health Organisation in their Health For All 2000 initiative[6]. The food industry in many countries is the largest manufacturing industry and, according to WHO, influences the consumption of foods more than any conscious nutrition education campaign[6]. This is particularly true for countries like the United Kingdom, where only 15% of food is purchased in the form of unprocessed raw products[7].

Given the complex array of influences upon diet, it is essential to tackle the food and health issue from a variety of angles. Although nutrition education is an essential component in any strategy intended to promote healthier eating, there is little point in giving people the knowledge and skills to choose a healthier diet if the necessary foods are not readily available, easily identifiable, and at a price they can afford. In addtion to public education, therefore, it is absolutely essential

Figure 1 **A Strategy for Dietary Change**

	EDUCATION	COMPOSITION	
Professional advice			Primary production (e.g. breeding programmes)
Community education			Preparation techniques (e.g. meat cutting)
Mass media			Product reformulation/ New products
Consumer/ customer programmes			Purchasing specifications
Award schemes	RECOGNITION	ACCESS	Food retail shops
Product labelling			Catering outlets
Menu identification			Pricing policy

to address the issues of food recognition, product composition, and consumer access (Figure 1).

The retail food sector

The role of the retail food sector in this strategy is crucial. Retailers can have an impact on every aspect of human food supply and, at the same time, are also able to influence consumer choice. As either caterers or shopping outlets, they act as the interface between supply and demand in the food consumption model.

From the public education point of view, they are ideally placed to advise and inform the millions of consumers who avail themselves of the food industry's services every day. Following the initial campaign by Tesco, most supermarket chains now provide healthy eating literature, often backed up by advisory centres in the larger stores, staffed by qualified home economists. Within the first year and a half, Tesco had distributed 21 million leaflets, many of which ended up in the project books of local schools undertaking nutrition related activities. Increasingly, the major supermarkets are also introducing consumer kitchens, where customers can not only learn about the principles of healthy eating, but also acquire some of the cooking skills as well. There is an increasing trend to provide specific recipes for customers' future reference.

The move towards healthy eating advice is not restricted just to the larger retail shops. Backed by their industry boards, a number of smaller retailers have engaged in high profile campaigns of low fat product promotion, linked to public education. Perhaps the most notable is the Lean Choice Scheme operated by service butchers with the support of the Meat and Livestock Commission, initially piloted in six centres around the country and now available to any butcher nationwide.

Caterers can also play a significant role in public education, particularly those responsible for feeding large numbers of people at their place of work each day. They have a largely captive and, just as importantly, usually receptive audience. Company attitude surveys in the United States have shown that 'in-house' nutrition programmes are viewed by the workforce as a valued, tangible employee benefit[8]. Such activities not only contribute to health, therefore, but also generate a positive image for the employer and contribute to harmonious labour relations.

From knowledge to choice

Public education without product recognition is of little value. The move towards nutritional labelling has grown rapidly over the past two or three years. Retailers are able to exert considerable pressure on manufacturers and distributors. As such, they are frequently able to specify their public information requirements on packaging, and this has led to many products exhibiting a quantified statement on composition. The most successful schemes, however, are those that also provide a simple visual cue as to the nutritional status in comparison with other, similar products, for example, 'high fibre' or 'low fat'. Product information can sometimes be augmented by shelf labelling to identify those food groups which would be considered essential to improved nutrition.

Caterers have also played their part in identifying those foods likely to contribute to a healthier diet. Healthy eating has been a growth industry for caterers in recent years, with restaurants, fast food outlets, workplace caterers, and the school meals service all playing a part. There has been a move away from the early labelling schemes, which used a traffic light colour coding approach, and most caterers now adopt a simpler method, merely identifying the 'healthier' dishes on the menu. The Heartbeat Award scheme, launched in Wales in 1986 as a collaborative exercise between Environmental Health Departments and Heartbeat Wales, has been particularly successful and now operates in many parts of England as well.

Compositional changes

Side by side with the introduction of consumer information is the need to provide products which meet the nutritional guidelines promoted by NACNE[2] and the COMA Report[3]. The large food retailers are able to use their immense purchasing power to alter product composition. Within the first eighteen months of the Tesco Healthy Eating Campaign, 400 existing products were reformulated. Furthermore, large scale retailers, because of their high turnover, are in a position to commission new low fat products as an alternative to traditional product lines.

Mass caterers can also exert a similar influence upon food processors and manufacturers through the tight control of purchasing specifications to ensure that they comply with current nutritional recommendations. It is here that the public sector could play a major role. The civil service, local authorities and the NHS between them provide far more meals each and every day than any other organisation in Britain. Although influential in their own right at the local level, as either individual establishments or regional consortia, the full opportunities afforded by the collective public sector buying power have yet to be realised.

Promotion and marketing

At the end of the day, the highly competitive commercial world of food retailing is guided by marketing strategy. Driven by the profit ethic, commercial organisations must perceive a benefit to their support for the healthy eating message, either in the form of increased media coverage, overall public relations, improved turnover, or better market share.

Marketing takes many forms, ranging from company public relations, product development, advertising, market research and pricing policy. As the concept of healthy eating diffuses through the population at large, food retailers are recognising that pricing policy is of increasing importance for those consumers who accept the principle, but have yet to alter their purchasing behaviour. Frequently, retailers will test the market by lowering their profit margin for a limited period in order to assess the incentive value of a reduced price. Pressure from the health lobby can sometimes encourage such a development, particularly if it is clear that health professionals will be supporting the move within the community.

Television advertising is usually undertaken on a regional or national basis, whereas local radio and press are often employed to support specific promotional campaigns within a small geographical area. Advertising falls into three categories. Many supermarket chains place their main emphasis on company promotion, each one endeavouring to convince the public that it is more concerned with the public health than the competition. However, the industry marketing boards, such as the Milk Marketing Board or the Meat and Livestock Commission, pursue commodity advertising, the intention being to increase the overall volume of sales of their particular range of products. Finally, individual manufacturers engage in brand advertising, designed to increase their share of a specific commodity market.

The role of the primary health care team

The health sector has a crucial role to play in promoting change within the food industry. Clearly, the four national health promotion agencies have the prime responsibility for negotiating product reformulation with the industry boards, major manufacturers, and multi-outlet retailers. However, much progress can also be made at the local level, particularly by primary health care teams working with the support of their health authority health promotion department.

Members of the PHCT can relatively easily identify which local food outlets have a food and health policy, and lobby those in the immediate practice locality which do not. Every team should ensure that all of its catchment schools, sports centres, supermarkets, butchers, restaurants, and 'take-aways' provide some clearly identified 'healthy' options on either their menus or in their product ranges. In pursuing this, local consumer and interested voluntary organisations should be encouraged to lobby for change. Subject to the limitations of time, health care professionals should offer to update those in the food industry on contemporary nutritional recommendations and, in return, invite the local retailer to identify those products that are currently available which meet the guidelines. Such collaboration will enable both to offer a more explicit and comprehensive service to their customers or patients.

The local GP, Health Visitor or Practice Nurse is often ideally placed to contribute an article to the area's freesheet or participate in a 'phone-in' on the radio. They have credibility in the eyes of the public and local knowledge, but rarely offer themselves to the local media, although they would undoubtedly be well received. Given that only 12% of men and 15% of women have fat intakes which meet the COMA recommendations[9] and in the light of the Government's proposed strategy to improve the nation's health[10], such an involvement must be at the top of the Primary Health Care Team's agenda.

Co-operation not compromise

Health professionals have frequently resisted any close association with commercial organisations on the grounds that their professional standards might be compromised. The ethical acceptability has sometimes been questioned, although the experience to date would suggest that there is absolutely no foundation for these concerns. In acknowledging the evidence that education by itself has a limited impact upon the population's dietary patterns, one has to ask if it is ethical not to adopt the more effective and beneficial approach of forming a partnership with the food industry.

References

1   Parish R., Catford J., and Nutbeam D., (1987) 'Breathing Life into Wales: Progress in the Welsh Heart Programme'. *Health Trends*, Vol 19.

2   National Advisory Committee on Health Education. (1983) *Proposals for Nutritional Guidelines for Health Education in Britain*. Health Education Council, London.

3   Department of Health and Social Security. (1984) *Diet and Cardiovascular Disease: Report of the Panel on Diet in relation to Cardiovascular Disease*. HMSO, London.

4   Department of Health. (1991) *Dietary Reference Values for Food Energy and Nutrients for the United Kingdom. Report of the Panel on Dietary Reference Values of the Committee on Medical Aspects of Food Policy'*. HMSO. London

5   Department of Health. (1991) *Dietary Reference Values – A Guide*. HMSO. London

6   World Health Organisation. (1987) *Targets for Health For All*. WHO Regional Office For Europe.

7   British Medical Association. (1986) *Diet, Nutrition and Health*. Chamelion Press Ltd. London.

8   American Dietitic Association et al. (1986) *Worksite Nutrition: A decision maker's guide*. ADA, Chicago.

9   Gregory J., Foster K.,. Tyler H. and Wiseman M. (1990). *'The Dietary and Nutritional Survey of British Adults*. HMSO. London

10   Secretary of State for Health. (1991) *'The Health of the Nation: A Consultative Document for Health in England.'* HMSO. London.

16   Heartbeat Wales
John Catford and Don Nutbeam, Health Promotion Authority for Wales

Introduction

Heartbeat Wales is a major national demonstration project to promote good health amongst the three million population in Wales, and is particularly directed towards reducing the risks of cardiovascular disease throughout the whole of the Principality. Its major priorities include promoting non-smoking, good nutrition, regular exercise, stress management, health screening and first aid for heart attacks. The long-term aim of the programme has been to develop and evaluate, as a pilot venture, a regional strategy that will contribute to a sustained reduction in the incidence of coronary heart disease, morbidity and mortality in the general population of Wales, and in particular those under the age of 65.

The programme was publicly launched on St. David's Day, 1 March 1985, for an initial five-year period, and has since attracted considerable lay, professional, political and media interest[1]. Initially, core funding was provided by the Health Education Council and the Welsh Office, and the project administered through the University of Wales College of Medicine. From April 1987 these responsibilities were passed to the Health Promotion Authority for Wales, who under its new 'Health for All in Wales' Strategy intends to continue the programme at least until 1995[2]. Considerable additional support is also provided to Heartbeat Wales by statutory, commercial and voluntary agencies as well as the general public in Wales. In total, expenditure is of the order of 50p per person per year.

Research and evaluation

Evaluation of the effectiveness and efficiency of the programme is necessary so that others can learn from the experience, and a full range of evaluation methods are being used[3]. Like community-based interventions elsewhere assessment of outcome has been undertaken using a quasi-experimental design with the intervention population in Wales (treatment) being compared with a similar, reference population in another part of the UK (control). Experience in Wales and in other countries has shown this design as having the best potential to demonstrate the success of programmes when combined with studies which help explain the process of change among individuals and individual networks in communities[4].

To establish a baseline of information for evaluation and monitoring, the Welsh Heart Health Surveys were planned and carried out during 1985 and 1986. Table 1 provides a summary of the key information for Wales derived from an initial analysis of a large questionnaire survey (The 'Community Survey') of 22,000 Welsh people aged 12-64, and information collection from medical examinations of a 10% sub-sample (the 'Clinical Survey'). The data show the extent of the challenge faced in Wales in the very high proportion of the population who fall into the various categories of risk. Of particular note is the fact that, the substantial majority of adults aged 35-64 falls outside of the desirable range for blood cholesterol (less than 5.2 mmol/L), and that a relatively high proportion of the population are smokers. In addition more than half of adults aged 35-64 are overweight, and the great majority have relatively inactive lifestyles.

Further details and analysis of the data are available through a series of published reports[5,6]. The large database for Wales also allowed analysis of the health status of the population area by area. Individual reports for each county and health authority have been produced together with a special study of social class differences[7]. An interim monitoring survey was carried out in 1988, and a major five year follow up survey in Wales and the reference area in 1990, after which a more substantial analysis of change during the five years of Heartbeat Wales will be possible.

As well as assessing the outcome of the intervention, great emphasis is also placed on process evaluation to determine how and why the changes were achieved. The evaluation strategy for the programme sets out a number of approaches, which include measuring organisational change, particularly in hospitals, schools and the workplace[3]. Other evaluation projects include a study of changes in health promotion practice among general practitioners and health visitors, as well as a series of market research surveys which provide regular feedback and more sensitive monitoring of national initiatives, particularly those involving the mass media.

Intervention strategies

The key elements of the intervention strategy were based on the recommendations of two WHO Expert Committees[8,9] which emphasised an approach focussed on achieving change within the total population. This 'population approach' would normally be supported by strategies, such as risk factor screening, designed to reach those at high risk.

The experiences of other community-based cardiovascular risk reduction programmes were also utilised, particularly the North Karelia Project in Finland and the Stanford, Minnesota and Pawtucket heart disease prevention programmes in the USA[10,11,12,13]. These have indicated that for the successful achievement of long-term risk factor changes, social-psychological theory and principles need to be central to programme planning. The main theoretical frameworks used in the Heartbeat Wales intervention are summarised in Figure 1.

Figure 1

Theoretical frameworks for intervention

Theory	*Key Elements*
Social learning	- role models/social cues - observational learning - feedback on progress
Diffusion of innovations	- role models - professional and lay opinion leaders
Community development	- needs assessment - participation and partnership - ownership and self-determination
Organisational change	- finding common ground - providing incentives - instituting monitoring systems - training
Social marketing	- consumer orientation - recognition of costs and benefits - focus on promotion and placement

Social learning theory emphasises the great importance of not only providing individuals with information and motivation to make change, but also the personal skills and social reinforcement necessary to sustain change in lifestyle. The importance of positive role models is particularly emphasised[14]. Diffusion of innovation theory combines with these approaches, emphasising the techniques which can be used to speed up the process of change in communities through the actions and example of key opinion leaders (such as GPs and nurses)[15]. Principles of community development, adapted from experiences in the past two decades, emphasise the need to promote a strong sense of participation, partnership and self determination when establishing 'community-based' programmes (e.g.[9]). Management theories to promote organisational change have also been utilised in programme planning and execution for promoting policy and service developments within the NHS and large employers in Wales (e.g.[16]). Finally, social marketing principles have been adapted to provide an overall framework to the programme, emphasising the need for utilising good quality 'consumer' information in planning and targeting the delivery of programmes designed to reach large numbers of people (e.g.[17]).

These theories have been developed into a sequential model which has guided planning and priority setting in the Heartbeat Wales Programme[1]. This model, presented in Figure 2, illustrates the sequential process of achieving and sustaining change, drawing upon key themes from the theories above. It can be applied equally to individuals, groups and organisations, and explicit recognition is given to the fact that individuals or organisations will be at different points in this developmental sequence at any one time. In this sense all elements of the model may be operating at one time, and the skill required of programme managers is to find the right balance of activities at any one time. A more developed discussion of the model has been presented elsewhere[1].

Although the promotion of a healthy lifestyle among individuals is at the core of the project, drawing upon such a broad theoretical base has ensured that an important part of the strategy is to achieve environmental, organisational, structural and policy changes within Wales that will support healthy choices. Examples include restricting smoking in public places, better food labelling, increasing availability of 'healthy' foods in shops, workplace canteens and restaurants, and changing work practices amongst health and education professionals.

Action programmes

Heartbeat Wales was established as a community-based project which drew substantially on intrinsic resources from within the varied communities and organisations in Wales. As a consequence the intervention, guided by the model above, has comprised of a wide range of locally organised projects together with centrally led initiatives.

The importance of participation by the many communities in Wales was recognised at the outset. Considerable energy was directed to meeting key individuals and agencies throughout Wales during the early months, in order to plan a programme that would meet the interests of Welsh people and generate support. This culminated in the publication of a detailed consultative document

Figure 2   **The Choice-Change-Champion process for health promotion**

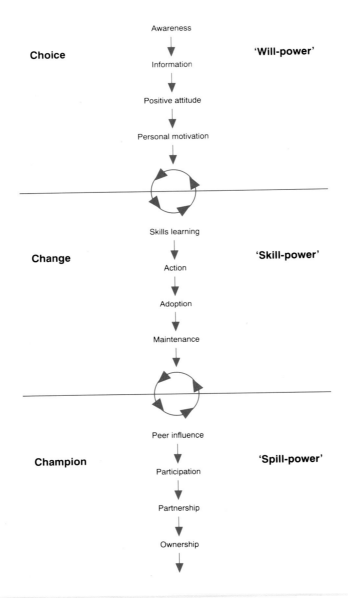

which outlined the proposed strategy and described the conceptual framework[18]. The document generated an overwhelming response from health authorities, family practitioner committees, and individual health professionals, as well as the many other organisations targeted in the documentation. Almost without exception the comments supported the proposed strategy.

Raising public and professional awareness, interest and commitment to the programme was a major goal during the first twelve months. The print and broadcast media were both employed extensively, to raise awareness about the need for community action and to enlist the support of the public, the professionals and politicians. The Welsh language is used extensively in certain parts of Wales, so a bilingual policy was adopted at the outset which included all public materials including health education literature and press releases.

A commitment was also made *not* to use paid advertising as a part of our intervention. The Programme would be newsworthy in itself if it was succeeding in its goal of community involvement. In the event, extensive coverage of the Programme has been achieved by providing attractive stories and material to the local and regional press, local radio, and national and regional television. The mass media activities during 1985 culminated in an extremely successful six-part television series on BBC Wales entitled 'Don't Break Your Heart', shown during peak viewing time. Since then Heartbeat Wales has collaborated with independent television and the BBC in the production of a number of other health related television programmes. The most recent have been the 'BBC Diet Programme' and 'Psst - the really useful guide to alcohol'.

Wales is a nation with a strong tradition of county shows and events, particularly during the summer period. As part of the process of raising awareness and community involvement, Heartbeat Wales, in conjunction with the health authorities, has had a presence at most of the major county and agricultural shows during the five year period 1985-90. Follow up studies have shown that the reach of these mass communication initiatives was very high such that the vast majority of the population in Wales know about and supported the aims of Heartbeat Wales within one year[19].

Following detailed discussion and consultation with key organisations in Wales a number of pilot projects at local level were set up in 1985. Each health authority established a 'Heart Action Team' for the planning and implementation of local initiatives and through these a wide programme of local action has been launched.

Each health authority received financial support from Heartbeat Wales, providing that grants were matched with new resources at local level. More than fifty projects have now been set up across a wide range of sectors. Funding came from various sources including health, education and local authorities, private industry and Heartbeat Wales.

At national level the Heartbeat Wales team was also instrumental in stimulating and supporting a number of important health promotion initiatives. These include:

- Food labelling and health education programmes with major Welsh supermarkets (e.g. Tesco)
- Lean meat merchandising schemes with the meat retail trade and the Meat and Livestock Commission (e.g. Lean Choice Award Scheme in 120 butchers in Wales)
- Low fat milk promotions with Unigate and the Dairy Trades Federation
- Heartbeat Awards - a restaurant/canteen award scheme implemented by 26 local environmental health departments (e.g. in Pubs, Schools, Restaurants, etc)
- No smoking policies in collaboration with health and local authorities, British Institute of Management and trade unions
- Food and Health Policies (in collaboration with health authorities and school meal services)
- Heartbeat Ways - more than 30 exercise 'trim' trails built by local authorities, youth training programmes, and young offenders schemes
- Well Welsh - Heartbeat Wales own health screening and education programme
- HeartStart Wales - community first aid training for heart attacks
- Training of health professionals, teachers and other key groups (e.g. GP Training Days, Practice Nurse Training Workshops)
- Development and dissemination of health education curriculum materials to schools
- Pulse - a special participative 'health club' for primary school children
- A network of Look After Yourself classes particularly in support of the 'Lose Weight Wales' Campaign
- Make Health Your Business - a joint venture with CBI Wales to encourage commerce and industry to participate in health promotion activity through a prestigious competition and award scheme
- Quit and Win - a smoking cessation project in South East Wales, in which prizes are used as incentives for smokers to trigger attempts to give up.

Behavioural change

Three years after the Programme was launched, a follow-up interim questionnaire survey of 8,500 adults aged 18-64 was carried out in the summer of 1988. This showed that large numbers of Welsh people were reporting important behavioural changes. Just over a third of daily smokers reported trying to give up smoking in the previous year, a third of these attempts lasting a month or more. Overall, reported smoking prevalence has fallen from 37% in 1985 to 33% in 1988.

The interim survey also revealed changes in the dietary patterns of adults in Wales which indicated a trend towards healthier eating. For example, both men and women reported eating fruit and vegetables more often and foods high in saturated fats less often than in 1985.

Both these findings were supported by data from regular tracking surveys of 1,000 adults across Wales carried out every six months. The most recent, in March 1990, showed that 27% of respondents said they had successfully lost more than 5lbs in weight in the last year, while 24% reported increasing their level of exercise by at least 60 minutes per week. Fifty seven per cent reported having had their blood pressure checked in the past year. The changes were observed in both sexes, all ages and social groups, and throughout the whole of Wales.

Once data from the 1990 surveys have been collected and analysed, and the process evaluation studies completed a fuller understanding of the importance of these findings will be possible.

Conclusions

Heartbeat Wales was established as a demonstration project for the rest of the UK to determine how best to implement current knowledge on reducing coronary risks within a population. Even at this relatively early stage in the evaluation it can be seen that this objective has been met. Many projects at national and local level have either been modelled on, or have drawn extensively from the ideas and experiences of Heartbeat Wales. Regular Visitors Weeks and conferences have helped to disseminate findings, and scientific publications and materials have been widely distributed. The diffusion has not been limited to the UK and already programmes in Europe have been greatly influenced by the Welsh experience. There is even now a Heartbeat New Zealand developing along similar lines. Such progress has not gone unnoticed by other commentators (e.g.[20,21,22]).

Following the analysis of the 1990 survey and the process evaluation studies, careful consideration will be given to what worked, what did not, and to how activities could be improved. Although the detailed assessment of individual projects will be useful, it will be a set of principles and approaches on how to win commitment and achieve change that will be the major lessons for health promotion from the Heartbeat Wales experience. Figure 3 summarises some of the key steps that seem to have been important in the development of this project to date. Vision, enthusiasm, courage and compassion are perhaps the most important ingredients for successful prevention of coronary heart disease.

Figure 3   **Key steps in health promotion action**

1   Recognising the problem, by
        - defining health risks and challenges
        - assessing the barriers to progress
        - communicating the findings
        - raising awareness
2   Developing alliances, by
        - knowing the community
        - understanding the key providers
        - appreciating ongoing work
        - looking for the common ground
        - finding the right entry point
3   Agreeing a strategy, by
        - studying past experiences
        - adopting a comprehensive approach
        - determining priorities
        - setting goals, objectives and targets
        - allocating tasks
        - winning resources
4   Implementing action programmes, by
        - creating an identity
        - going for early successes
        - providing mutual support
        - responding to vested interests
        - monitoring progress
        - broadcasting achievements
        - using the power of information
        - assimilating action into the community

Table 1

Prevalence of major risk factors for coronary heart disease in Wales, 1985

		18-34	**35-64**
% Population who smoke	M	38.5	42.8
	F	34.0	33.0
% Population cholesterol level > 5.2 mmol/L	M	40.6	76.4
	F	41.1	74.1
% Population cholesterol level > 6.5 mmol/L	M	7.3	29.5
	F	6.2	31.3
% Population blood pressure			
diastolic 90-100 mm/Hg	M	15.5	26.4
systolic 140-160 mm/Hg	F	1.8	18.3
diastolic > 100 mm/Hg	M	N/A	9.9
systolic > 160 mm/Hg	F	N/A	5.0
% Population overweight or obese			
BMI > 25 (men)	M	37.7	57.1
> 23 (women)	F	30.2	53.5
% Population exceeding safe alcohol consumption			
> 21 standard units (men) per week	M	30.5	20.5
> 14 standard units (women) per week	F	8.0	3.3
% Population minimally active or sedentary			
Exercise < 2 x per week (moderate	M	21.4	43.0
or strenuous)	F	61.5	79.4

Sources: Welsh Heart Health Surveys (WHPD 1986(a), 1987)

References

1   Catford J., Parish R. (1989). 'Heartbeat Wales: New horizons for health promotion in the community', in Seedhouse D., Cribb A. (eds) *Changing ideas in health care.* John Wiley, New York.

2   Health Promotion Authority For Wales. (1990). *'Health for All in Wales: Strategies for Action'.* Health Promotion Authority for Wales, Cardiff.

3   Nutbeam D. and Catford J. (1987). 'Welsh Heart Programme Evaluation Strategy. Progress, Plans and Possibilities', *Health Promotion,* 2.1, 5-18.

4   Nutbeam D., Smith C., Catford J. (1990). 'Evaluation in health education: a review of possibilities and problems.' *Journal of Epidemiology and Community Health,* 44, 2, 83-89.

5   Welsh Heart Programme Directorate. (1986a). 'Pulse of Wales: Preliminary Report of the Welsh Heart Health Survey 1985.' *Heartbeat Report No. 4.* Health Promotion Authority for Wales, Cardiff, UK.

6   Welsh Heart Programme Directorate. (1987). 'Hearts of Wales: Results from the Welsh Heart Health Clinical Survey.' *Heartbeat Technical Report No. 16.* Health Promotion Authority for Wales, Cardiff, UK.

7   Welsh Heart Programme Directorate. (1986b). 'Pulse of Wales: Social Class Analysis.' *Heartbeat Report No. 5.* Health Promotion Authority for Wales, Cardiff, UK.

8   World Health Organisation. (1982). 'Prevention of Coronary Heart Disease.' Report of a WHO Expert Committee, *Technical Report Series No. 678.* World Health Organisation, Geneva.

9   World Health Organisation. (1986). 'Community Prevention and Control of Cardiovascular Diseases.' Report of a WHO Expert Committee; *Technical Report Series No. 732.* World Health Organisation, Geneva.

10 Puska P., Nissinen A., Salonen J.T., Tuomilehto J., Koskel K., McAlister A., Kottke AT., Maccoby N., Farquhar J. (1985). 'The Community Based Strategy to Prevent Coronary Heart Disease: Conclusions from the Ten Years of the North Karelia Project.' *Annual Review of Public Health.* Annual Reviews Inc, U.S.A., Vol 6.

11 Farquhar J., Fortmann S., Maccoby N., Wood P., Haskell W., Barr Taylor C., Flora J., Solomon D., Rogers T., Adler E., Breitrose P., Weinder L. (1984). 'The Stanford Five City Project: an Overview'. In Matarazzo J., Weiss S., Herd J. et al (eds) *Behavioural Health: A Handbook of Health Enhancement and Disease Prevention.* John Wiley, New York.

12 Lasater T., Abrams D., Artz L., Beaudin P., Cabrera L., Elder J., Ferreira A., Kinsley P., Peterson G., Rodrigues A., Rosenberg P., Snow R., Carleton R. (1984). 'Lay Volunteer Delivery of a Community Based Cardiovascular Risk Factor Change Programme: the Pawtucket Experiment.' In Matarazzo J., Weiss, S., Herd J. et al (eds) *Behavioural Health: A Handbook of Health Enhancement and Disease Prevention.* John Wiley, New York.

13   Blackburn H., Luepker R., Kline R., Bracht N., Carlow R., Jacobs D., Mittelmark M., Stauffer L., Taylor H. (1984). 'The Minnesota Heart Health Programme: a Research and Development Project in Cardiovascular Disease Prevention'. In Matarazzo J., Weiss S., Herd J. et al (eds) *Behavioural Health: A Handbook of Health Enhancement and Disease Prevention.* John Wiley, New York.

14   Bandura A. (1986). *Social Learning Theory.* Prentice Hall, Englewood Cliffs, New Jersey.

15   Rogers E. (1983). *Diffusion of Innovation.* Macmillan, London.

16   Kanter R.M. (1983). *The Change Masters.* Allen and Unwin, London.

17   Lefebvre R.C. and Flora J.A. (1988). 'Social Marketing and Public Health Intervention.' *Health Education Quarterly,* 15.3, 299-315.

18   Welsh Heart Programme Directorate. (1985). *Take Heart: A Consultative Document on the Development of Community-based Heart Health Initiatives within Wales.* Health Promotion Authority for Wales, Cardiff, UK.

19   Welsh Heart Programme Directorate. (1986c). 'Heartbeat Wales Awareness and Recall Survey Report'. *Heartbeat Report No. 6.* Health Promotion Authority for Wales, Cardiff, UK.

20   Whitehead M. (1989). *Swimming Upstream. Trends and prospects in education for health.* King's Fund, London. 1989, Vol. 1, March 4th, p 511.

21   House of Commons: Committee of Public Accounts. (1989). *Coronary Heart Disease.* HMSO, London.

22   Report by the Controller and Auditor General. (1989). National Health Service: *Coronary Heart Disease.* HMSO, London.

17 Look After Your Heart

Paul Lincoln, Programme Manager,
Health Education Authority

Look After Your Heart (LAYH) is the national Coronary Heart Disease (CHD) prevention programme for England. LAYH is jointly funded and managed by the Health Education Authority (HEA) and Department of Health. It was launched (in April 1987) as a campaign and has now been extended as a broad based, comprehensive and systematically planned programme from 1990-1995. This chapter outlines the development of LAYH, its aims and objectives, components, and activities, a brief summary of progress to date is given. Also discussed is the philosophy and approach that underpins the programme.

The main aims

The main aims of the LAYH programme are:

a) To contribute towards a substantial reduction in the premature death caused by Coronary Heart Disease. This will be achieved by contributing to a reduction in the major risk factors causing coronary heart disease by

- promoting public awareness and understanding of the lifestyle changes required
- equipping individuals with the knowledge and skills to make those changes
- initiating, stimulating and supporting CHD prevention and health promotion activities through mass media, the workplace, local government, industry and commerce - through joint activities between the HEA and the National Health Service (NHS).

b) To contribute towards a reduction in the variations in CHD mortality and morbidity between social groups, geographical regions and ethnic groups.

c) To contribute towards a reduction in the social and economic costs of CHD.

d) To promote healthy living.

The essential components of LAYH

It was a basic tenet from the outset that health education about heart disease should concentrate on helping people to understand the known principal risk factors and equip them with the knowledge and skills required to take personal and collective action. LAYH therefore concentrates on:

- smoking and tobacco use
- diet and nutrition
- control of blood pressure
- promotion of physical activity

The first three years (1987-1990)

Initial activity was concentrated on three broad areas:

- mass media and publicity
- community based activity
- the workplace

Within a relatively short space of time, much has been achieved under the LAYH umbrella. For example:

- 82% of the general public are now aware of the LAYH programme advertisements
- 100 percent of health authorities are involved in LAYH prevention activities in some form or another. Over 60 percent are involved with LAYH projects, 50 percent have CHD prevention programmes; all use LAYH publications
- 41 percent of local authorities are involved in the LAYH programme and over 1000 Heartbeat Awards have been made to local restaurants
- 360 major national organisations, covering 2.9 million employees, are actively involved with the LAYH Workplace Project
- 270 community projects have been funded by LAYH at a cost of £700,000
- many of the 'healthier food' producers and retailers are involved in co-promotions with the LAYH programme
- 13 million LAYH publications have been distributed to the general public.

Progress has not, however, been uniform across the whole country and in all sectors. Projects are well developed in some areas; in others they are only in their early stages. Nevertheless, the list of achievemens demonstrates that LAYH has succeeded in its initial objective of promoting a generally greater awareness of CHD.

The 1990-1995 Strategy

Preparation of this five year strategy has taken account of the extensive consultation carried out in 1988 by the HEA on how the programme should be developed, the comments of the National Audit Office and Public Accounts Committee and detailed comments from a wide number of organisations including the Forum of CHD Prevention Agencies and the Coronary Prevention

Group have been taken into account. It also takes account of and builds on those activities in the first phase of the programme which have proved successful and draws lessons from those which were not so successful. The overall strategy sets out the systematic basis for developing work on a broader front in all the key sectors of society.

Development of the second phase of the Look After Your Heart programme is quite consciously moving from what has previously been regarded as an 'opportunistic campaign' to a comprehensive and systematically planned programme of activity.

The (1990-1995) Strategy:

- sets clear priorities
- takes forward the work to develop major targets
- emphasises the development of partnerships
- sets out plans for the effective integration of national and local CHD prevention activity
- increases support for local CHD programmes
- encourages health authorities to monitor progress in implementing CHD prevention programmes through their review and planning mechanisms

The strategy is built around a number of separate, yet interlinked initiatives and approaches. It takes the best and most successful of current activity, develops it further and adds a number of new dimensions, having regard to the multifactorial nature of CHD and the multisectoral activity needed to address it.

The building blocks

The LAYH strategy may be seen as having six main building blocks:

- Look After Your Employee (workplace projects)
- Look After Your Customer (commercial co-promotions; Heartbeat Award)
- Look After Your Patient (primary care projects)
- Look After Your Community (community based projects)
- Look After Yourself (public education project, mass media publications, promotional activity)

The strategic objectives

To achieve the broad aims of the programme, eight major objectives have been set. These take into account the national umbrella nature of the programme and the need to build the foundations of LAYH around the development of local CHD prevention activity.

The eight major objectives are:

1   to promote greater public awareness and understanding of the lifestyle changes required to reduce the incidence of the CHD risk factors and to promote a healthy lifestyle

2   to disseminate good practice through effective working partnerships with the NHS and other organisations in the field

3   to keep CHD prevention high on the agenda of government and professional organisations

4   to develop a comprehensive range of special projects on specific CHD risk factors and healthy living

5   to develop, under the broad LAYH umbrella, specific projects targeted at those sections of the population at greatest risk of CHD

6   to develop CHD prevention initatives for the ethnic minority communities

7   to make the market work for health, so that the promotion of a healthy lifestyle is seen to become economically and socially more attractive to producers and consumers

8   to evaluate and monitor the efficiency and effectiveness of the LAYH programme and its constituent projects.

Partnerships - their central role

The development of co-operation and partnerships will be a central element of the next five years. The aim of LAYH is to establish a wide range of high quality projects, wherever possible developed jointly in partnerships and by identifying local need and innovation. The national LAYH programme is intended to complement and support local programmes of CHD prevention, developed independently from, or in conjunction with LAYH by regional and district health authorities, jointly with local authorities and other organisations concerned to improve the health of the population they serve.

The success of such community based activities will depend largely upon the ease with which the national programme activities can be adopted and adapted to suit local circumstances. Over the strategy period, it is therefore intended that the amount of LAYH resources available for local activities should be progressively increased. It is also hoped that local agencies will reciprocate by increasing the level of their own investment.

The first steps towards this goal have already been taken with the appointment of two full-time LAYH programme officers in each health region -

a total of 28 officers in all. These officers will establish new channels of communication to ensure that the national and local programmes are synchronised and jointly planned.

Advisory group

A special group has been formed to advise on the development of the LAYH programme. It consists of representatives from:
- The Department of Health
- The Health Education Authority
- The Joint Consultative Committee of District Health Education Officers
- The National Forum of Coronary Heart Disease Prevention
- The Coronary Prevention Group
- The Ministry of Agriculture, Fisheries and Food
- The British Heart Foundation.

As the LAYH programme progresses, representatives from other relevant organisations and government departments will be invited to join the advisory group.

Research

The direct budget for LAYH in 1990-1991 is £4.9 million. The benefits from commercial co-promotions and other partnerships are considerable and augment the level of LAYH resources. This strategy is based on the assumption that the budget will at least be maintained at its current level in real terms, and will in practice continue to increase.

The future

LAYH is one of the few truly national CHD prevention programmes in the world. The 1990-1995 strategy is ambitious but realistic. Success will depend upon building partnerships and jointly developing winning projects and activities in all of the key sectors of our society. The umbrella nature of the LAYH programme allows national and local agencies to work together towards the common goal of making a major contribution to a substantial reduction in the incidence of premature death by CHD in England.

The new (1990-1995) strategy for the programme is available from the LAYH office at the HEA, Hamilton House, Mabledon Place, London WC1H 9TX. Telephone: 071 383 3833.

The Good Hearted Glasgow Campaign

18

Philip Hanlon, Director of Health Promotion, Greater Glasgow Health Board

Introduction

The case for a successful coronary heart disease (CHD) prevention programme in Greater Glasgow is unequivocal. Forty-five per cent of all deaths in Glasgow are due to coronary heart disease or stroke and these diseases account for an estimated 1300 beds daily of which 400 are in the acute sector[1]. The Standardised Mortality Ratio from CHD in Scotland ranks among the highest in the world for both men and women but, within Scotland, Glasgow fares particularly badly with a ten per cent higher mortality from CHD than would be expected on the basis of the Scottish national figures[1]. Morbidity relating to CHD is correspondingly high and the population is known to have high levels of known CHD risk factors[2].

The Good Hearted Glasgow Campaign

The troubled history of the Good Hearted Glasgow Campaign, which was launched by the Greater Glasgow Health Board in May of 1986 with the aim of reducing the incidence of heart disease and stroke in Glasgow by 10%, is of interest because it illustrates many points which are relevant to the current debate over appropriate methods for CHD prevention.

The Good Hearted Glasgow Campaign was designed with three components:

1　A community-based education campaign directed at specific risk groups by providing nutritional advice and reinforcing the existing anti-smoking campaign (Glasgow 2000).

2　An individually-based screening/advisory campaign, organised through the primary care system. Patients were invited to a free health check which included family history, medical history and smoking history, together with measurement of weight, height, blood pressure and cholesterol. The health check was carried out by the Health Visitor attached to the practice using an interactive microcomputer programme which also calculated the risk of premature heart disease. Once the relevant facts had been collected, advice

181

was given on a wide range of lifestyle issues. The role of the GP was to recruit patients opportunistically for the health check and follow up those found to have risk factors which required medical intervention.

3   A population-based mass media campaign to raise awareness of Good Hearted Glasgow and to encourage the population to adopt a more healthy lifestyle.

The type and scope of intervention employed by the Campaign was to a large degree determined by the results of a baseline survey of beliefs and attitudes which was carried out on a random sample of 3,000 individuals stratified in such a way as to include all geographical areas of the city. It is clear that at the time of the survey in late summer 1987 the average Glaswegian was well aware of the major CHD risk factors. For example, 84% of the sample recognised that there were certain things they could do to reduce their chance of a heart attack and, when presented with a list of risk factors, the following proportion of respondents considered the risk factor mentioned to be very important (Table 1).

Table 1

Percentage of the population aware of coronary risk factors

Risk Factor	% Aware
Overweight/obesity	97%
High blood pressure	95%
Stress	95%
Cigarettes	95%
Alcohol	89%
Lack of exercise	85%

It was thus clear to the programme planners that lack of awareness was not the problem. Providing the motivation, opportunity and supportive environment for change was the major challenge.

The Good Hearted Glasgow Campaign was, therefore, planned so that the media campaign would attract people to the 'free health check' where the novel presentation of risk scores through the microcomputer programme, allied to individual counselling, would provide the motivation for change. It was also intended that the community programme would provide the means by which the motivation for change, created through individual advice and counselling, could be sustained.

Early problems

In the event, the Good Hearted Glasgow Campaign faltered before it had really gathered momentum and matters came to a head in April of 1987, only one year after the launch, when the campaign came under review by the Board's managers who were concerned about the poor level of recruitment as, at that time, the average screening/advice session was achieving a throughput of only one to two people against a target figure of seven per half day session.

Good Hearted Glasgow staff argued that the campaign had not been given sufficient time to prove itself and was still in its pilot phase. Others pointed to the lack of funds for publicity and the fact that, as a matter of policy, the campaign had started in the city's most deprived areas where recruitment was likely to be difficult.

The third group with a distinct point of view on the campaign was Health Education Officers many of whom felt ill at ease with the 'top down' strategy employed by Good Hearted Glasgow. In particular, those working in community development expressed the opinion that the 'bottom up', holistic approach to health promotion was more likely to be succesful in the long term. In short, a debate raged over philosophy, strategy and cost effectiveness.

Reasons for poor recruitment

An evaluation of the Good Hearted Glasgow Campaign was carried out towards the end of 1988 in three of the health centres where it had been established longest. This evaluation included, among other activities, a questionnaire survey through street interviews of a stratified sample of approximately 200 patients from each of the three health centres and a parallel survey among equivalent numbers of patients while they were attending their respective health centres (1,200 subjects in all). The results revealed that awareness and knowledge of the campaign was surprisingly high. 70% of health centre patients interviewed in the street survey and 91% of those interviewed while visiting the health centre knew of the campaign and only 14% of those who had heard of the campaign were unable to give a reasonable description of it.

There were no important differences in awareness and knowledge among the three health centres surveyed despite the fact that one had achieved much higher recruitment figures than the other two. This result suggested that lack of awareness of the campaign did not account for the poor recruitment figures.

Posters and leaflets were the main reported source of knowledge about the campaign, while the family doctor was the main source of personal information. In the centre which had achieved comparatively good recruitment, 47% of patients interviewed had received from their GP a personal recommendation to be screened compared with only 26% and 17% in the two centres with poorer recruitment. It seemed likely, therefore, that G.P.s had an important role to play in recruiting patients.

All G.P.s, Health Visitors, Nurses and Receptionists in each of the three centres were also interviewed. There was general support for the basic strategy of the campaign among all staff groups but almost all identified operational problems with the programme. Lack of publicity, lack of central support, lack of staff and underfunding were the most common complaints.

A small but significant minority of G.P.s thought the emphasis of the campaign was inappropriate for people living in areas of multiple deprivation where issues like smoking and diet were relatively low on the personal agenda of many of the population.

The review of the Good Hearted Glasgow Campaign led to the following conclusions:

1   No programme will succeed unless the potential recipients want it. Consultation and participation are important prerequisites for effective health promotion.

2   Any programme must be flexible and rapidly adaptable to changing need.

3   Organisers and participants must be enthusiasts.

4   Built in process and outcome evaluation is mandatory.

A change in direction

The review of the Good Hearted Glasgow Campaign described above took place against the background of other significant developments. Firstly, the Scottish Home and Health Department was conducting a review of heart disease prevention in Scotland which subsequently recommended that CHD prevention should be approached through a general, or holistic, health promotion strategy allied to other more focussed preventive activities[3]. Secondly, and concurrently, the Greater Glasgow Health Board was developing a comprehensive Health Promotion Strategy which sought to balance the need for broad-based health programmes with the more specific and targeted activities which had been developed by the Good Hearted Glasgow Campaign.

The Health Board's new Health Promotion Strategy is now being implemented. As part of the Strategy, screening/counselling is being offered to all Glasgwegians aged 20-65 through a variety of outlets including G.P. surgeries, health centres and open access centres. In addition, peripatetic teams are taking the screening programme into workplaces and community settings to support ongoing health promotion activities. The workplace and community programmes are proving particularly successful in as much as they are attracting large numbers of clients and stimulating other changes (e.g. increased exercise activities and greater demand for healthy menu choices).

The new G.P. contract is also causing important changes to occur. A survey conducted in Glasgow early in 1990 indicated that there will be a dramatic increase in the number of General Practitioners who will be offering health promotion sessions with a coronary prevention emphasis under the terms of the new contract. Consequently, the Good Hearted Glasgow team will, in future, concentrate its activities in the workplace and at open access sites, while General Practitioners will offer an individualy based service for their own patients. The remaining components of the Board's broadly based health promotion strategy ensure that CHD prevention is integrated with other health promotion activities.

Evaluation of these activities will be crucial. For example, cholesterol measurement remains a part of the Good Hearted Glasgow Campaign despite the recommendations of the Kings Fund Cholesterol Consensus Conference[4] but this can only be justified if the possible motivational effect of cholesterol measurement in encouraging people to accept and act on dietary advice is formally assessed as part of the programme.

Conclusion

This very brief history of the Good Hearted Glasgow Campaign illustrates some of the operational problems associated with CHD prevention programmes. However, many of the difficulties have now been overcome and the programme has been relaunched in the context of a broader and more integrated health promotion strategy. Time will tell whether this new approach will prove more successful.

References

1   Information Services Section, Department of Public Health Medicine, Greater Glasgow Health Board.

2   The WHO MONICA Project. (1988). 'Geographical variations in the major risk factors of coronary heart disease in men and women aged 35-64 years.' *World Health Statistics Quarterly.*

3   *Prevention of Coronary Heart Disease in Scotland. Report of the working group on Prevention and Health Promotion.* (1990). HMSO, Edinburgh.

4   'Blood Cholesterol Measurement in the Prevention of Coronary Heart Disease. Consensus Statement.' *The Sixth King's Fund Forum.* (1989) King Edward's Hospital Fund for London.

The South Birmingham Coronary Prevention Project

Deidre Fee, Dietitian, and Sally Ferris, Clinical Psychologist, South Birmingham Coronary Prevention

19

The South Birmingham Coronary Prevention Programme (CPP) was launched in 1985 with the aim of reducing premature deaths and disability from Coronary Heart Disease (CHD) within the South Birmingham Health District. Each year almost 800 people die from CHD in South Birmingham, a figure which represents 25.9% of all deaths. Of these, a quarter are under 55 years old.

The impetus for the Programme stemmed from a conference held in Canterbury in 1983. This recommended that the pandemic of premature death and disability from CHD could be prevented by district based coronary prevention strategies.[1]

South Birmingham's strategy

Following the conference, South Birmingham Health Authority decided to allot 0.1% of the district budget to coronary prevention and the Programme was set up. It has now been operational for six years.

The prevention team

The team is responsible to the Unit General Manager of the Family Services Unit, and consists of a Primary Care Facilitator, Dietitian, Psychologist, Health Promotion Officer and General Administrative Assistant. Individual members are advised by their managers and a Consultant in Public Health Medicine.

The team is based in its own set of offices with additional training rooms nearby. They have at their disposal a non-pay budget of £16,000 per annum for equipment and educational resources.

The Role of CPP team members

All programme members are involved in awareness raising events, staff training, the provision of health education material and evaluation.

Primary Health Care Facilitator

The Primary Health Care Facilitator's role is to establish and support health checks with a particular focus on Coronary Heart Disease within GP surgeries. Part of this role involves the evaluation of health checks through audits and organising regular training meetings for practice nurses.

Dietitian

The Dietitian gives advice aimed at the reduction of serum cholesterol and the management of obesity. Patients with cholesterol levels in excess of 6.5 mmol/L are referred by the GP or Practice Nurse and a protocol of treatment has been developed. Cholesterol tests are carried out locally.

The Dietitian has direct access to a lipid clinic, where individuals who do not respond to dietary advice can be further assessed and a decision made regarding drug treatment. Diet is always tried as a first line management for a minimum of three months.

Psychologist

The clinical psychologist provides stress management training for those who have mild hypertension or who have stress-related symptoms. Therapy consists of training in relaxation and cognitive aspects of stress with modification of 'type A' behaviour where appropriate.

The Psychologist also co-ordinates smoking cessation groups. Tutors have been trained to lead groups of 10-12 people for six sessions of an hour and a half. Each session is semi-structured and is based on a detailed package produced by the team.

One to one sessions are available for those clients who would not benefit from or who would not feel happy with a group approach.

Health promotion officer

The main role of the Health Promotion Officer is to assist the Facilitator in supporting Primary Health Care personnel. There is also involvement in providing smoking cessation groups and the promotion of exercise. The Health Promotion Officer has also co-ordinated media events, displays, and has had an input to schools.

General Administrative Asssistant

The Assistant carries out all the administrative duties and helps the Facilitator to carry out audits in the GP practices.

Primary care

The Programme is based in primary care. Members of the public between the ages of 35-64 are screened via a health check for coronary risk factors.

The health check consists of a practice nurse conducting a 20-30 minute interview with the patient. Information is sought on the primary risk factors, e.g. diet, smoking, exercise and stress. Blood pressure is taken routinely and cholesterol levels are measured either on request or when other risk factors are present. In some practices cholesterol testing is carried out routinely.

Where risk factors are identified, patients are offered the choice of counselling by the Practice Nurse, referral to their GP and/or direct referral to members of the CPP.

The immediate and long term impact of the health check is currently being evaluated using a lifestyle questionnaire, comparing health-related behaviour before and after the health check. Comparisons are being made with a control group.

CPP - achievements

To date, 21 out of a potential of 50 GP practices within South Birmingham are involved in the Programme. Several others are waiting to be included. Communication links remain strong via monthly practice nurse meetings and visits to individual GP practices. These venues provide opportunities for regular training input by team members. A resource facility is available for nursing staff to collect referral forms, equipment, books and health education literature.

Several leaflets, including dietary information and advice on stress management, have been produced by members of the Programme. These leaflets, together with the Smoking Manual, can be purchased by other Districts.

In relation to smoking prevention, non-smoking has been actively encouraged particularly amongst NHS staff. There has also been support for school-based education initiatives to encourage those who do not smoke not to start smoking and motivate those who do smoke to give up.

Tutors have been trained to run smoking cessation groups and members of the Primary Health Care Teams (particularly practice nurses) have been encouraged to offer advice on a 'one-to-one' basis. One-to-one counselling has also been provided for highly dependent smokers who want to give up smoking but who have not responded to practice based initiatives.

In the field of nutrition, the District Food and Health Policy has been supported and developed; in particular the virtues of a low fat, high fibre diet have been promoted. Specific dietary advice has been provided for individuals with raised blood cholesterol and the avoidance and alleviation of obesity has been encouraged by the support of weight reduction clinics run by practice nurses and the provision of individual counselling when necessary.

Very close working relationships have also been established with the Environmental Services Department of Birmingham City Council, particularly in respect of the 'Heartbeat Awards' Scheme and the City's involvement in the 'Look After Your Heart' project.

In the field of exercise promotion, exercise classes have been arranged for NHS staff, and the health check system has been used as a way of promoting sensible levels of physical activity. The role of exercise in the alleviation of stress has also been highlighted.

The health check system has also promoted the importance of early detection and treatment of hypertension. This has been achieved by the measurement of blood presure of all those aged 35 to 64 years at a minimum of five yearly intervals.

As a response to the importance of compliance with antihypertensive medication in the prevention of strokes, education has been offered to the general public. Mild hypertension has been successfully treated by stress management, relaxation and meditation.

The future

Plans to expand the scope of the Programme are now being discussed, and particularly in the current climate there will be an ongoing need to develop and foster links with other bodies, both statutory and voluntary.

The NHS White Paper and the new GP contract will dictate a number of changes in the area of Health Promotion/Disease prevention. The indications are that the scope and freqency of screening will be extended beyond those previously recommended by the Programme. Thus, from 1 April 1990 the Programme has extended the current age range of 35-64 years to 17-74 years to come into line with the NHS White Paper recommendations. Liaison with the local Family Health Services Authority will be essential for a co-ordinated interpretation of the recommendations to ensure a quality service across the South Birmingham district.

The increase in the number of health checks carried out within South Birmingham suggests that there will be a greater demand for services offered by the Programme. This is expected to come from those practices already involved with the Programme who will be screening more people. In addition, recent enquiries suggest that there will be a demand for services from several of the remaining 29 practices, who are not currently involved with the Programme.

The potential increase in the number of referrals will mean that team members will have to take on an increasingly consultative role. More time will be spent training and supporting members of the Primary Health Care Teams to produce effective clinical practice.

In addition, given the current resource limitations of the Programme it is uncertain whether the increased workload will necessitate an increase in the number of staff or perhaps require limitations to be placed on the referral criteria or the prioritisation of certain high risk groups.

Adoption of the latter suggestions may take various forms. It may lead us into industry to target particular occupations known to be at high risk of CHD. Links with occupational health services would need to be developed, together with a plan to initiate screening and mass education for employees including the running of smoking cessation and stress management courses on site and the provision of healthy food choices and advice to canteens. Alternatively it may lead us to foster a closer working relationship with colleagues on coronary care units and those working in the field of cardiac rehabilitation.

References

1   *Coronary Heart Disease Prevention – Plans for Action.* (1984) Pitman, London.

The Oxford Prevention of Heart Attack and Stroke Project

20

Elaine Fullard, National Facilitator Development Officer

The Royal College of General Practitioners report 'Prevention of arterial disease in general practice' published in February 1981[1] gave the impetus for this project. This report concluded that 'about half of all strokes and a quarter of deaths from coronary heart disease in people under 70 are probably preventable by the application of existing knowledge'. Among the report's recommendations was that major risk factors for arterial disease should be identified in general practice in patients under 65 as they consulted by:

1   measuring the blood pressure at least every five years;

2   recording smoking behaviour;

3   measuring people's weight and height esepcially of those who looked fat.

Though the report recognised that obesity has a small independent effect on the risk of arterial disease, obesity nevertheless remains as a good visual indicator of increased lipid levels. These measures were thought to be the first step towards prevention of arterial disease in general practice. In May 1982 the Oxford Prevention of Heart Attack and Stroke Project began as a research study to test wether the recommendations of the report could be implemented. The research had four main objectives:

1   To test the feasibility of implementing the recommendations without undue disturbance or extra cost to general practice.

2   To look at the contribution which a Facilitator working for the Health Authority can make in helping general practitioners and their primary health care teams expedite the amount of preventive medicine already practised.

3   To provide a model which is widely adaptable.

4   To extend collaboration between Family Health Services Authorities, Health Authorities and General Practice.

Method

Three experimental and three control practices in Oxfordshire were chosen. These were matched for similarities in practice size, population and in interest in research. Intervention practices were chosen because they were typical of other

193

practices but did not have a systematic approach to screening. For example, the first practice comprised two doctors working from a semi-detached house. Control practices were matched for location, structure and size of practice. The socio-economic profiles of all six practices were similar.

Intervention

In order to raise the level of identification of major risk factors for arterial diseases, the Facilitator encouraged the General Practitioners to appoint a practice nurse to share the extra work load of screening their patients. If there was already a nurse in post they encouraged the nurse to allocate some 'protected time' for prevention. The receptionists were trained and initially helped by the Facilitator to invite patients in for a health check or what was nick-named a human 'MOT', as the patients consulted their doctor for any other reason. This opportunistic approach was based on the fact that 75% of the population consult their General Practitioners within any one year, 85% within three years and over 90% within five years. There were, of course, no postal expenses to consider, nor was a age/sex register or computer necessary. The Facilitator (EF) had been a health visitor and health education officer and she acted as a temporary guest and catalyst in the intervention practices helping to set up and support the screening and audit of records.

First Audit

The first step was to establish the extent of recording of risk factors in the medical notes. The first audit was conducted and the medical notes in the three experimental practices were reviewed to obtain a base line of information to establish the percentage of women aged 35-64 who, in the preceding five years from April 1982 had had:

a) a record of their blood pressure recorded in the notes

b) smoking habits recorded

c) a record of weight or an indication of obesity

This audit of 7,000 records in the three practices was conducted with the permission of the General Practitioners and with strict adherence to a protocol of confidentiality.

Facilitator

The Facilitator also trained the nurses in the conducting of the health check and, for example, acted as their resource for revision of methods of blood pressure

Figure 1

	HEALTH CHECK RECORD		
	Name	Date	
	Occupation	Age	M
			F
	Partners Occupation	DOB	

History	Personal	Family
Heart Disease		
Cerebrovascular Disease		
Hypertension		
Diabetes		

Exercise		Alchohol		Units/Week
Diet		Stress		

Smoker	Cigs	/Day	Pipe	Cigars	Total years smoked
Non Smoker	Never		Gave up 19........		
Date	1		2	3	Mean, if applicable
Blood Pressure					
Tetanus Date	1		2	3	Booster

HT.	CMS FT	Smear Date	Result		
Ideal WT.	KG ST				
WT.	KG ST				
Urine					
Cholesterol		Rubella Immune	Yes	No	Date
Date		Vaccination	Date		
Comment:-					

measurement and how to counsel about smoking and dietary habits. She acted as a resource in, for example, designing a health summary card (figure 1) and in providing blood pressure protocols (figure 2) and offering training courses.

The health check

The health check took about 20 minutes and was either included in the surgery consultation or especialy allocated to what are now known as Health Promotion Clinics.

The nurse asked about relevant family history and diabetes, recorded blood pressure, height and weight, diet, alcohol consumption and, where appropriate, oral contraception and smoking habits.

Enquiry about exercise, tetanus injections and cervical cancer screening was included. A protocol was designed so that patients who had sustained blood

Figure 2   **Protocol for blood pressure treatment**

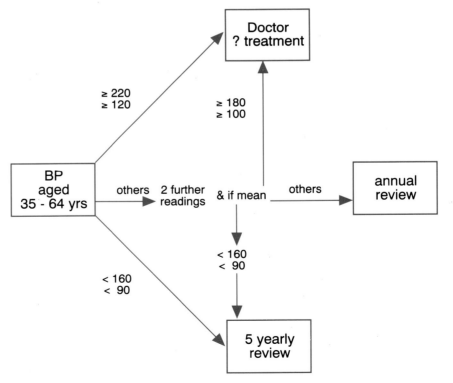

Adapted from Hammond and Garfinkel[35] and reproduced with permission

pressure at or above 180/100 were referrred to the doctor for consideration of treatment. Those patients with blood pressures below 160/90 were told that another check would be needed within five years. If either the systolic or diastolic pressures were at or above 160/90, then the patients were told that the blood pressure was slightly higher than normal, and were asked to return to the nurse for further readings at approximately weekly intervals. If the average of these three blood pressures was such that the blood pressure was at or above 160/90 and yet below the 180/100, the patient was asked to come back in a year's time for annual review. A three-way system was used to ensure that the patient was followed up:

1 The nurse tagged the records with the date of the next recommended review
2 The patient was asked to record that appointment in his or her calendar or diary
3 The recording was highlighted on the computer recall system or in a manual box file system, so that if the patient did not attend, he or she would be followed up.

Other non-pharmacological ways of reducing blood pressure were discussed and health education materials such as the Health Education Authority educational leaflets were supplied and a height/weight chart (figure 3) was used. Cholesterol levels were only taken on patients who had a direct family history of premature heart attack or stroke and patients who had multiple risk factors. A random non-fasting sample was taken, with a full lipid profile being taken if this was found to be raised. The nurse had the option of discussing any patient she was concerned about with the General Practitioner. Patients who smoked, were overweight, and others who needed dietary counselling were also followed up.

Results

A second audit was made in both the experimental and control practices to establish the change in recording of risk factors in patients notes. This second audit was carried out two and a half years later than the initial audit.

The controls were not told that they were part of the trial until the intervention was completed in order to avoid the possible effect of a change in behaviour. The second audit in the control practices was therefore retrospective. The recording of risk factors in the patient's notes was chosen as a measure of professional behaviour. There was no attempt to determine whether there had been a decrease in the number of strokes and heart attacks since the numbers in the population were too small for significant alternations to be likely over a short period of time. Instead, the evidence from large epidemiological trials with longer intervention and follow-up times was relied on[2,3].

Audit results

There had been a team effort by General Practitioners and Practice Nurses in identifying risk factors.

Practices which had been helped by the facilitator showed a highly statistically significant rise in their risk factor recording[4]. Altogether, 1,033 extra people had had their blood pressure recorded, an extra 2,327 their smoking recorded and an extra 2,158 their weight, or an indication of obesity recorded in the three intervention practices, compared with the three control practices. Likewise in 80 patients hypertension was newly detected with blood pressures of sustained readings at or above 180/100 and this included three patients with sustained measurements more than 220/120.

Patient reactions

The offer of a health check proved very popular and many others were checked informally by their General Practitioner. Only 107 (3%) of the first 4,000 offered a health check actively declined the offer. These patients were either checked then by their General Practitioner or asked for a health check at a later date. These high levels of acceptance had been replicated in the National Lipid Study, in which 97% of patients accepted the offer of a health check that included measurement of their cholesterol[5].

Many patients made positive observations:

'I think it is a marvellous idea; the NHS should have been doing this a long time ago.'
'Yes I should be pleased to have my blood pressure checked, I do have a check at work but I would like my family doctor to have it on his records.'
'I'm unemployed so would miss out on check ups at work.'
'I'm glad the men are not being forgotten, my wife always seems to be the one who gets all the attention.'

Since women consult their practitioners twice as often as men, women were encouraged to ask their husbands to make an appointment. Several couples came in together to see the nurse.

General Practitioner reactions included:

'We are doing the obvious, we should have done this before. We just needed somebody to get us organised and give us a bit of help'

'We just needed a "kick" to get us going.'

'I feel it is a team effort, it has crystallised what we have been trying to do.'

Receptionists reactions included:

'I think it shows concern by the practice.'

'I enjoy asking people; it is nice to offer something positive, rather than saying "I'm sorry there are very few appointments left".'

'The men are as proud as Punch when they have been back to see the nurse having lost weight and their blood pressure has dropped.'

'It is extra work at first but well worth while I think.'

Nurses reactions included:

'I enjoy meeting the patients whom I do not normally see.'

'If we could at least delay the onset of strokes it would make a tremendous difference to my workload.'

'The men seem a bit shy of letting the General Practitioner know that they are worried about having a heart attack and so they don't ask for him to take their blood pressure.'

'It is nice to have the General Practitioner next door if I do find somebody with a very high blood pressure. I then just ask him or her to see the patient.'

'Mr X hasn't smoked a single cigarette since he saw me last month.'

Successes and some of the problems encountered in the Oxford Project

The most exciting development in the Oxford Project has been the development and extension of the practice nurse's role. Practice nurses undertook the major part of the screening and follow up and with the April 1990 GP Contract the numbers employed for preventive medicine and health promotion have increased to a Royal College of Nursing estimate of 17,000 (1991). The health visitors and district nurses very often acted in a complementary role and in some practices health visitors have undertaken health checks alongside the practice nurses. In other practices district nurses and health visitors have been the key members in recruiting patients. Health visitors have very often developed practice profiles encouraging the practice to look at the local community needs. With the plans for a modular training course for practice nurses, all practice nurses should have training for health promotion.

Primary care facilitators

The original Oxford model has been widely adopted by other Health Authorities and Family Health Services Authorities. There are currently 172 (January 1991) Facilitators in the UK, 50% of whom are funded jointly by Family Health Services Authorities and Health Authorities (figure 4). Primary Care Facilitators help practices in the following ways:

a)   Recruitment of practice nurses.

b)   Co-ordination of training of practice nurses.

c)   Providing resources for practice team protocols, guidelines for health promotion clinics, suggestions on methods of recruiting and follow up of patients, advice and sometimes practical help with audit of records to establish progress towards screening targets and ongoing support.

The role of the primary care Facilitator has been adopted by other countries, such as the Netherlands, who are employing four Facilitators funded by the Dutch Heart Foundation where they are working in a very similar fashion to their British counterparts. The Facilitator is in effect a new health professional, giving a career path for many practice nurses, health visitors and district nurses[6].

'Rent An Audit'

The Auditing team who reviewed the records in the six research practices have since offered their help to other practices in Oxfordshire. They charged a fee of about £25 to do a 10-20% sample of the records. Many other Facilitators have also provided this way of giving feedback to the practices to assess the quality of care[7].

Problems in Screening:

Nurses were assessed on how well they had followed up the hypertensives identified by their blood pressure protocol. The results showed that follow up at a year was good (80%) but the follow up of dietary and smoking advice was far less good. The study[8] emphasised the need to develop formal protocols for dietary and anti-smoking interventions. Further research[9] was also conducted to obtain information on the dietary knowledge of the primary health care team workers. All participants offered health checks and promoted prevention in primary care. The study questionnaire focused on issues relating to managing patients with moderate hypercholesterolaemia. Results show important gaps in the health workers' knowledge. For example only 91 of the 128 interviewed understood that dietary intake of polyunsaturated acids as a proportion of total fat intake should

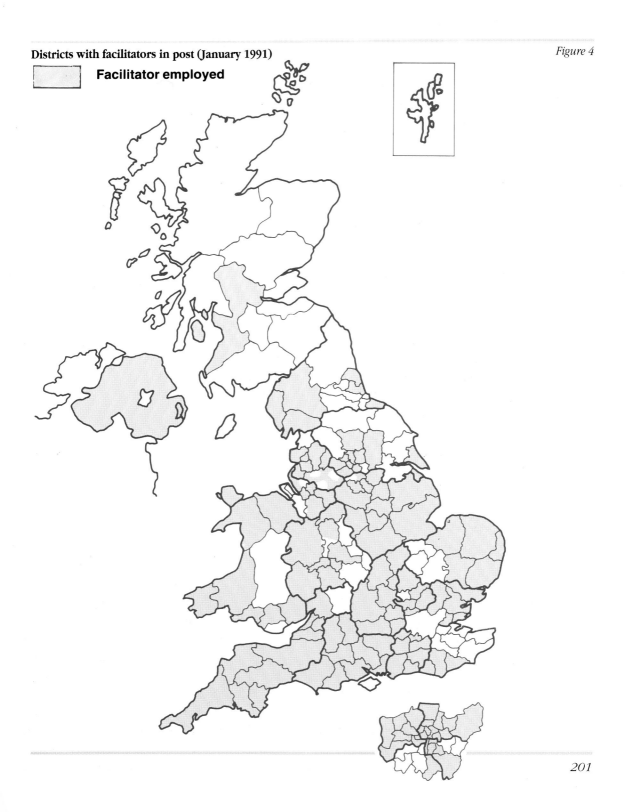

Figure 4

Facilitator employed

Figure 5

Extract from nurses log book

No.	Name	Male or Female	D.O.B.	Normal B/P	Previously Undiagnosed Hypertensive	Controlled Hypertensive	Uncontrolled Hypertensive	B/P 1	2	3	Mean of 3
NURSES LOG BOOK											
	Totals										

Smoker	Overweight	Family History	Diabetes	Urine	Oral Contraception	Cervical Smear	Tetanus Injection	D.N.A.	Recall	Remarks

be increased in a diet designed to reduce serum lipid levels. Gaps in the primary health care team workers' ability to give practical and appropriate dietary advice were also identified. Thirty gave advice that would have led to the patient losing weight, although his history indicated that he was not overweight, and twenty seven gave only negative advice offering no suggestions about substituting healthy food for unhealthy foods. The conclusion of this study was that since the demand for primary health care workers to give dietary advice is increasing, and is likely to increase further if a national screening programme for cholesterol levels is recommended, then there is an urgent need for improved dietary education and training for General Practitioners, nurses and primary care Facilitators.

Cost effectiveness of health checks

The Oxford Project relied on the results of several large trials on which to base the intervention, but there is a need to assess the effectiveness of nurses conducting health checks and the overall costs and benefits of screening. The 'Ox Check Trial' involved five practices in Bedfordshire measuring the intervention of nurses on cholesterol levels, blood pressure and smoking. Early resul on workload have been published[10].

Translation of the Oxford model

The low cost, low technology approach of the Oxford Project has proved widely adaptable and feasible in general practices throughout the U.K. The model has been able to be adopted in small inner-city single handed practices who are not as yet computerised. The opportunistic method of invitation is appropriate in highly mobile areas within inner-cities. The April 1990 G.P. contract has widened the age group of screening and shortened the interval of screening. Computerisation has made both identifying patients who need to be invited for health promotion clinics easier, and facilitated the recording of risk factors. Data initially recorded in a simples nurses' log book (figure 5) with minimal additional paperwork can be used in practice reports. The opportunistic method can likewise be used for assessments of the elderly.

The Oxford Project is now based within the Health Education Authority Primary Health Care Unit in Oxford and has been renamed the National Facilitator Development Project and provides a network of support and training opportunities for primary health care teams in England.

An Association of Primary Care Facilitators has been formed. The nutrition programme and the multi-disciplinary training workshops that the Health Education Authority Primary Health Care Unit staff offer is complementing what

Top twenty causes of death in Oxfordshire Health Authority, 1989, Age range 35-74 (OPCS) men & women

Figure 6

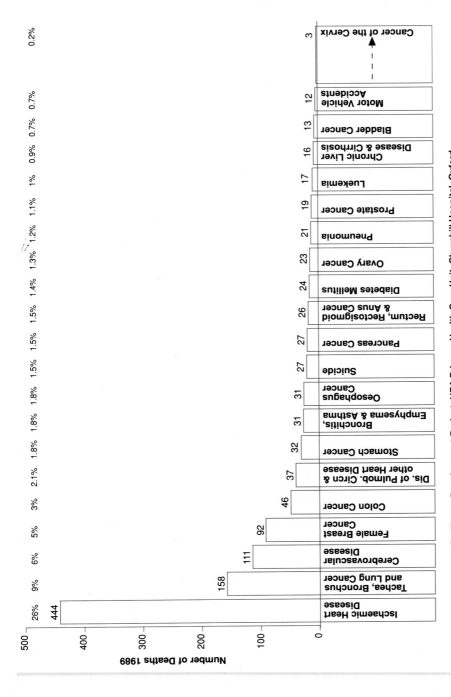

Facilitator Development Project, HEA Primary Health Care Unit, Churchill Hospital, Oxford

the Oxford Project set out to achieve. The Office of Population Censuses and Surveys data on the Top Twenty Causes of Death in a district is available from Health Authority Information Officers and could be used by the practice to assess yearly changes (figure 6).

The Oxford Project set out as a pioneering research study in six general practices. It is now very much part of the national scene, both in facilitator development and in development of screening and follow up.

If Primary Health Care team members can increase their involvement in preventive medicine to enable their patients to feel motivated and enabled to reduce their risk from premature strokes and heart attacks, then the aims will have been achieved.

Acknowledgements are due to the Chest, Heart and Stroke Association who funded the initial research and who continue to fund the National Facilitator Development Project.

References

1   Royal College of General Practioners. (1981) 'Prevention of Arterial Disease in General Practice.' *Report from General Practice No 19.* RCGP, London.

2   Hypertension Detection and Follow-up Co-operative Group - Five year findings of the hypertension detection and follow-up programme: Reduction in mortality of persons with high blood pressure, including mild hypertension.' (1979) *JAMA.* 242, 2562-2571.

3   Australian National Blood Pressure Study Management Committee. 'The Australian Therapeutic trial in mild hypertension.' (1980) *Lancet.* (i), 1251-1257.

4   Fullard E.M., Fowler G.H., Gray J.A.M. (1987) 'Promoting prevention in primary care: controlled trial of low technology, low cost approach.' *British Medical Journal.* 294, 1080-1082.

5   Mann J.I., Lewis B., Shepherd J., Winder A.F., Fenster S., Rose L., Morgan B. (1988) Blood lipid concentrations and other cardiovascular risk factors: distribution, prevalance, and detection in Britain.' *British Medical Journal.* 296, 1702-1706.

6   Astrop P., (1987) 'Facilitator - The Birth of a New Profession.' *Health Visitor* (1988) 61, 311-312.

7   McKinlay C., 'Rent-an-Audit: An educational exercise facilitating change.' *European Newsletter on Quality Assurance.* 4 (1), 5.

8   Mant D., McKinlay C., Fuller A., Randall T., Fullard, E. (1989)Three year follow up of patients with raised blood pressure identified at health checks in general practice. *British Medical Journal* 298, 1360-1362.

9   Francis J., Roche M., Mant D., Jones L., Fullard E. (1989) Would primary health care workers give appropriate dietary advice after cholesterol screening? *British Medical Journal* 298, 1620-1622.

10 Imperial Cancer Research Fund OXCHECK Study Group. (1991) Prevalence of risk factors for heart disease in OXCHECK trial. Implications for screening in primary care. *British Medical Journal* 302, 1057-1660.

Printed in the UK for HMSO

Dd 294057 C 20 1/92